Hunting Tito

Hunting Tito

A History of Nachtschlachtgruppe 7 in World War II

LOVRO PERŠEN

Edited by Nick Beale & Mario Ragúž

Dedication
Para Monica

Library of Congress Control Number:
2014940173

Type set in Zurich & Times New Roman

Cover photo: Dinko Predoević: Formation of the Heinkel He 46 aircraft of the Störkampfstaffel Südost over Bosnia and Herzegovina in 1943.

ISBN: 978-0-7643-4632-3
Printed in China

Published by Schiffer Publishing, Ltd.
4880 Lower Valley Road
Atglen, PA 19310
Phone: (610) 593-1777
Fax: (610) 593-2002
E-mail: Info@schifferbooks.com

Back cover images: Ognjan M. Petrović

Table of Contents

Acknowledgments

Two girls that have a special place in my heart need to be recognized. I would like to thank my wife Monica for all the love, support, understanding, and useful advice I received. I would like to express my gratitude for her being patient with me during the time I was writing this book and not sufficiently dedicated to her. I apologize for every time the word *aircraft* was mentioned in our house. I would also like to thank my teenage daughter Dora for her love and smiles during the last 17 years.

First and foremost: immense credit and my great thanks to Nick Beale, author of *Ghost Bombers* and a "veteran" of NSGr research for materials, advice, and patience in answering the hundreds of e-mails I sent him. Thanks also for sharing his contacts. A partial list of the help I received from Nick includes: his English, work on the unreadable draft of my book, and the preface he agreed to write. Without Nick this book would probably be only a newspaper article.

One other man requires special acknowledgment. Great credit goes to Mario Raguž for all the time he spent editing this book, for the many photos that contributed to its attractiveness, and his contacts, as well as for the knowledge he passed on me. Mario wrote two paragraphs based on his earlier research that are entirely integrated into this book. Thanks for his patience and friendship.

I express my sincere gratitude to another "veteran" of NSGr research, Dr. Christian Möller, who provided me with many flying log books and his research materials from the Bundesarchiv. Specific thanks to Dr. Möller for letting me publish his integral aircraft availability tables that shortened my work by several weeks, and for permission to use some of his summaries of the aircraft of NSGr 7 as the basis on which I created the tables at the end of this book.

A sincere thank you is extended to Dinko Predoević for sharing photos from his personal collection, which represent almost half of the images in this book. Many thanks to Tomislav Haraminčić for all the archive materials and photos that he shared with me. Many thanks to Tomislav for being a proofreader, as well. Thanks to Boris Ciglić for the advice, photos, and materials he provided to me.

This book would have been impossible without the help of the following people, and to them I am sincerely grateful: Tomislav Aralica, for photos and history lessons; Nemanja Baćković, for photos; Sven Carlsen, for understanding how the Luftwaffe worked and help with SG 151; Robert Čopec, for photos and advice; Ferdinando D'Amico, for help with Italian MM; Hans Peter Eisenbach, for photos; Mario Jelušić, for photos; Ralph Markert, for his German; Ognjan Petrović, for profiles and research in Serbia; Dejan Savić, for photos and contacts; Dragan Savić, for the Partisan Morane; Radovan Živanović, for data about the Caproni from Lič and his contacts; Garry Staffo and the 99th Bomb Group Historical Society (BGHS) for their help with 99th BG missions over Croatia; the Military Museum in Beograd; and the Initiative for the Preservation of Croatian Aviation Heritage (Inicijativa za očuvanje hrvatske zrakoplovne baštine). I would like to express gratitude to Christophe Cony, who published my first article and somehow encouraged me to keep on searching and writing. Thanks again to all the unknown friends of friends who answered questions and gave clues, papers, and advice.

Glossary & Abbreviations

15th Air Force	U.S. formation of four-engine bombers operating within MAAF (Američka formacija četveromotornih bombardera koja djeluje u sklopu MAAFa)
AA	Anti-aircraft - Protuzrakoplovna
Abwehr	German Intelligence - Njemačka obavještajna služba
Agram	Zagreb
B4	German 87-octane fuel - Njemačko 87-oktansko gorivo
Beobachter	Observer - Izviđač
Bordschütze	Air Gunner
BG	Bomber Group (U.S.) - Bombarderska pukovnija (SAD)
BS	Bomber Squadron (U.S.) - Bombarderska eskadrila (SAD)
Cardinal Directions	In the text, only four main points of the compass are given in their full name. All other (12) directions are given by abbreviations, i.e., NE is North East, SSW is South South West, etc.
Chetnik*(s)*	Serbian quisling movement led by Dragoljub Draža Mihailović that collaborated with German and especially with Italian fascist forces, showing particular brutality towards Croatian and Muslim civilians
EK	Eisernes Kreuz - Iron Cross (I & II Class) - Željezni križ (1. i 2. klase)
FFS A/B 123	Flugzeugführerschule A/B 123 - Pilots school A/B 123 in Zagreb, later in Graz - Pilotskaškola A/B 123; u Zagrebu, a kasnije u Gracu
FG	Fighter Group (U.S.) - Lovačka regimenta (SAD)
Fliegerführer Kroatien	Aviation Command Croatia - Zrakoplovno zapovjedništvo Hrvatska
Fliegerführer Nordbalkan	Aviation Command North Balkans, named for Fliegerführer Kroatien on 28 August 1944
Flugbuch	Flying Log Book - Letačka knjižica
FS	Fighter Squadron (U.S.) - Lovačka eskadrila (SAD)
Gruppe	Group - Pukovnija njemačkog ratnog zrakoplovstva
Gruppenkommandeur	Regiment Commander - Zapovjednik pukovnije njemačkog ratnog zrakoplovstva
Home Guard	regular Army of the NDH - Domobran;
JG	Jagdgeschwader - Fighter Wing - Lovačka pukovnija njemačkog ratnog zrakoplovstva

Kette	Three aircraft usually flying in "V" formation; a tactical formation in the Luftwaffe
KG	Kampfgeschwader - Luftwaffe Bombardment Wing - Bombarderska pukovnija njemačkog ratnog zrakoplovstva
Luftflotte	Air Fleet - Zračna flota
MAAF	Mediterranean Allied Air Forces - Savezničko mediteransko ratno zrakoplovstvo
MM	Matricola Militare - Unique numeric code that identifies Italian military aircraft
NAGr.	Nahaufklärungsgruppe - Close Reconnaissance Regiment - Regimenta za blisko izviđanje
NASt Kroatien	Nahaufklärungsstaffel Kroatien - Tactical Reconnaissance Squadron Croatia - Eskadrila za taktičko izviđanje Hrvatska
NDH	Nezavisna Država Hrvatska - Independent State of Croatia
NLAPDY	National Liberation Army and Partisan Detachments of Yugoslavia - Narodnooslobodilačka vojska i Partizanski odredi Jugoslavije - NOV I POJ; official name of Tito's Army from November 1942 until 1 March 1945, when it was renamed the Yugoslav Army (YA). Before November 1942, the name was Partisan Detachments and Voluntary Army of Yugoslavia
NSGr 7	Nachtschlachtgruppe 7 - Night Harassment Gruppe 7 - Pukovnija (skupina) za noćno uznemiravanje 7
OKL	Oberkommando der Luftwaffe - Supreme Command of the Luftwaffe - Vrhovno zapovjedništvo njemačkog ratnog zrakoplovstva
POW	Prisoner of War - Ratni zarobljenik
RAF	Royal Air Force - Kraljevsko ratno zrakoplovstvo (Velika Britanija)
Rotte	Pair of aircraft consisting of leader and wingman; a tactical formation in the Luftwaffe
SAAF	South African Air Force - Južnoafričko ratno zrakoplovstvo
SD	Sprengbombe Dickwand - Thick-walled fragmentation bomb - Avionska fragmentacijska bomba
Semlin	Zemun
Squadron *(RAF and dominions)*	Eskadrila Kraljevskog ratnog zrakoplovstva
Staffel	Squadron - Eskadrila
Staffelkapitän *or* **StaKa**	Squadron Commander - Zapovjednik eskadrile

Stammkennzeichen	Luftwaffe four-letter factory registration code—Luftwaffe; jedinstvena tvornička registracijska oznaka zrakoplova koji se sastoji uvijek od četiri slova
Störkampfstaffel Kroatien	Harassment Squadron Croatia - Eskadrila za uznemiravanje Hrvatska
Störkampfstaffel Südost	Harassment Squadron South East - Eskadrila za uznemiravanje Jugoistok
Technicher Offizier	Technical officer - Tehnički časnik
Ustasha	Croatian quisling paramilitary movement led by Dr. Ante Pavelić, which was brought to power in Croatia by Germany and Italy after the breakdown of Yugoslavia. Showed particular brutality against Serbian and Jewish civilians. Should not be confused with the Homeguard (Domobran), which was the regular army.
ULTRA	Allied security classification for decrypted German machine ciphers - Saveznička sigurnosna klasifikacija za dešifrirane njemačke poruke kodirane Enigmom
Verbandskennzeichen	Luftwaffe; an operational code of four characters; a combination of letters and numbers - Luftwaffe; operativna registracijska oznaka zrakoplova koji se sastoji od četiri znamenke i kombinacija je brojeva i slova
W.Nr.	Werk Nummer - Production serial number - Proizvodni serijski broj
z.b.V.	zu besonderer Verwendung - Special purpose - Za posebne namjene
ZNDH	Zrakoplovstvo Nezavisne Države Hrvatske - Air Force of the Independent State of Croatia

Preface

by Nick Beale

I first found the Luftwaffe's Nachtschlachtgruppen fascinating simply because there was so little information about them; just a few brief sentences in books or a mention in passing that a particular type was also used in the night harassment role. The "D3" unit code NSGr. 2 was among the first things I found through research that I had never seen in a book. In time, I was able to meet and correspond with many veterans of NSGr. 9 and to write a book about them and their unit. At an NSGr. 9 reunion I met Christian Möller, whose efforts to discover his grandfather's fate while serving with NSGr. 2 gave him an unrivaled range of contacts with veterans of the harassment units. His Ph.D. thesis (which became a book) examined NSGr. 1, 2, and 20's operations against the Anglo-Americans in the West in 1944–45. Now a new author has stepped forward to tell the story of another of the Nachtschlachtgruppen.

In writing this history of NSGr 7 and its forerunners, Lovro Peršen has opened up new territory. The Gruppe's war was a very different war from that fought by its counterparts in the West or across the Adriatic in Italy; rather than fighting regular mechanized armies by night, this was a battle against Partisans on land and sea, largely conducted in broad daylight. The men of NSGr 7 flew low in aircraft that were very often slow and always extremely vulnerable to ground fire; their frequent losses in action were compounded by the Western Allies' bombing of their bases. The majority of the Nachtschlachtgruppen fought only on the Eastern Front and were formed expressly to combat Partisans. This was NSGr 7's role from first to last, and Lovro Peršen is the first author to document so thoroughly this neglected area of the war in the air, showing that far from a one-sided fight, this was a highly dangerous assignment for the aircrews involved.

Introduction

Ante Pavelić in the Croatian Parliament in April 1942. (Peršen)

Hitler and Nazi Germany's allies attacked the Kingdom of Yugoslavia on 6 April 1941 and brought it to its knees in several days. Yugoslavia was broken down to several occupation zones and some parts of the country were directly adhered to Bulgaria, Germany, Hungary, and Italy. On the territory that is today Croatia, Bosnia, and Herzegovina, and parts of Vojvodina, the puppet Independent State of Croatia (NDH) was created by Hitler and Mussolini. NDH was commanded by the Fascist regime of the Ustasha political movement led by Ante Pavelić.

Each of the two main Axis forces kept some military units of secondary importance, with a minimum of air power, while the NDH was to build an army and air force to suppress possible resistance within its borders. Two months after the crushing of Yugoslavia, the first organized anti-fascist military unit in the territory of Yugoslavia was created near Sisak, South of Zagreb, on 22 June 1941. The Sisak Partisan Detachment, as it was named, started its armed struggle immediately, followed two weeks later by an uprising in Serbia that was brutally crushed by German and quisling Serbian forces. After the collapse of rebellion in Serbia and the local strength of the Chetniks, it was impossible for Tito to raise the number of his Partisans and gain wide national support in Serbia for his cause at that time. He switched his operations towards the territory of the Independent State of Croatia (NDH), especially in the area that is today Bosnia and Herzegovina, and by the end of 1941, constant harassment by Tito's forces made the German and Italian commands engage more inadequately trained and equipped forces on heavy and unknown terrain. In early 1942, the National Liberation Army and Partisan Detachments of Yugoslavia (NLAPDY), under Tito's leadership, put the main accent of their

Luftwaffe parade in Zagreb on 5 April 1942. (Peršen)

operations in East Bosnia and Herzegovina, and this growing force kept on pushing their actions further to western Bosnia and Herzegovina and Croatia.

Since the end of 1941, the German army stationed in the Independent State of Croatia had been asking the Oberkommando der Luftwaffe for air support in its anti-guerrilla operations. These repeated requests were successfully resisted until 1942. The German military historian of the SE command, E. Wisshaupt, states that on the basis of a request from the Wehrmacht CO of the SE front, the commander of the Luftwaffe agreed on 1 August to form combat detachments from schools already stationed in Zagreb and Zemun, so they could "be engaged in the ground battles using machine guns." (Wisshaupt is referring to FFS A/B 123, stationed in Zagreb since 10 May 1941; and BFS5, stationed in Zemun since 31 May 1941.)

This fighting detachment was disbanded on 4 August because "there are not enough adequate targets" and the aircraft were reintegrated into the schools mentioned above, exclusively in the training role.

Later that month, X. Fliegerkorps received another request, but this was refused with the approval of Oberkommando der Luftwaffe on the pretext that they did not have enough aircraft because of their tasks in the Mediterranean and North Africa.

Meanwhile, a paradoxical situation existed on NDH territory that was creating the context for the creation of an anti-Partisan unit. The Croatian Ustasha and the Home Guard (Domobran) army fought other ethnic Croatians and Serbs among the Partisans, as well as the Chetniks. Serbs from Chetnik units fought Croatians and Serbs in the Partisans and Croatians of the regime. The Germans and Italians fought Partisans, and the Germans from 1943 tried to dismantle the Chetniks. The Ustasha regime didn't like Italians. Germans and Italians did not like Croatians and disliked the Chetniks even more. The Allies, especially Great Britain, were providing aid to Chetniks to fight their other ally Tito until mid-1943, when they provided aid exclusively to Tito to fight the Chetniks, among others, as it was proven that the Chetniks were dealing with the Germans and Italians. In 1945, Ustasha, Chetniks, and Germans fought systematically shoulder to shoulder against Partisans.

Tito saw his chance to succeed in this melting pot. By fighting in Bosnia and Herzegovina and Croatia, he attracted many Serbs from Croatia and Croatians opposed to the NDH regime to join his units. With the aid of the USA, UK, and Soviet Union, Tito won the war.

Chapter One: Störkampfstaffel Kroatien

As part of the response to the Wehrmacht's demands, in November or December 1942, it was decided to create Störkampfstaffel Luftwaffenstab Kroatien in Zagreb with aerodromes in Zalužani, near Banja Luka, and Sarajevo. In some sources, this unit can be found as Einsatzstaffel Fliegerführer Kroatien, but it is certain that this refers to the same formation.

Group photo of the Störkampfstaffel Kroatien in Sarajevo in the spring of 1943. Note the official headgear of the Muslim fez similar to that of 13 Waffen SS division "Handschar." This is the only Luftwaffe unit that wore this hat as part of its uniform. (Peršen)

There are indications that the Luftwaffe conducted ground attacks earlier in 1942 with He 46 aircraft, and Mikić, in his book about German aviation in Yugoslavia, attributes these actions to FFS A/B 123. It is impossible to confirm this from the available flight log books and archive materials from FFS A/B 123. It is known that during the "Battle of Kozara" in 1942, some He 46s and/or Hs 126s made sorties from Borongaj aerodrome against the Partisans, but is hard to establish which units these machines belonged to. The newly-formed Staffel would became one of the most important Luftwaffe units in the Wehrmacht's continuing struggle to break down Tito's war effort and his Partisan "army" in NDH (and beyond). There is very little information about the early days of this unit, except that it was equipped with Heinkel He 46 and Henschel Hs 126 aircraft. Its main task was harassment of Partisan forces, daily reconnaissance, support of the ground troops, and to pinpoint anti-Partisan operations. This would not change for the rest of the war.

Rajlovac aerodrome as seen on 15 September 1942. In front is a Croatian Blenheim Mk I and a Croatian Do 17K-1 with Gnome Rhône engines. (Raguž)

Hauptmann Buss (right) with an unknown Luftwaffe officer at Rajlovac aerodrome. Buss is wearing the Croatian pilot's insignia below the German one. In the background is He 46 "White 6" of the Störkampfstaffel Kroatien (left) and an Hs 126 (right) of NASt Kroatien. (Peršen)

On 21 January 1943, German aircraft were used intensively in armed reconnaissance of the hills around Bosanski Petrovac, where Partisans were clashing with Axis forces. Exactly one month later, one Hs 126 attacked a railway transport that contained wounded Partisans and staff of the Petrovac Partisan hospital.

Again on 14 March, a few He 46s were engaged in Operation Fall Weiss (Case White), attacking retreating Partisan columns in the area between Jablanica, on the river Neretva, and lake Boračko, South of Konjic in Bosnia and Herzegovina. Fall Weiss was an Axis plan in three phases (starting on 20 March) to destroy Partisan forces in Bosnia and Herzegovina throughout two months of intensive fighting.

Some historians argue that Fall Weiss, the so-called Battle of the Neretva in Yugoslav historiography, was a German attempt to destroy Chetnik formations while also inflicting heavy casualties on the Partisans. Hitler issued the order for the Chetniks to be disarmed, fearing they would change sides should the Allies land on the Adriatic shore. The issue here was that Chetniks were directly supported by the Italians and could not be openly disarmed by the Germans without causing a dispute between the two Axis allies. For that purpose, Germans let the Partisans pass over the Neretva river, so the majority of the Partisan forces were able to withdraw to the east bank, which was held by Chetniks, and there the Partisans entered into a frontal clash with them. Hoping that exactly this would happen, the Germans channelled the retreat of Tito's forces straight toward the main Chetnik forces while the Luftwaffe and Croatian Air Force did not touch the bridge nor retreating columns in the last phase of the battle. There is also speculation that Tito and the German HQ agreed that air power should not touch the bridge over Neretva because at the same time Tito ordered the Slavonian Partisans not to touch the Zagreb-Beograd (Belgrade) railway, which was the artery for German survival in Greece and the Balkans as a whole.

A day later, on 15 March, Störkampfstaffel Kroatien was officially transferred to the Independent State of Croatia, with its first base at Sarajevo. It is quite possible that parts of the Staffel were operating in Croatia as early as December 1942. The Staffel had been formed earlier that month from KBS 3 Tutow, but was based in Schwerin (both small cities in North Germany), with Hptm. Heinz Buss as its first Staffelkapitän.

Its first strength report can be found for 20 March, when the unit reported a paper strength of 16 Heinkel He 46 aircraft, while actual field strength was nine, of which eight were serviceable.

Group photo of the men of Fliegerführer Kroatien in 1942. (Peršen)

On 26 March 1943, Generalleutnant Wolfgang von Chamier-Glisczinski was moved to Zagreb from his post of commander of the Große Kampffliegerschule (KampfBeobachterschule 3—KBS3) in Tutow, to become commander of the Fliegerführer Kroatien. Fliegerführer Kroatien (Feldpost 52466) was a small formation composed of:

- one Staffel of Ju 88 of the Einsatzkampfgruppe Ju 88/General der Fliegerausbildungs (Eins. KGr. Ju 88/Gen. d. Fl. Ausb.), based in Zemun,

- IV.(Erg.)/StG 3,
- 15. (Kroat.)/KG 53, using Dornier Do 17s at Pleso near Zagreb,
- NASt Kroatien, equipped with Hs 126s at Borongaj aerodrome with different detachments during the war,
- and Störkampfstaffel Kroatien, with several He 46s at Zalužani aerodrome. The latter was headed at the time by Hptm. Heinz Buss, who was awarded the Medal of Poglavnik Ante Pavelić for Bravery (Kolajna poglavnika Ante Pavelića za hrabrost) the day after creation of Fliegerführer Kroatien.

The Heinkel He 46 which, in its variants C and D, was the unit's main aircraft from its very beginnings, was a parasol-winged aircraft of mixed construction equipped with a nine-cylinder, single-row, air-cooled Siemens-Halske SAM 22 B3 engine of 592hp at take-off. This engine was denominated later to the Bramo 322 series, of which most common variants used on the He 46 were the B1 and J1. This engine gave an operational ceiling of 6,000 meters (19,685 feet) and a maximum speed of 250kph (155mph). Fully armed and loaded, the aircraft attained a far lower speed. The He 46 was armed with one MG 15 7.92mm machine gun in the observer's position and it could carry up to ten SD 10[1] bombs or an equivalent weight of SD 2[2] bombs on the rails, or using container dispensers.

Generalleutnant Wolfgang von Chamier-Glisczinski in Sarajevo in 1943. In the background is an Hs 126, probably of NASt Kroatien, which cooperated closely with Störkampfstaffel Kroatien and from which later Second Staffel of NSGr 7 was formed. (Peršen)

The unit's first recorded loss was He 46 WNr. 403, coded VF+UC (100% damage), which crashed near Bosanski Petrovac on 11 April 1943. In Croatian archive material, the unit was referred to as Störkampfstaffel Banja Luka. The pilot, Ogefr. Heinz Rennberg, and Gefr. Josef Hansen, his Beobachter, were both killed.

From the end of March to 20 April, the Staffel on average disposed of nine operational He 46 aircraft from the nine on strength.[3] On the last day of April, the Staffel was already at almost full establishment strength with 15 out of 16 Heinkels, 12 of them operational.

As already stated, daily activities consisted of harassment of Tito's growing forces and reconnaissance for the Army. Sometimes these aircraft were used on supply missions to encircled Axis garrisons together with obsolete Croatian Air Force (ZNDH) aircraft. On 22 May 1943, Störkampfstaffel Kroatien lost another of its He 46s (WNr. 339), which crashed in Central Bosnia and Herzegovina at an unknown location with damage estimated at 80%. Pilot Uffz. Erich Kaldyik and Beobachter Gefr. Edmund Elei (elsewhere named as Uffz. Erich Kaleyt and Gefr. Edmund Klei) were wounded (according to some sources they were killed). Another Heinkel (WNr. 331) was badly damaged (60%[4]) at Rajlovac aerodrome when the landing gear collapsed on landing after a mission. The crew survived the accident but were hurt. Dr. Möller's research materials indicate that this He 46 was damaged 100%.

He 46 WNr. 331 in flight over Bosnia and Herzegovina in 1943. (Predoević)

While attacking Partisans in Eastern Bosnia and Herzegovina on the last day of May 1943, He 46 WNr. 12 was hit by small arms fire and crashed NW of the village Ustikolina; Uffz. Hermann Caspers was killed.

The strength of the Störkampfstaffel Kroatien from May to June 1943 was as follows:

Date	Total/on number (operational)	Type
10.05.1943	16/15(11)	He 46
20.05.1943	16/15(11)	He 46
31.05.1943	16/13(9)	He 46
10.06.1943	16/11(10)	He 46

Four photos of Hptm. Buss and his men inside their barracks at Rajlovac aerodrome near Sarajevo, playing Skat. These almost idyllic photos were probably taken in the summer of 1943. Many of these aviators will not live long enough to see the end of the war. (Predoević)

Four photos of Hptm. (Continued)

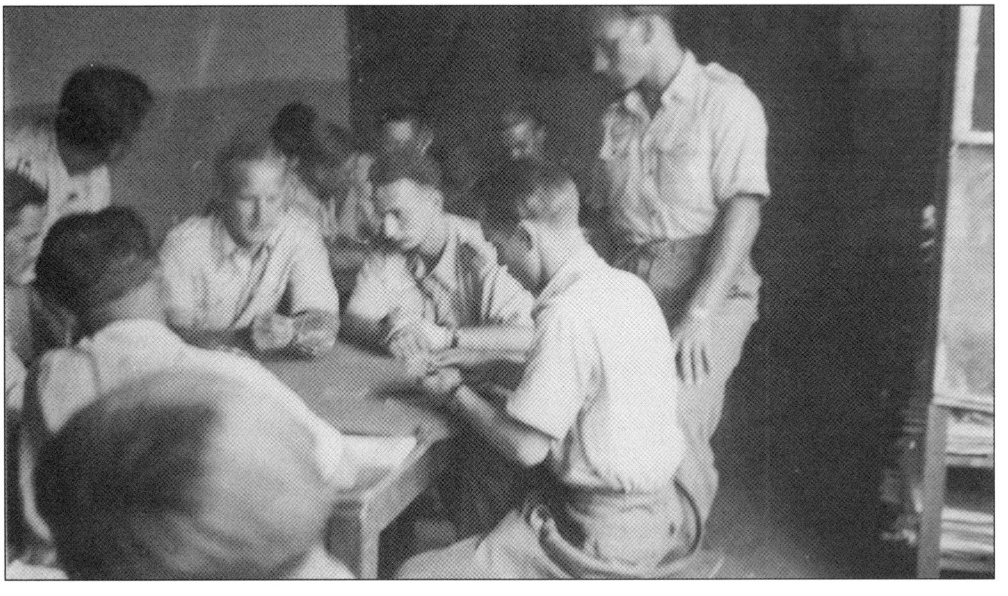

Chapter Two: Störkampfstaffel Südost

At the beginning of June 1943, Störkampfstaffel Kroatien was redesignated Störkampfstaffel Südost (Feldpostnummer L53512) or 1. Störkampfstaffel Südost, and Hptm. Buss kept his position as Staffelkapitän. His Flugbuch for Störkampfstaffel Südost starts on 21 June 1943. Between 15 May and 16 June German, Italian, Ustasha, and Chetnik forces tried to surround and destroy Partisans in Eastern Bosnia and Herzegovina. Operation Schwarz (Black), as the Germans called it, was yet another attempt to crush the Partisans, who had managed to escape and withdraw to the mountains of Montenegro during Fall Weiss, and was its logical continuation. For this operation, the Germans assembled a force of 160 aircraft that pounded the retreating Partisans.

Pilots of 1. Störkampfstaffel Südost in Banja Luka, 1943. (Peršen)

On a sunny 20 May, the Luftwaffe conducted 27 bombing and strafing sorties, mostly attacking inhabited villages in front of the SS "Prinz Eugen" division spearhead. One of the attacks resulted in a direct hit on a Partisan ammunition depot, which blew up. German attacks intensified and two days after, despite the rain and low clouds, German aircraft carried out 39 sorties concentrated on the Tara river canyon. After morning reconnaissance, bombardment of both sides of the Tara river continued the next day with a total of 46 sorties reported. On 26 May, aircraft bombarded Partisans in support of the 118. Jäger-Division with 75 combat flights. The following day the weather deteriorated, so that only 13 sorties were flown, mainly along the 118. Jäger-Division's line of advance. Further deterioration of the weather on 28 May meant that only nine flights were made in the Gradac area, where 369. (Kroatische) Infanterie-Division/"Teufels-Division" (369th Croatian Infantry Division, "The Devil's Division") was battling stubborn resistance from Tito's forces. Two days later, on 30 May, meteorological conditions ameliorated and more sorties were flown. Summary reports give the day's total as 10 armed recce, two supply, and 24 bombardment sorties. The Heinkels' flights were concentrated on the area Gradac - Žabljak - Dobri Do,[5] in which Partisan troop concentrations and inhabited places were targeted.

Rajlovac aerodrome in spring/summer of 1943. Three Do 17Z-1s of 15. (Kroat.)/KG 53—note the coat of arms of the unit under the cockpit. The aircraft in the middle is coded A1+SZ—this is the only known photo of it—while behind it is A1+OZ or CZ. The Ju 52 under repair is marked ??+PU and could be the unit's transport aircraft. In the right corner is an Hs 126 of NASt Kroatien. (Peršen)

During the battle of the Sutjeska river (operation Schwarz), the commander of the 3rd Krajiška Brigade (3. krajiška brigada), Nikola Karanović, wrote in his diary for 7 June 1943:

> This march is harder and more exhausting than any other because of its length and the general fatigue of the combatants, as well as because of the mountainous terrain. Harder than anything was enemy aviation, which was present in the sky throughout the second day of the march. It bombarded our columns that were marching through the open terrain, but also the ones that were marching through the woods, causing casualties among them. The sky was full of different types, from black Stukas which were diving on our columns with a terrifying sound of sirens and delivering their deadly load, to Dornier, Messerschmitt, and Storch types. I don't remember that we were followed and attacked earlier by so many aircraft. From numerous explosions and shooting, everything around us is boiling and shaking like in hell. We are in a hurry, and this rush of ours looks to me like crawling.[6]

On 9 June, other Luftwaffe and Croatian Air Force units, including Dornier Do 17s of 15.(Kroat.)/KG 53, Ju 87s of IV.(Erg.)/StG and Heinkels of Störkampfstaffel Südost, attacked the Sutjeska river valley and Ozren mountain in several waves. The first attacks made early in the morning were on the elite 4th Proletarian Brigade, and during these the brigade's CO, Vasilije Vako Đurović, was killed.

Aircraft of Störkampfstaffel Südost in flight over Bosnia and Herzegovina. First Heinkel 46 is WNr. 331. Its code is partially visible as +IN. (Predoević)

The most horrible day for the groups of Partisan wounded was 9 June, when their columns and the Piva River crossing came under attack by German aviation. Partisan officer Obrad Cicmil, who was there, wrote: "...then aviation and artillery attacked. Wounded and their bearers were often directly hit by the shells and bombs. Everything was torn up in pieces and flying through the air: arms, legs, crutches, stretchers, and rags. Falling back, many of these things stuck in the branches of the trees."[7]

Savo Burić, Commander of the 3rd Division (Treća divizija), had these impressions: "All day, almost without a break, the river crossings were under air attack. Bombs were falling in the river bed and on the banks of the canyon. Many combatants were injured by direct explosions and broken stone, especially the wounded and Partisans with typhus."[8] Later that day, the same units bombarded the heights of Mount Ozren, where Tito and his HQ were positioned east of the peak. During the bombardment by Luftwaffe aircraft, one bomb fell near Tito. He tried to take cover behind a tree when the attack started, but was hit above the elbow by a piece of shrapnel from a bomb. Several people were killed during this attack, among them Tito's adjutant, Đuro Vujović Španac, the British liaison officer to Tito's HQ, Capt. Bill Stewart, and several Partisans from the HQ battalion. Tito's German shepherd, which was near him, was killed too. Besides these events, Axis planes managed to destroy an improvised bridge over the Sutjeska and a mortar position. Altogether, in a probably incomplete report, the Luftwaffe reported six bomber and four recce sorties for the day, besides two on supply and two for medevac. Several Luftwaffe aircraft were damaged by strong AA fire.

The next day, 10 June, bombs continued to fall on seven Partisan brigades of the 1st and 2nd Proletarian Divisions that were pushed into the small area Lučke Kolibe, on Mount Zelengora. As a result, losses among Partisans were very high.

The Commander of the Partisan 2nd Proletarian Brigade (2. Proleterska brigada) wrote in his diary: "All day aviation is heavily bombarding the tight space we are in. The Germans are persistently attacking. They occupied Ljubin Grob. Psychosis is very heavy. There is a specially heavy situation among the wounded. It is the longest day since the beginning of the fighting. Aircraft are causing casualties to the 4th Brigade and among the wounded. Comrade Stari (eng. Old) is wounded in the arm."[9]

A Heinkel He 46 coded B?+O?, of Störkampfstaffel Südost in 1943. (Predoević)

On 10 June, He 46 WNr. 394 was hit by small arms fire, later crashing and exploding near the village of Vrbnica, near Tjentište, on the Sutjeska river.[10] Pilot Gefr. Heinrich Fuchs and Beobachter Gefr. Helmut Gödecke were burned in the wreckage of their aircraft. According to Vladimir Dedijer's[11] war diary, this plane was shot down by Dragoljub Stojić, commander of the auxiliary weapons platoon of the 2nd Proletarian Brigade. Allegedly he dismounted the machine gun from the crashed Heinkel and continued to shoot at other Luftwaffe aircraft.

Three days later, 48 combat and eight recce sorties were flown by the Luftwaffe. The 369. (Kroatische) Infanterie-Division was involved in heavy fighting with the Partisans. With the 369th Division unable to penetrate Partisan lines, the Luftwaffe attacked positions in front of it in support of its efforts. Luftwaffe airmen reported high casualties in men and animals among the Partisan forces. Aircraft also observed a direct hit on the Partisan ammunition dump, which resulted in an immense explosion and columns of smoke rising into the sky.

According to Yugoslavian sources, the estimated number of Partisan casualties in the operation was between 6,300 and 7,800, while German sources state Partisan losses at 11,000 soldiers out of a total strength of around 19,500 on the eve of the battle. It is interesting that not a single Partisan was captured by Axis forces during operation Schwartz, or, more accurately, did not survive capture.

A Do 17Z-1 of 15. (Kroat.)/KG 53 camouflaged at Zemun aerodrome in the summer of 1943. This unit was stationed here only during the "battle of Sutjeska," when Tito was wounded by shrapnel from a bomb. (Peršen)

Staffelkapitän Heinz Buss's favorite Heinkel, PR+NM White 1, at Banja Luka airfield. The second Heinkel is CQ+HP White 2. Note the rails for the SD 2 bombs. (Peršen)

Overall, during Operation Schwarz the Luftwaffe made 1,300 sorties during the 32 days of the offensive, while ZNDH added another 700.

On 15 June, the German air force was supporting the SS Division "Prinz Eugen" and the Brandenburg Division on Zelengora mountain in clashes with Partisan forces.

On 28 June, Hptm. Buss made three armed reconnaissance flights from Rajlovac in an He 46 coded PR+NM: from 10:50–12:05; from 13:15–14:05; and from 18:50–19:45. Next day, he flew the same aircraft to Banja Luka at 09:10, landing there at 09:55. He came back to Rajlovac the same day, starting from Zalužani at 16:15 and landing at Rajlovac at 17:05. June 30th was very busy for Buss, as he made no fewer than six sorties with PR+NM, and on the seventh sortie he flew an He 46D coded CW+AW. Sorties started early in the morning at 08:50 and landing at 10:10, while his last flight was at 19:40 with a landing at 20:15. Next day, he flew CW+AW for 40 minutes from 12:05.

Heinkel He 46 coded PR+NM (White 1) taking off from Rajlovac in 1943. (Predoević)

Two days later, Buss was again in the air for half an hour starting at 18:40 from Rajlovac aboard He 46 PR+NM. The Staffelkapitän flew two types of aircraft on 4 July. His first flight of the day was a Fiesler Fi 156 PO+AL (WNr. 601) both ways between the Sarajevo aerodromes Rajlovac and Butmir. Later in the evening, he flew Heinkel PR+NM, taking off and landing from the same airfields. It seems that the flight back from Butmir to Rajlovac was a direct one with no activities against the enemy, as it lasted only seven minutes.

Next day, the same Storch was flown on a reconnaissance sortie to Banja Luka, leaving Rajlovac at 12:50. Buss returned to Rajlovac at 19:00, being among his men in Banja Luka for three hours and 40 minutes. Flight log entries 21 to 34 were made on Fiesler Fi 156 PO+AL at Rajlovac airfield from 2:30 to 3:40 hours, with durations of three to six minutes. They involved five different copilots and seem to be some kind of familiarization or training flights.

On 7 July, a test flight was made in Storch PO+AL from Rajlovac to Zalužani, lasting 3 hours and 7 minutes. On 8 July, Hptm. Buss was in Banja Luka. There he flew four sorties in PO+AL and was back at Rajlovac on 9 July at 10:45 aboard He 46 PR+NM. In his Flugbuch, this sortie is described as a test flight. Next day, he flew a combat sortie in the same Heinkel that lasted 1 hour and 20 minutes.

Between 22 and 24 July, the StaKa flew his favorite Heinkel (PR+NM) five times on sorties against Partisans in Bosnia and Herzegovina. He accumulated 5 hours and 55 minutes of combat flights, undertaking all these missions from Sarajevo. After one day without activities

A rare view of complete installations of the Rajlovac aerodrome in 1943, seen from an He 46. (Peršen)

Three Heinkel aircraft at Rajlovac. The one with the tail number White 4 is being armed with SD 2 bombs. (Predoević)

he was in the air again on 26 July. Four more combat sorties were added to his account by 28 July, three of them flown in PR+NM and one aboard an Fi 156 coded GF+YN, all from Rajlovac. Another aircraft was lost on 27 July, during a combat sortie near Podgar,[12] in Bosnia and Herzegovina. This was Heinkel He 46D (WNr. 33, CW+AW), whose engine failed and whose crew was obliged to make an emergency landing. The aircraft was 70% damaged and was written off. Both the pilot, Ogefr. Kurt Ilker, and his observer, Gefr. Erwin Weiser, were injured. Over the next five days Buss made test flights from Banja Luka to Sarajevo and back.

The Grand Mufti of Jerusalem, Muhammad Amina al Husayni, visits Rajlovac at the beginning of April 1943. In the background are three Dornier Do 17K and E of the Croatian Air Force. Most of the Croatian Dorniers were destroyed in a Partisan attack on 10 August 1943. The first Dornier in the photo is probably ZNDH, registration 0313, from the 13th Squadron of the 5th Air Base, which defected with its crew to the Partisans on 17 November 1943. This aircraft was later destroyed by a Hs 126 of 2./NSGr 7 at Livno airfield when Partisan commander Ivo Lola Ribar lost his life. (Peršen)

On 10 August 1943, Partisan 1st Krajiška Brigade attacked Rajlovac airfield near Sarajevo, causing havoc among the German and Croatian planes. Around 21:00 hours, the aerodrome crew was informed by the local population that a Partisan attack on the base was imminent. At that time protection of the aerodrome consisted of 240 German soldiers with 14 machine guns and 450 Croatian soldiers with 32 machine guns. These forces were supported by 12 mortars and one crew with an AA gun. Around 110 German soldiers were positioned on the peaks outside of the base due to the configuration of the terrain. The 1st Krajiška Brigade attacked at its full strength of around 1,000 Partisans at 22:00 and the 369. (Kroatische) Infanterie-Division "Teufels-Division" was in charge of reinforcing the airfield's defenses in case of such an attack. The Divisional HQ was only alerted at around 22:40, and the first reinforcements arrived around 23:30, when the 1st Krajiška Brigade withdrew leaving chaos, fire, and smoke at the aerodrome.

At the time of the attack, Störkampfstaffel Südost had at least seven He 46 aircraft and about 40 men at Rajlovac. Hptm. Buss organized his men, who fiercely defended their aircraft against several Partisan attacks, including using the machine guns mounted on their Heinkels. The Störkampfstaffel lost one man, but all the aircraft were intact, although other Luftwaffe and ZNDH units suffered heavily. The 1st Krajiška Brigade had six dead and six seriously and two slightly wounded men. Gefr. Horst Wagner, observer and gunner, was the unit's only loss, and he was buried in a Sarajevo cemetery. In order to destroy aircraft, the Partisans mostly used Molotov cocktails to cause fires. While the report of the 1st Krajiška Brigade stated that in this attack they destroyed 30 aircraft, the true number was smaller, but nonetheless tragic. The Luftwaffe lost one Do 17Z-3 (WNr. 3478) belonging to 15. (Kroat.)/KG 53; Junkers W 34 WNr. 3195, belonging to Verb.St. 58 (based in Zagreb); two Junkers Ju 52s belonging to FFS C. 1, namely WNr. 539 and 555; and another Ju 52 of an unknown unit and WNr.

This photo gives a good overview of ground installations at Rajlovac just before Partisan attack in August. In the foreground, a Croatian Air Force Do 17E coded 0319 which had crash landed there on 4 July 1943 with its crew: pilot Sergeant Luka Kirola, observer Pilot Officer Drvodelić, radio Corporal Krhatlić, and mechanic Leading Aircraftman Ugarković. Note a "spot" on the left wing which is over-painting of the earlier German cross and can be found on many Croatian aircraft of German origin, as Croatian aircraft had their coat of arms on the right wing only. (Raguž)

One of two Croatian Blenheim Mk. Is destroyed at Rajlovac on 10 August 1943. Standing on the left is Croatian pilot Tomislav Kralj. (Raguž)

The Croatian Air Force lost 10 of their Dornier Do 17s (coded 0305, 0306, 0308, 0321, 0322, 0323, 0324, 0325, 0327, and 0328) and two Blenheim Mk. Is (coded 1504 and 1508). For the disaster of that night, German General Werner Pfafferott, commander of the German troops in Croatia, blamed the Croatians, who apparently did not put enough effort into defending their aircraft.

Lieutenant General Wolfgang von Chamier-Glisczinski decorating Leutnant Jessat with the Eiserne Kreuz 2nd Class at Rajlovac aerodrome, 1943. (Peršen)

To confirm the rule that disaster does not strike singly, the following day, 11 August, Generalleutnant Wolfgang von Chamier-Glisczinski died in an accident near Sisak when his Ju 52 (coded G6+KS [of 8./TG 4]) entered a storm and crashed. He was returning from an inspection of the Rajlovac aerodrome attack, and besides him ten more officers of Fliegerführer Kroatien and crew members were killed. He was replaced by Generalleutnant Wolfgang Erdmann on 26 August as commanding officer of Fliegerführer Kroatien.

The strength of the unit around the dates of attack was as follows:

10.08.1943 .... 16/11(8) .... He 46
12.08.1943 .... 16/7(?) .... He 46

On 12 August, the Staffel was still based in Rajlovac with 40 people on strength. The next day, Hptm. Buss flew one of his only two combat sorties of the month, piloting an He 46 coded SA+HW on his 67th mission since joining the unit. On 22 August, he flew Heinkel CA+CI for 75 minutes against Partisans in Bosnia and Herzegovina.

During the last few days of August, Störkampfstaffel Südost lost two more He 46 aircraft. The first was WNr. 732, which was lost near Bihać on the 29th due to Partisan small arms fire. It seems that its Beobachter was from the Croatian Air Force and was wounded, while the plane was damaged 70% during the ensuing crash landing. The same day, another German aircraft was damaged by small arms fire from the ground, but no other information is available on this event. The second Heinkel (WNr. 510) was lost two days later when it force landed

Aerial view of Rajlovac aerodrome from one of the unit's He 46s. On the right-hand side is an Hs 126 and He 46 White 3 coded BB+CI; more unidentified aircraft are parked in front of the hangar with open doors. (Peršen)

Lieutenant General Wolfgang von Chamier-Glisczinski, holder of the Ritterkreuz and Commanding Officer of Fliegerführer Kroatien (Südost), decorating Hauptmann Heinz Buss with the Eiserne Kreuz 1st Class at Rajlovac, 1943. (Peršen)

after being damaged by AA fire. According to a report of the Podgrmeč Partisan detachment, it was shot down by the members of 2nd Batallion and crashed near the school in the village of Hadrovci. All four crew members of both planes came back on foot to their own troops unharmed. Due to unknown causes, another Heinkel was lost on 2 September, crashing to the ground and burning near Bihać, in the area Prijeboj—Poljanak. One crew member was killed and the other wounded. According to a report from the HQ of the 8th Partisan Division, Partisans from 2nd and 4th Batallion of the 1st Brigade shot down this Heinkel with small arms fire. Before it was shot down, the Luftwaffe aircraft managed to bombard the Partisans; one of them was killed and two more were wounded during the attack.

The German Army in the Independent State of Croatia (as well as the Partisans) began preparing for Italy's eventual capitulation and withdrawal from the war well before this actually happened on 8 September 1943. With this in mind, the German army, in collaboration with Flughafenbereich (Aerodrome Regional Command) Zagreb 6/XVII, entered Zadar before the capitulation. On 28 August 1943, the Germans prepared an auxiliary airfield in Škabrnja, near Zadar, in case Luftwaffe intervention was needed. Some days later, on 10 September, a German-reinforced motorized battalion entered Zemunik aerodrome and occupied it without resistance. Zemunik would became a very important base for detachments of NSGr 7 in its struggle against the Partisans. A day later, Luftwaffe attacks on Dubrovnik were noted at 16:00 and 18:00 hours, but without details of the participating units; only that bombs were used and one ship was sunk, while an Italian torpedo boat marked T-8 was damaged and its crew perished. Italian sources report that the attackers flew Ju 87 dive bombers.

Men of the Störkampfstaffel Südost at Rajlovac aerodrome in 1943. (Predoević)

After Italy capitulated, the Partisans moved quickly to Split and held it for several days. During the German recapture of Split on 26 and 27 September, besides the Ju 87 several He 46s provided ground support to German and Croatian forces attacking Partisan units around Mount Klis. By the end of September, the Germans had managed to secure the Dalmatian coast and disarm more than 30,000 Italian soldiers stationed there. There are several Partisan reports in which it is said that aviation was constantly attacking them during the operations around Split. On 21 September, the 1st Proletarian Assault Division (1. Prva proleterska udarna divizija), preparing for attack on Sinj and Dicmo, near Split, was a victim of numerous air assaults. Next day, the 3rd Proletarian krajiška brigade (3. Proleterska krajiška brigada) was attacked by aircraft in the vicinity of Sinj. There was an auxiliary airstrip at Sinj that the Germans used to transport men of the Prinz Eugen SS division from Mostar by three-engined aircraft from 9 September onwards.

On 25 September, another He 46 was lost between Kupinečki Kraljevec and Zdenčina, SE of Zagreb, around 17:00 hours. This Heinkel (WNr. 882) was hit by small arms fire and made a forced landing; its crew was saved, though injured, but Partisans looted the plane and set it ablaze. Pilot Ogefr. Peter Schmidt was treated in the infirmary in Banja Luka, while Ogefr. Karl Heinz Lorenz died from his injures there and is buried in Banja Luka cemetery.

On 29 September, Oblt. Willy Rümmelin, Technical Officer of NASt Kroatien, was named Staffelkapitän of the newly-created 2. Störkampfstaffel Südost, which was to become the second Staffel of the new Nachtschlachtgruppe. The base of the newly-formed unit was Banja Luka (Zalužani airfield), and its Feldpost number was L 54364.[13]

Wing of He 46 E-2 coded BB+CI (White 3) being loaded on an Opel Blitz truck after a forced landing in the vicinity of Banja Luka, 1943. (Peršen)

Known bases of Störkampfstaffel Südost include the following:

xx.03.1943 - 15.03.1943 .... Schwerin, Germany
15.03.1943 - 22.03.1943 .... Sarajevo
22.03.1943 - xx.05.1943 .... Banja Luka
xx.05.1943 - 23.08.1943 .... Sarajevo-Rajlovac (10km [6.2 miles] West of the city)
xx.05.1943 - 26.08.1943 .... Sarajevo and Banja Luka
23.08.1943 - 22.09.1943 .... Banja Luka
26.08.1943 - 10.10.1943 .... Zagreb
27.09.1943 - 10.10.1943 .... Zagreb

Formation of He 46s over Bosnia and Herzegovina in 1943. Although outdated, the He 46 proved very useful against Tito's forces. (Predoević)

Pilot of Störkampfstaffel Südost in front of his He 46 at Rajlovac aerodrome in 1943. (Predoević)

Between 22 September and the renaming of his unit on 10 October 1943, Staffelkapitän Buss flew various different Heinkels from Borongaj against Partisans in Croatia. In total, twelve more combat sorties and two test flights were made in this period; he was flying the "usual suspect" He 46 PR+NM, as well as CQ+HP, DB+ZC, DB+AO, CN+HJ, and PR+NL.

In order to reinforce the unit, the Luftwaffe withdrew pilots and Heinkels from 1./ Störkampfgruppe Luftflotte 4, sending them to the area which was becoming more and more important, as Tito's forces grew in strength and endangered the rear of the German army in Greece. This growth in Partisan activity, supported by Allied material aid, posed a threat to the supply route carrying vital raw material for the Reich's war industries. Yugoslavia and the Balkans in general are full of metal ores such as bauxite, which Germany did not possess.

From the Flugbuch of Lt. Hermann Gade, it can be clearly seen how reinforcements of Heinkels to the endangered part of Balkans were organized. Lt. Gade was a member of 1./ Störkampfgruppe Luftflotte 4, just like StaKa Buss had been, and this unit was renamed in October 1943 to 1./NSGr. 4.

In the last few days of September, some of the aircraft and the crews of 1./Störkampfgruppe Luftflotte 4 were withdrawn from the Eastern Front, transferring into East Prussia and on through Germany by several stops. Lt. Gade flew his He 46 (1K+CH) to Wien-Aspern on 1 October 1943. Three days later he was airborne, heading from Wien to Zagreb with an intermediate stop in Graz from 12:00 to 14:40 hours. Finally he reached his destination—Zagreb—at 15:40, after exactly one hour's flight from Graz.

His first combat sorties on the new battleground were made using the Heinkels of 1./ Störkampfgruppe Luftflotte 4 from Borongaj aerodrome; the aircraft still bore their old unit codes (Verbandskennzeichen). Lt. Gade flew Heinkel 46 1K+CH at 11:40 for 80 minutes and 1K+EH at 16:35 for 70 minutes on 6 October. Next day, he flew a "native" Störkampfstaffel Südost He 46 coded BB+CI for 75 minutes, taking off from Borongaj at 16:00 hours. On 8 October, he added two more combat sorties to his account, flying SA+HW and 1K+EH and landing in Zagreb at 12:15 after 105 minutes and 17:40 after a 70-minute flight, respectively. On the first mission his observer was Gefr. Reischle, while on the second it was Fw. Ernst.

Group photo of Störkampfstaffel Südost men in spring or early summer 1943 at Rajlovac aerodrome. (Peršen)

Just before the official re-designation of Störkampfstaffel Südost to NSGr 7, in the first few weeks of October, the unit was operating from Zagreb with detachments in Banja Luka and Rajlovac. Partisan sources mention the use of German aircraft against Partisans:

- on the island of Preko in front of the town of Zadar, two aircraft on 1 October
- in the area of Ludbreg, near Varaždin, on 3 October. In two waves, numerous aircraft attacked the Partisan brigade "Braća Radić" from 11:30 to 13:00 hours. The Partisans ran away from their positions due to the aerial attack, and the positions were overrun by Croatian infantry and tanks. According to Partisan sources, in this attack nine Stukas, seven Dorniers, and ten "school planes"[14] were used. These school planes were probably aircraft from 1./NSGr 7.
- On 5 October, around 17:30 hours, in the area of the city of Varaždin, five aircraft bombarded and attacked Partisans with MG fire.

A series of photos of Störkampfstaffel Südost's 1000th sortie celebration at Rajlovac in July 1943. Hptm. Buss is carried on the backs of his men, while the Heinkel in question is probably PR+NM. On the paper is written "Zum 1000. Feindflug herzlichen. Glueckwunsch!", or: "For the 1000th flight against the enemy. Congratulations!" (Peršen, Predoević)

Störkampfstaffel Südost's 1000th sortie celebration (Continued)

Störkampfstaffel Südost's 1000th sortie celebration (Continued)

Störkampfstaffel Südost's 1000th sortie celebration (Continued)

Störkampfstaffel Südost's 1000th sortie celebration (Continued)

Chapter Three: Aircraft Markings

Markings of the Störkampfstaffel Kroatien and Störkampfstaffel Südost

There was no uniform way of marking the aircraft of Störkampfstaffel Kroatien and Störkampfstaffel Südost, as they received their machines from many other units. For example, He 46 from 1./NSGr. 4 arrived with the 1K+ unit marking and were used with the same code in NSGr 7. Prior to the renaming of Störkampfstaffel Kroatien and Störkampfstaffel Südost to NSGr 7, these Staffeln did not have their own unit code. One will find many different factory codes (Stammkennzeichen) and operational codes (Verbandskennzeichen) in the two units with no connection or obvious logic applied.

As with many other NSGr. units, the aircraft carried a fuselage marking, plus a number on the fin. In NSGr. 2 for example, the fin number corresponded with the individual aircraft code letter, so D3+AH would have "1" on the fin, D3+BH would have "2," and so on.

Both the Störkampfstaffeln in question used this style of marking the aircraft, but again, without any systematic reference to the individual aircraft code letter or fin number, as there often was none. We find for instance that PR+NM had fin number "White 1" (perhaps because it was the Staffelkapitän's machine); CQ+HP had "White 2"; BB+CI "White 3"; and so on as a provisional marking. All the fin numbers had one common characteristic: they were white. Often it can be found that aircraft coming from another unit did not follow the "NSGr. way"; for example, TP+AC from NSGr. 4 was "White 14."

Heinkel He 46D WNr. 735 (coded BO+FX), photographed at Rajlovac aerodrome in December 1943. (Eisenbach)

Markings of NSGr 7 Aircraft

The Group code was 4X. The third letter was the individual code letter for the aircraft (A, B, C, and so on), and this code letter would be in color: the 1st Staffel letter was white, the 2nd Staffel letter was black, and the 3rd Staffel letter was yellow. These 3rd Staffel codes are seen in the photo of the Caproni Ca. 314 4X+BL or profile of the C.R. 42 4X+HL in Chapter six.

The fourth letter represented the Staffel: B for the Stab, H for the 1st Staffel, K for the 2nd Staffel, and L for the 3rd Staffel.

The individual fin number would correspond to the individual aircraft number: A would be 1 in the Staffel color, B would be 2 in the Staffel color. Here are some examples:

4X+AH may be read as: 4X is an aircraft of NSGr 7, AH is the 1st aircraft of the 1st Staffel, and its fin number should be "White 1."

4X+CK may be read as: 4X is an aircraft of NSGr 7, C is the 3rd aircraft of the 2nd Staffel, and its fin number should be "Black 3."

4X+BL may be read as: 4X is an aircraft of NSGr 7, B is the 2nd aircraft of the 3rd Staffel, and its fin number should be "Yellow 2."

From available archive sources, photos, and flying log books, it is apparent that this norm was generally respected, though some exceptions exist, especially in the 1./NSGr 7.

Also, later in this book the aircraft are mostly referred to by their colored fin number, as archive sources, especially for 1944 and 1945, as well as log books, do not state their factory or operational code, but rather their tactical fin number and WNr. Usually they are referred to as "Yellow 12," "Black 9," and so on, with the corresponding factory serial number (WNr.). Though valid, doubt will remain until any new evidence appears, as there is no evidence that the Gruppe abandoned 4X+ style codes, nor that they kept the 4X+ style codes and eventually adopted fighter-style markings. Photos of C.R. 42s in Austria in 1944 and 1945 seen by the author show that these aircraft retained the 4X+ style of marking, but the photos of destroyed Falcos around Zagreb from 1945 do not give a clear answer to this question, as they were cannibalized or heavily damaged.

Respecting the general principle of marking the Gruppe's aircraft, set out below is part of the author's table reconstructing operational codes. It must be emphasized that this is a speculative aid to understanding the fin numbers, and as such assumptions have been avoided elsewhere in this book:

Type Inferred	Verbandskennzeichen	Known WNr.	Known Fin number	Known Affiliation	Remarks
C.R. 42	4X+LH	5623	White 12	1./NSGr 7	Dam. 50% 21.9.1944
C.R. 42	4X+IK	9199	Black 9	2./NSGr 7	Dest. 10.10.1944
C.R. 42	4X+HH	9768	White 8	1./NSGr 7	Dest. 14.10.1944

Chapter Four: Nachtschlachtgruppe 7

Croatian Do 17 burning at Zalužani aerodrome near Banja Luka in 1943. (Peršen)

On 10 October 1943, Nachtschlachtgruppe 7 (NSGr 7) was officially formed in Zagreb. Gruppenkommandeur was Major Theodor Blaich, and his adjutant was possibly Oblt. Shrenz. The Stab section was formed from Stab./Sch.G. 1 with a new Feldpost number (L 53890). Stab./Sch.G. 1 was officially disbanded on 18 October 1943, so it seems that the new unit was not fully equipped until mid-November. Major Blaich took command of the Group, coming from Stab./Fliegerführer Kroatien, and he stayed in this position until 10 September 1944, when he was replaced by Major Klaus Ostermann, who led the unit until it was disbanded on 13 March 1945. Stab./NSGr 7 was originally equipped with Ju 87Ds, subsequently exchanging them for Fiat C.R. 42s in October 1944.

The 1./NSGr 7 was formed from Störkampfstaffel Südost, and the 2./NSGr 7 from parts of Nahaufklärungsstaffel Kroatien, flying Hs 126s and Do 17s—both keeping their existing Feldpost numbers. The 2. Staffel flew these types from the time of its formation until at least 20 December 1943, and possibly even until 10 January 1944, when the first official reports that they were equipped with C.R. 42s can be found. For this period, actions by Do 17s and/or Hs 126s will be included in this book, insofar as the aircraft concerned are not clearly identified by the author's sources as belonging to other units.

Hauptmann Buss in the hangar at Rajlovac with his men in 1943. In the background is an He 46 of the unit. (Peršen)

The Henschel Hs 126 was a parasol wing reconnaissance aircraft liked by its crews for its short take-off and landing abilities and maneuverability, together with its low speed performance. It was powered by a Bramo Fafnir 323 R nine-cylinder, single-row, air-cooled engine; this was a development of the SAM 22 engine from the He 46. It developed 950hp, which allowed a maximum speed of 356kph (221mph), a ceiling of 8,550 meters (28,051ft), and a theoretical range of 1,000km (621 miles). The aircraft was equipped with a Revi C/12 C reflex sight installed in the semi-enclosed pilot's cabin and used in conjunction with the forward-firing synchronized MG 17, 7.92mm machine gun. In the observer's open cockpit was a flexible MG 15 machine gun of the same caliber. A total of 150kg (330.6lbs) of various bombs could be carried, including SD 2, SD 10, SC 50, SD 50, etc., on fuselage and underwing racks. The Hs 126 was equipped with different kinds of cameras, such as the M.G. ESK 2000 (synchronized to the machine guns) and the 20cm photo camera using the FK 30 film cassette for 30 x 30cm images, etc. The aircraft could be used to lay down smoke screens and for that purpose was equipped with the S 200 system fixed on the port side of the fuselage.

Known bases for Stab./NSGr 7 include:

10.10.1943 - 02.06.1944 ....Zagreb, Borongaj
02.06.1944 - xx.11.1944 ....Zagreb-Pleso (10km SE of Zagreb)
21.10.1944 ....Zagreb-Lučko (12km SSW of Zagreb)
xx.11.1944 - xx.01.1945....................Zagreb-Lučko
xx.01.1945 - 04.04.1945 ....Zagreb-Gorica (10km SE of Zagreb)
21.04. & 03.05.1945...........................Zagreb-Gorica (disbandment)

A Dornier Do 17Z-1 of the 2nd Staffel at Banja Luka airfield. (Peršen)

Group strength on 10 October 1943 was:

Unit	Full strength	Available	Operational	Type
Stab	2	0	0	
1 Staffel	20	25	16	He 46 (15/10), Hs 126 (10/6)
2 Staffel	20	18	14	Hs 126 (14/11), Do 17 (4/3)

Hptm. Buss flew his first combat mission after the unit was renamed in He 46 PR+NM from Zagreb for 90 minutes on 12 October. Flying alongside was Lt. Gade in He 46 BB+CI, which took off at 13:35 and landed back at 15:05; his observer was Fw. Ernst. Hptm. Buss landed five minutes before his comrade. Next day, Lt. Gade was again in the air for 105 minutes in the same plane, landing at Borongaj at 12:35.

On 16 October, Lt. Hermann Gade was airborne again, flying He 46 VA+AC from 15:37 to 17:25, and the next day was in the air in the company of Uffz. Karl Nemitz as observer in the same aircraft. They were up for 81 minutes, landing at Borongaj at 11:25. On 16 and 17 October, Croatian and German forces fought Partisans around Varaždin, in NE Croatia, and it is quite possible that these flights were made against Partisans in this area, since they correspond in duration of flight as well as with reports of the 1st Ustasha Transport Brigade that Luftwaffe aircraft engaged Partisans in the area of Lepoglava. Two more sorties were flown by Lt. Gade on 19 October aboard He 46 1K+JH, with Uffz. Keller as observer, and later on another Heinkel (1K+BH), constituting his 934th and 935th missions of the war and his 14th and 15th since operating in Croatia against the Partisans. Again, presumably, these sorties were in the area of Lepoglava, where Partisans were attacked by GP bombs, incendiaries, and machine gun fire.

Men of NSGr 7 at Rajlovac aerodrome in a rare moment of leisure. (Predoević)

The same day, Lt. Gade, with Uffz. Nemitz as observer, flew He 46 PR+NN from Zagreb to Bihać, arriving there at 10:50 hours. After refuelling the aircraft in Bihać, they flew four reconnaissance flights in the area during the day. Their fifth and last sortie of the day was a return to Zagreb at 17:25, after accumulating 2 hours and 34 minutes of flight in less than four hours of their stay in Bihać.

Partisans of the 2nd Brigade reported an attack by one high-winged aircraft with bombs and machine gun fire on 26 October in Margetići, between Sarajevo and Vlasenica, in Bosnia and Herzegovina. Its Command, hospital, and the 4th battalion were the target; two Partisans were wounded and four horses were killed.

A photo of the He 46 of Störkampfstaffel Südost taken against the sun. (Predoević)

The day after his official nomination as Fliegerführer Kroatien, Generalleutnant Wolfgang Erdmann assigned 2./NSGr 7 as aerial support to the 1st Cossack Division[15] during Operation Wildsau (Wild Boar) in Bosnia and Herzegovina. This took place from 26 to 29 October 1943, and aimed to destroy Partisans in the area Tuzla-Zvornik-river Drina. For this purpose, the same command formed Einsatz Kommando Semlin from different units in the area, intended to support the operations of Wehrmacht units as they crossed to the far bank of the Sava river and then to be disbanded. All aircraft and crews from Nahaufklärungsstaffel Kroatien equipped with Hs 126s that had been part of Einsatz Kommando Semlin were ordered to fly to Banja Luka, where they were to be integrated into 2./NSGr 7. Nahaufklärungsstaffel Kroatien never ceased to exist, but parts of it became the 2nd Staffel of Nachtschlachtgruppe 7.

Men of the German 1st Cossack Division in Bosnia and Herzegovina. Cossacks were ruthless towards the civilians; they were "known" for burning villages, raping, and stealing. (Raguž)

For his part, Lt. Gade was again in the air on 21 October, flying He 46 1K+BH South of Zagreb from 10:35 to 12:05. The same afternoon he made another armed recce flight Zagreb-Bihać-Zagreb in Heinkel PR+NN with Uffz. Weiser as observer. They landed in Bihać at 15;48 and were airborne again only 27 minutes later, landing back at Zagreb at 17:25 after spending 142 minutes in the air between the two cities.

Almost immediately after their creation, the unit's Stab and first Staffel were sent to "work" in what is today Slovenia, in support of the 2nd SS Armoured Corps during Operation Wolkenbruch (Cloudburst), aimed at clearing Slovenia of Partisans. This operation was executed in four phases, from 21 October to mid-November 1943.

Group strength on 20 October 1943, on the eve of operation "Wolkenbruch," was:

Unit	Full strength	Available	Operational	Type
Stab	2	0	0	-
1 Staffel	20	25	22	He 46 (16/13), Hs 126 (9/9)
2 Staffel	20	16	10	Hs 126 (13/8), Do 17 (3/2)

He 46 White 14 (TP+AC) of 1./NSGr 7 over Bosnia and Herzegovina in 1943. The photo was taken from another He 46. (Predoević)

Formation of He 46s in flight over Bosnia and Herzegovina in 1943. (Predoević)

On 22 October, Lt. Gade made two reconnaissance flights NE of Zagreb aboard the Heinkel coded 1K+BH. Next day, he flew a combat sortie in an He 46 coded TY+NC. On 25 October, he attacked Partisan positions East of Ribnik, in modern Bosnia and Herzegovina. He landed back at base in Zagreb after a 100-minute flight at 15:40 hours.

On 26 October, Lt. Gade was very active: for the day's first sortie he was flying Heinkel TY+NC from 09:20 on an armed recce mission in the area of Žužemberk, Slovenia, NW of his home base Zagreb. Gade landed back at Zagreb at 11:00, and an hour later he was airborne on a reconnaissance flight SE of Zagreb, flying one of the "old friends" from NSGr. 4, call sign 1K+EH, for 85 minutes. After three hours of rest, his last flight of the day was a reconnaissance mission East of Zagreb for one hour, finally landing his He 46 coded 1K+BH at 17:10 hours.

Next day, Oberkommando Der Luftwaffe communicated its intention to create another Staffel equipped with Caproni Ca. 313 and Ca. 314 aircraft; meanwhile, the 1st Staffel continued intensive flying from Borongaj. The same day, He 46 coded BB+CI, with Lt. Gade at the controls, attacked Partisans 40km (24.85 miles) NE of Zagreb from 16:10 to 17:10. On 28 October, he flew another of the same type coded TY+NC in action 10km (6.2 miles) SE of Karlovac. Staffelkapitän Buss flew a morning combat sortie in Heinkel PR+NM lasting 1 hour 20 minutes. On 29 October, the 1st Staffel recorded several more combat missions. Lt. Gade logged two sorties, the first in the morning from 10:00 to 11:40 hours in Heinkel 1K+BH, 130km (81 miles) ESE of Zagreb, and the second in the afternoon, when several aircraft of the 1st Staffel attacked Partisans around Lepoglava, North of the Croatian capital. This attack took place from 16:03 to 17:00 hours and was led by Hptm. Heinz Buss personally, flying He 46 VA+AC. Buss had also been active that morning, flying PR+NM from 11:05 to 12:25 against an unknown target.

On 30 October, the duo was again in the air; Buss was flying He 46 VA+AC and Gade was in 1K+BH from 10:05. The aircraft were back at Borongaj between 11:05 and 11:10 hours. Lt. Gade was in the air again for 70 minutes during the afternoon. Both flyers continued their

Attacking Partisan positions in Bosnia and Herzegovina with an He 46 in 1943. (Predoević)

activity on the last day of October, but separately: Buss undertook one combat sortie from 14:30 in the same aircraft as the previous day (VA+AC), while his Leutnant was airborne on harassment sorties twice: during the morning commanding Heinkel VH+AC and another (1K+EH) in the afternoon. The last three sorties were against the same target, whose names are identical but not fully legible from Lt. Gade's Flugbuch. As best the author can understand from Gade's handwriting, the target was in the area of Trebnje, in Slovenia.

Group strength on 31 October 1943 was as follows:

Unit	Full strength	Available	Operational	Type
Stab	2	0	0	
1 Staffel	20	19	17	He 46
2 Staffel	20	11	9	Hs 126

On 7 November, an HS 126 of 2./NSGr 7 (WNr. 3371) was brought down by flak near Trogir during an armed recce mission, since heavy fighting between Partisans and Axis forces had continued in Dalmatia since Italy's capitulation. The shot down crew set their aircraft on fire. Later on, another Hs 126 (WNr. 2928) of the same Staffel was damaged during a strafing and bombardment mission and made an emergency landing at Banja Luka airfield. It was damaged 50% and Uffz. Rudolf Fuhr, Bordfunker, was injured. That same day, the German 264th Infantry Division requested support from the Zadar detachment of 1./NSGr 7 for operations on the island of Šolta for 2 and 3 December 1943, against Partisans who had landed there. Lt. Jessat, CO of the detachment, got his instructions about planned actions from Fliegerführer Kroatien even before the request by the 264th Division arrived on his desk. Flying He 46 1K+BH, Lt. Gade made one of his longest missions while flying for 1./NSGr 7; he took off from Borongaj at 11:25, landing back there at 13:25 hours.

Assembly of He 46E-2 BB+CI, WNr. 1234, tail number White 3 near Banja Luka in 1943. (Peršen)

Ultra decrypt CX/MSS/R. 14 (B) includes a communication signed "Feldluftgau-Kommando Zadar" (probably to Flugfuhrer Kroatien), advising that two Fiat Falco (WNr. 5664 and 9198) "are available to pick up." Though incomplete or only partially understandable, this is significant, as it is the first recorded information regarding re-equipment of NSGr 7 with the type. From the message it is not clear where those two aircraft are—at a depot or a specific aerodrome? From later German communications, it can be deduced that Zemunik aerodrome was probably used as a dispatch center for Italian aircraft passing to the Luftwaffe and Croatian Air Force in the region. It seems likely that those two planes belonged to the 2nd Staffel, which was the first element of NSGr 7 to operate the type.

Bosnia and Herzegovina from the perspective of an NSGr 7 pilot. (Predoević)

The Gruppe reported two more losses on 9 and 12 November. The first was He 46 WNr. 160 of 1./NSGr 7, which crash landed East of Zagreb due to an engine malfunction and was damaged 65%. On 12 November, at around 12:30 hours, ten allied fighter bombers attacked the airfield Jasenica, near Mostar. During the attack, 2./NSGr 7 lost Henschel 126 WNr. 3297 (100% damage). Other losses were an unknown Dornier 17 and an Hs 126 with an unknown WNr. belonging to NASt Kroatien. Next day, two more He 46s were damaged at Borongaj aerodrome when WNr. 150 rammed and damaged WNr. 144 during take-off on a combat mission. Both aircraft suffered 20% damage.

Group strength on 10 November 1943:

Unit	Full strength	Available	Operational	Type
Stab	2	0	0	
1 Staffel	20	19	16	He 46
2 Staffel	20	11	7	Hs 126

On 21 November II Fliegerkorps, following orders from 27 October, dispatched three aircraft mechanics from IV./KG 76 to Udine for the setup of 3./NSGr 7. The same day brought yet another loss: Hs 126B-1 (WNr. 4297) of 2./NSGr 7 crashed in flames near Sisak around 15:00 hours. This loss did not result from any enemy action, but the aircraft was totally destroyed. Two days later, KG 76 sent mechanics, who arrived in Udine on the 24th of the same month. The same day, Buss was attacking Partisans aboard He 46 PR+NM, his flight lasting about an hour. The reported strength of 1st Staffel for the day was 16 Heinkel 46s, of which 15 were operational. On 22 November, the second Staffel was based in Banja Luka, still flying Hs 126s and Do 17s.

From 23 to 29 November, strong Partisan forces attacked Glina and Čazma, and the positions of the Axis forces in the area were critical. Čazma fell into Partisan hands on the 29th around 9:00 hours. In order to help defending forces keep their positions and resist the Partisan attacks while reinforcements came, all available German and Croatian aircraft were engaged in attacks

Aerial view of Sarajevo from an He 46 in 1943. (Peršen)

An He 46, probably coded 4X +VH (White 9), of 1./NSGr 7 over Glamoč field in 1943. (Military Museum Belgrade via Dejan Savić)

on the Partisans. From surviving pilots' log books, it is known that NSGr 7 was active in the area on these dates. On 24 November, the 2nd Brigade was attacked by several "low flying enemy aircraft" at 15:00 hours. Partisan units were attacked and reported that these aircraft "managed to disorganize and break down our [Partisan] units in those positions." One Partisan cannon was destroyed by a direct hit from an aerial bomb. Partisans mention that three big bombs of up to 200kg (440lbs) were dropped on their artillery positions, which leads to the conclusion that some Ju 87s or even Do 17s were engaged in these attacks. Aerial attacks stopped around 16:00 hours, and as a result, the planned attack of the 2nd Brigade was postponed until late at night, instead of at dawn that day. On 25 November, the Headquarters of the Partisan 7th Division reported a powerful attack by four aircraft around 13:00 hours using bombs and machine gun fire. This attack, carrying the typical signature of NSGr 7, lasted till 17:00 hours. Again, men of the 2nd and 3rd Partisan Brigade panicked and left their positions.

On 27 November, Hptm. Heinz Buss, StaKa of 1./NSGr 7, made an emergency landing behind enemy lines 1km (.62 miles) South West of the village of Babče when his He 46 (1K+FH) was hit by small arms fire while attacking Partisans in the area of Čazma and Glina at 12:55. Hptm. Buss and his Bordfunker, Fw. Hartmann, rejoined German units in the area by foot and were unharmed. The crash-landed He 46 was a newcomer to 1./NSGr 7 from 1./NSGr. 4 and is mentioned for the first time on 18 November. Some other He 46s arrived at the first Staffel from 1./NSGr. 4: 1K+BH, first mentioned on 7 January 1944; 1K+CH, first mentioned on 12 November 1943; 1K+HH, first mentioned on 19 December 1943; and 1K+GH, first mentioned on 27 December 1943.

The attack described above was carried out by six Heinkels of the 1st Staffel and all were hit by ground fire. This was Buss's second sortie of the day (and his 119th since joining the Staffel), both flown from Borongaj. Fliegerführer Kroatien received reports that Čazma was fully under Partisan control and sent several He 46s on armed recce. On the first sortie of the day, Hptm. Buss led a group of Heinkels (probably four) to the same area from 10:10 to 11:10 hours.

Men of NSGr 7 loading an Opel Blitz truck with sand. With characteristic dark glasses in the center is Hptm. Buss. He wore the same type of glasses later on in NSGr 9. (Predoević)

A report of Fliegerführer Kroatien mentions that eight aircraft were hit by AA fire during the actions that day, but it does not specify what damage was done to the Partisans. A Partisan report mentions that the 17th Assault Brigade (17. Udarna brigada) shot down two "Heinkel 126"[16] aircraft on 29 November, while another report mentions two Henschel aircraft without specifying the type. In the German records, only one loss is mentioned for 29 November; an He 46E-2 of 1./NSGr 7 (BB+CV, WNr. 1247) made an emergency landing between Koprivnica and Čazma, and Partisans again misinterpreted the aircraft type. The same day, one of the Hs 126s of 2nd Staffel bombed Partisans South of Beočin in Fruška Gora.

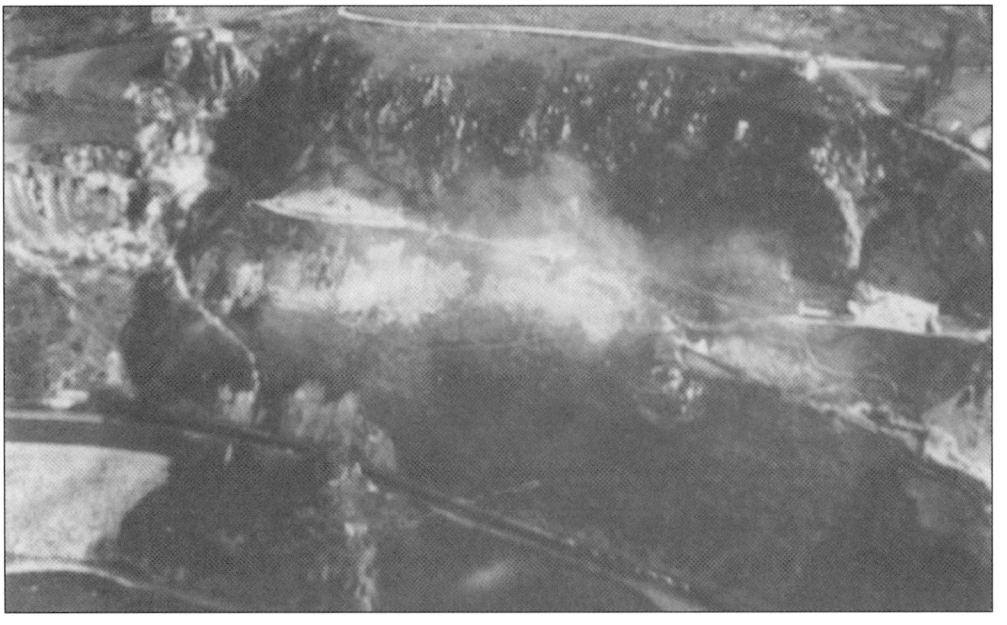

Attack by an He 46 of NSGr 7 on Partisan positions somewhere in Bosnia and Herzegovina. (Predoević)

Also that day, the 2nd Staffel dispatched four of their Hs 126s on armed recce missions to Senj, Glamoč, Glina, and Mitrovica. As a low-flying Hs 126 arrived over the airfield of Suhopolje, near the village of Čosije—on Glamoč field, where the Partisan 1st Air Base and airstrip was situated—a Partisan Do 17E-2 was about to take off. The Dornier was attacked by bombs and machine guns in several passes and caught fire, resulting in its complete destruction. The Henschel, taking off from Zalužani, dropped four 50-kg (110-lb) bombs altogether.

Ex-Luftwaffe Do 17E-2 NN+DA, WNr. 2067 (ZNDH 0313), destroyed by Hs 126s of NSGr 7 at Glamoč field. (Raguž)

Major Krešimir Boras in the uniform of the Royal Yugoslavian Air Force. (Raguž)

The Dornier in question was ex-Luftwaffe NN+DA (coded 0313 by the ZNDH) WNr. 2067, which had been flown to the Partisans some time ago by its defecting Croatian crew. That day, the crew was headed by Captain Krunoslav Kulušić (former ZNDH) as the observer; pilot Lieutenant Džemil Bukovac; copilot Major Krešimir Boras; and radio operator Corporal Petar Hercigonja (former ZNDH). According to Boras's logbook, aircraft flew in to Glamoč from Livno after a 25-minute flight at an altitude of 1,200 meters (3,937 feet).

Their precious load was three British liaison officers to Tito's HQ, namely Lieutenant Colonel Donald Night, Major Robin Hetherley, and Captain Deakin; and high-ranking officials of the National Liberation Army and Partisan Detachments of Yugoslavia, including Miloje Milojević, Milentije Popović, Vladimir Velebit (later to become Minister of Foreign Affairs of Yugoslavia and Executive Secretary at the UN European

Economic Commission), and Ivo Lola Ribar. Ivo Ribar was one of Tito's closest collaborators and a rising star of the movement, the Secretary of Communist Youth and freshly-named the first Chief of the Partisan Military Mission to the Mediterranean Allied Command. Ribar and the other members of the delegation jumped out of the nearby bushes and had begun loading the plane immediately when the Hs 126 appeared. Lola Ribar, the two British officers (Night and Hetherley), and mechanics Hercigonja, Kuzmić, and Uršić were killed in the attack and some others were wounded. Corporal Petar Hercigonja died in the burning Do 17, firing the rear defensive weapon at the attacker until his end. On the ground, the Political Commissar of the 1st Air Base, Savo Kreković, and one Partisan were also killed. At the time of attack, the 1st Air Base operated the Dornier and an A.V.I.A. FL. 3 liaison plane (formerly ZNDH 8102), both previously in the inventory of the Croatian Air Force. The total strength of the base, according to the Abwehr, was 78 men, including 22 pilots, six reconnaissance officers, an engineer, a meteorologist, a radio officer, and numerous mechanics.

Men of the Partisan 1st Air Base in front of the Do 17E-2 destroyed by the 2nd Staffel. (Raguž)

This action is still the subject of many controversies today and there is a theory that Tito "sold out" his brilliant young commander to the Germans, as he felt threatened by Ivo Lola Ribar's popularity.

It is well known that in both General Rudolf Lüters's HQ and in Tito's a radio station was installed through which the two commanders could communicate directly as part of an agreement. Officially, these radio stations served to arrange the exchange of POWs. To history, these agreements are known as the March Agreements, as the relevant negotiations started in March 1943. There are also theories that a Croatian or German agent informed the Axis about the event. On the other hand, it is known that pilot Boras had flown the Dornier earlier in the morning and the delegation was about 20 minutes late for its scheduled embarkation. As they were belatedly boarding, the Henschel appeared and destroyed the aircraft, along with Ivo Lola Ribar.

Wreckage of the Partisan Do 17E-2 in which Ivo Lola Ribar lost his life. (Raguž)

The four Henschels dispatched, including the one that attacked the Do 17, used a total of 600 kilograms (1,322lbs) of bombs and 3,200 rounds of ammunition during these sorties.

On 29 November, the one serviceable Hs 126 and three serviceable He 46s based at Zemunik were very active. The Henschel was in action from 8:58 to 09:40 hours, on armed recce over the archipelago off the town of Zadar, but abandoned its mission due to bad weather. A Heinkel of the detachment was active SE of Zadar from 10:10 to 11:30 hours; departing at 12:10 hours, three He 46s bombed the islands of Molat and Ist. The Detachment reported that the Henschel had sunk one sailing boat of 300-500 tons using bombs, while the Heinkels reported two ships of between 200 and 300 tons sunk and one more damaged. Later that day, two He 46s carried out armed recce of the heights 12km (7.45 miles) NE and 7km (4.35 miles) SE of Biograd. They discovered new Partisan positions that were attacked with 1,000 rounds of ammunition. During the attack, one Heinkel received a hit in its fuselage from ground fire; due to a lack of spare tires, another He 46 was out of order in Zadar. On this date, the detachment disposed of five crews, of which one was in Drniš.

On the mainland, Heinkel He 46E-2 (BB+CV, WNr. 1247) was reported damaged 10% by ground fire and made an emergency landing between Koprivnica and Čazma. Its crew soon reached German positions on foot.

The Advanced Battlefield Headquarters (probably Sarajevo) informed Fliegerführer Kroatien of the day's actions: one Hs 126 from 8:40–11:00 in the area Višegrad-Pljevlja, four SC 50 bombs and 1,000 rounds of ammunition used; one Hs 126 from 8:45–10:15 in the area of Gacko, four SC 50 bombs and 400 rounds of ammunition used; one Hs 126 from 8:50–11:35 in the area of Travnik, four SC 50 and 300 rounds; and one Hs 126 from 13:10–14:00 in the area of Sarajevo, 96 SD 2 bombs and 300 rounds of ammunition expended. In the source documents, the unit(s) to which these Henschels belong is not given, so they may have been either from NASt Kroatien or the 2./NSGr 7. The Partisans gave SD 2 bombs the colloquial name "Krilašica", meaning "the one with the wings."

Formation of He 46s of the 1./NSGr 7 on a combat sortie. Note the MG in the observer post. (Predoević)

Several Heinkel 46s on the dispersal area around Sarajevo in 1943. Behind the He 46 with the tail marking White 11 is an armorer's wagon, around which a tent has been built. (Peršen)

The 1st Staffel's detachment in Zadar made only one sortie on 30 November and had one Hs 126 and two He 46s serviceable at the aerodrome there. One He 46 had ignition problems, while another had been in unserviceable condition at Drniš since the 29th of the month. The Detachment reported four crews in Zadar and one in Drniš. Retrieval of the unserviceable aircraft was in progress.

Meanwhile, intensive armed reconnaissance was underway in Bosnia and Herzegovina, and Luftwaffe units in the region reported strongly-fortified field positions at Prijevolje[17] and the heights around Višegrad. South of Sarajevo and North of the village of Ilovice, "50 guerillas" were sighted; a place called Grab,[18] 14.5km (9 miles) South of Sarajevo was on fire; and the road from Sarajevo to the South toward Dobro Polje[19] had been blown up. During the armed recce, 96 SD 2 and 12 SC 50 bombs were used together with 2,000 rounds of ammunition. The 1./NSGr 7[20] reported the strength of its detachment at Butmir as three serviceable Heinkel 46s. The beginning of December 1943 found 2./NSGr 7 at Banja Luka aerodrome.

For 1 December, the Detachment in Zadar reported two He 46 aircraft of 1./NSGr 7 and one Hs 126 serviceable, while two Heinkels were still unserviceable (this Hs 126 belonged to NASt Kroatien). "Nachtschlachtstaffel Butmir" disposed of three He 46s, while the next day, only two Heinkel aircraft were serviceable at Sarajevo Butmir; Nachtschlachtstaffel Butmir was in fact a detachment of 1./NSGr 7.

Men of the NSGr 7 at Rajlovac aerodrome, Sarajevo, in 1943. (Predoević)

For the same 1 December, another report stated that Hs 126 CY+RB was with the NSGr. (2./NSGr 7) and was given back to NASt Kroatien that day. The latter unit requested that the NSGr. hand back all logbooks (engine, airframe, etc.) and all spare parts from Banja Luka to Mostar. This request was sent via the command of NASt Kroatien in Zagreb, as no direct communication existed at the time between Banja Luka and Mostar. Three more Hs 126s are mentioned in that report: call sign TD+EI (there is doubt if this aircraft was given to the repair shop at Mostar, probably after brief service with 2./NSGr 7); TD+EJ of the NASt (to be loaded and sent to the Reich); and BA+HQ (serviceable in Mostar for NASt. in Sarajevo).

Due to the bad weather, He 46 WNr. 343 of the 1st Staffel made an emergency landing and was damaged 40% the second day of the month. On 3 December, Henschel 126 WNr. 3038 —coded GE+AR and piloted by the Staffelkapitän of the 2nd Staffel, Max Griewatsch, with Ofw. Roth as an observer—took off from Banja Luka at 10:00 hours for an operational flight to Brčko. It never arrived there, as it was shot down by Spitfires of No. 126 Squadron RAF NW of Dubrovnik after a long chase. Both crew members regained friendly lines without injuries.

An He 46 of the 1./NSGr 7 over Glamoč field in 1943. (Military Museum Belgrade via Dejan Savić)

Two pilots of the unit wearing fez, Sarajevo, 1943. (Predoević)

In the second week of December, 1./NSGr 7 had 11 He 46s available at Borongaj aerodrome in Zagreb and three more detached to Butmir, near Sarajevo. Two of the He 46s at Butmir were serviceable, while one had been awaiting a spare tire since the end of November. The Butmir detachment had six crews available at the beginning of December.

Hauptmann Buss's first mission after being shot down by Partisans took place on 7 December. Aboard He 46 CQ+HP, he made a lengthy combat sortie of 2 hours and 15 minutes from Borongaj. Next day, he recorded two more combat flights in the same aircraft with a total flying time of two hours and five minutes. Most probably, the sorties were in the same area due to very similar time spent in the air.

On 10 December, Oberkommando der Luftwaffe ordered II. Fliegerkorps to supply sufficient ammunition, spare parts, bombs, and tools for Ca. 314 aircraft to Fliegerführer Kroatien, and for the latter to send one experienced officer to II. Fliegerkorps to help with the establishment of NSGr. 9. In Ultra intercept T24/68, it is mentioned that "captured aircraft" are in Hörsching, Austria, with Nachtschlachtgruppe 111. The same day, the Staffelkapitän and his comrade, Lt. Gade, ferried two Heinkel He 46 aircraft from Borongaj to Banja Luka. Heinkels 1K+BH and 1K+HH landed at 15:00 hours after a flight of 55 minutes. At Zalužani, between 19 and 26 December, two serviceable Hs 126s of NASt Kroatien were stationed and at least two more He 46s of 1st Staffel: TY+NC and BB+CI. The latter was flown by Hauptmann Buss on missions 125 to 130.

The Luftwaffe command in Sarajevo reported 15 sorties on 24 December 1943 by the 1./NSGr 7 detachment at Butmir, near Sarajevo.

Regarding the actions in the air, the end of December brought a few more sorties. Buss flew He 46 NF+NC on 28 December from 10:00 to 10:50 and his comrade Gade again flew 1K+BH. Due to bad weather there was no flying on the 29th, but operations resumed the day after, when Buss and Gade flew side-by-side in Heinkels NF+NC and 1K+BH from 10:04, and later in the day from 12:25 hours, landing a few minutes apart each time. Lt. Gade flew another sortie of 71 minutes, finishing his eventful 30 December at 16:23 hours.

The Stuka pilots of the I./SG 3 stationed at Sarajevo in December 1943 called the sturdy He 46 "hochbeinigen Möbelwagen," or "long-legged furniture van." One of them, Friedrich Christian Eisenbach, made a picture of the plane, writing on the back: "Der Schrecken Titos auf dem Balkan," or in translation, "The nightmare of Tito in Balkans."

Heinkel 46E-2 BB+CI, WNr. 1234 (White 3) being recovered after an emergency landing. (Peršen)

On New Year's Eve, Partisans attacked Banja Luka and the aerodrome at Zalužani (Flugplatzkommando A 8/XVII). According to Ultra intercepts, the 2nd Staffel had its seven Hs 126s available on Zalužani, and from the Flugbuch of Hptm. Buss, it is evident that the 1st Staffel had at least three more He 46s (1K+GH, NF+NC, and DB+ZC) stationed there. Again, Hptm. Buss organized his men and successfully defended the unit's aircraft just as in Sarajevo a few months earlier. On the day of the attack he made two sorties: the first from 15:05 to 15:55 and the second one fifteen minutes later, landing at 16:10. The first day of 1944 started with much action: Buss was in the air four times that day and three more times the next. On 1 January, he flew He 46 NF+NC three times: from 10 to 10:43; from 11:25 to 11:43; and from 12:22 to 13:15, then finished the day in another Heinkel (DB+ZC) from 14:00 to 14:50. Lieutenant Gade added four more combat sorties against besieging Partisan forces: twice in Heinkel 1K+BH, taking off at 10:15 and 13:40 hours; in Heinkel 1K+GH from 14:07; and again in 1K+BH from 16:30 to 17:05 hours. There are reports that one plane of NSGr 7 was lost on 1 January, but there are no details of which aircraft this was.

The testimony of German and Croatian resistance at the airport is described in the summary report of the Headquarters of the Partisan 6th Division (6. NOU divizija) on their fighting in January 1944. The report states: "The 3rd Brigade took part in the fighting for Banja Luka. Brigade was attacking the aerodrome and was holding positions from Gradiška to Prijedor. As forces at the airport were too numerous, Brigade did not fulfill its task. It managed to damage several planes and during the entire operation blocked the taking-off of the aircraft from the airdrome."[21] As we can see, this report is not quite accurate, as not only were aircraft flying during the fiercest fighting, but also the aerodrome's garrison was barely 600 men, which was at least three times less than the strength of the brigade in question.

Heinkel 46 in flight with a background of Bosnian mountains. This is the typical configuration of the terrain in this theater of war. (Predoević)

The Command of the 13th Krajiška Brigade (13. Krajiška brigada), in its fifteen-day summary report to the higher Partisan Command of 13 January 1944, mentions that on 31 December, the brigade was attacked by six aircraft while approaching Banja Luka. Aircraft bombarded the Partisan columns and strafed them with machine gun fire. As a result, two fighters of the 13th Brigade were killed and six were wounded. These types of attacks bear the signature of the NSGr 7 and the NASt Kroatien.

The 3rd Proletarian Krajiška Brigade (3. Proleterska krajiška brigada) reported shooting down one aircraft of the "Pikavac" type (Cigarette Butt) in December. Headquarters of the 3rd Brigade, in their report dated 18 January, regarding the summary of operations around Banja

Luka, states that type of aircraft was shot down and it crashed as one wing fell off. It also claims that three crew members died in the crash. In continuation, it reports two Partisan dead and five wounded in the attacks by enemy aviation. The 3rd Proletarian Krajiška Brigade was constantly harassed by aircraft, which slowed down its advance towards the initial position for the attack on Banja Luka. Besides snow blizzards, this was the main reason the Brigade was late to undertake its attack scheduled for 22:00 hours.

Clouds seen from above are very rare scenery for NSGr 7 pilots, as they were flying very low. The photo was taken from an He 46. (Predoević)

"Pikavac" aircraft, as the Partisans called them, were actually Henschel Hs 126s, which can be seen from other Partisan reports during the war. However, during the study of the Partisan documentation for this book, it seems that the name was used for any parasol-winged German aircraft, including the He 46. This conclusion can be drawn from the fact that Partisans often tried to dismount the machine guns from shot-down enemy aircraft for use as infantry weapons. Sometimes in the reports they mention capturing two MG from a Pikavac, in which case it would have been an Hs 126. In other cases, they report the retrieval of one MG from a Pikavac, indicating it was an He 46.

On 2 January, Gade was in the air aboard He 46 DB+ZC from 15:30 to 15:45; from 15:55 to 16:05; and from 16:10 to 16:15 hours. In report 10/44 of 2 January 1944 from Fliegerführer Kroatien Advanced battle HQ (Banja Luka), a copy of which was dispatched to Wehrmacht XV mountain corps, it states: "Our forces coming from the North penetrated as far as the centre of the city. Fighting with Partisans 1km SW of the crossroads of the centre of the Partisan-occupied village. Head of 92nd Motorized regiment (Wehrmacht) observed in Batrina 27km West from Brod. Otherwise ground situation largely unchanged." The same day, four Hs 126s of an unknown unit made reconnaissance sorties in Bosnia and Herzegovina, observing a Partisan column marching eastwards with an estimated strength of 500 men and pack animals in the Medojevici-Zunovi-Krusevici (Olovo area, 10-12km [6.2-7.45 miles] SSE of the town). Subsequently, eight He 46s attacked this column SE of Olovo with "...good results." These Heinkels were no doubt NSGr 7 aircraft, but the airfield from which they took off is not known (it could have been Banja Luka, Rajlovac, or Butmir).

Two photos taken at Rajlovac airdrome in 1943. In the first photo, one Hs 126, probably of NASt Kroatien, is visible. In the second photo, Hptm. Heinz Buss is in the middle, Technical Officer Obfw. Trussek is on the right, and the Administrative Officer Fw. Ratzkow is on the left. Hptm. Buss is wearing the Croatian Pilot badge under the German one and Frontflugspange above the left pocket. It seems that the small ribbon is from EK2. Behind them are several Do 17s, one Ju 52/3m, and an Fi 156. (Predoević)

On 3 January, Gade added two more flights to his mission records at 14:10 and 16:30, flying the same DB+ZC. All except one flight of 90 minutes lasted from 20 to 40 minutes, meaning that attacks were conducted very close to the aerodrome, if not on the aerodrome itself. Aircraft were landing and often taking off after only seven minutes on the ground; enough to be rearmed and put back in the air.

Uffz. Wittan from 1./NSGr 7 reported continuing attacks by the unit against Partisans withdrawing from Banja Luka from 12:45 to 15:45 hours on the third day of 1944. Attacks were intense on the road from Banja Luka to Kola. All around the road abandoned material and disrupted Partisan columns were reported. In open country and on the roads horse-drawn vehicles were observed, and Partisan columns were seen fleeing toward the SW. To cover the withdrawal from Banja Luka, areas South and SW of there were strongly occupied by the Partisan forces, including one anti-tank gun on the road. In the mountain chain four to five kilometers (2.48 to 3 miles) from Ola,[22] there were especially heavy defenses established by Partisans on both sides of the road. The heights were "sprayed" with bombs and gun fire by Heinkels of NSGr 7. One of the Heinkels of the Staffel made a recce flight in a direction from Banja Luka to Prijedor, but no enemies were observed.

According to the report of the HQ of the 13th Krajiška Brigade (13. Krajiška brigada) from 5 January 1944, this brigade was attacked by four aircraft around 14:30 on 3 January, during the fighting within the town around a building in Banja Luka called Sokolana.

Aerial view of Banja Luka from a Heinkel 46 of NSGr 7 at the end of 1943. (Peršen)

The end of December 1943 and the first days of January 1944 brought additional Fiat C.R. 42 Falcos to replace the He 46s and Hs 126s, and in the first weeks seven more aircraft were delivered, raising the strength of 2nd Staffel to nine Fiats. The Fiat's C.R. designation was in recognition of its designer, Celestino Rosatelli. The new Technical Officer of the 2nd Staffel was Oblt. Wilhelm Baumgärtner, who remained in post until March 1945. During January, systematic strategic bombing by the 15th Air Force of targets in the Independent State of Croatia began, bringing a new type of danger for Nachtschlachtgruppe 7.

After a day's break, Lt. Gade was again in action on 5 January, twice during the afternoon for 55 and 65 minutes, respectively, while Hptm. Buss resumed his combat flying two days later, on 7 January, taking off from Banja Luka at the controls of Heinkel 1K+BH. Strength of 1./NSGr 7 was 17 He 46s with 46 SD 50 bombs in stock, as reported on the evening of 6 January.

The first bombardment of aerodromes used by NSGr 7 happened on 7 January, when 18 B-24s of the 449th BG and 24 B-24s of the 450th BG attacked Mostar in slightly cloudy weather.

They dropped 90.5 tons of 225-kg (500-lb) type D (fused .1 and .025) bombs from 13:45 to 13:50 hours from an altitude between 5,790 and 6,065 meters (19,000-19,900 feet). The bombers were escorted by P-38s of the 82nd Fighter Group.

Bombs fell on the North end of the hangar line, where bomber crews observed fire and smoke; few bombs hit the SE dispersal area. Bomber crews reported: "Anti-aircraft fire from heavy guns of medium intensity and of the aimed variety with accuracy as to altitude." Crews also reported four points of contact with flak: one each at the SE, SW, NE, and NW corners of the aerodrome. Minor damage in the form of small holes in wings and tail surfaces and in the fuselage was found on several Liberators after their return to the base.

Ground staff of Störkampfstaffel Südost in front of Heinkel 46 CQ+HP White 2 and PR+NM White 1 at Banja Luka. (Peršen)

Heinkel 46 1K+EH was flown to Zagreb on 8 January by Hptm. Buss, who came back to Banja Luka by other means of transport, as there is no return flight entered in his flying log. Ultra decrypts show that Lt. Jessat took off from Zadar the same day with He 46 SA+HV for Banja Luka, but he did not arrive there still on 11 January. On 9 January, one mission was flown by Lt. Gade from 13:36 to 14:45 with an aircraft marked DB+ZC, and two days later, two more missions were flown by him with Heinkels 1K+BH and 1K+GH. Strength of 1./NSGr 7 on 14 January was 17 aircraft, of which 14 were serviceable.

In the Allied bomber pilots' vocabulary, all missions to Croatia were "milk runs" in the first weeks of attacks; no fighters, almost non-existent flak, and no casualties. However, the attack on Mostar on 14 January would change that. That day, around two hundred B-24s and B-17s attacked the town area and the airfield. This was a preventive mission to deny use of this base to the Luftwaffe and Croatian Air Force in any possible plans to attack southern Italy, but also to deny its use for the interception of four-engine bombers on their way to the targets in Hungary, Croatia, and Serbia. P-38s provided escort throughout the missions and P-47s joined the bombers at the target to cover the flight back to their bases. Bomber Groups engaged were the following: the 2nd BG with thirty-five[23] B-17s, primary target aircraft dispersals; 99th BG with thirty-four B-17s, primary target aircraft dispersals; 301st BG with an unknown number of B-17s, primary target aircraft dispersals; 449th BG with thirty-two B-24s, primary target Mostar airfield; and the 450th BG dispatched 35 B-24s, whose primary target was the town of Mostar.

Sarajevo from the observer's cockpit of an He 46 of NSGr 7. (Predoević)

Aerodrome in Mostar. This photo was probably taken in summer 1943 from an He 46. Note that the entire aerodrome is the coat of arms of the Regia Aeronautica. (Predoević)

The aerodrome at Mostar was very important for both the Luftwaffe and Croatian Air Force, each stationing a significant number of aircraft there. Prior to the bombings, Luftwaffe forces at Mostar were composed of one squadron from IV./JG 27 with nine Bf 109Gs, Henschel Hs 126s of Aufklärungs Staffel Agram-Semlin[24] (probably yet another name for a detachment from NASt Kroatien) 13./SG 151, with seven Junkers Ju 87s, and the 2nd Staffel of Nahaufklärungsgruppe 12[25] with 14 Bf 109s and five Fi 156s. Besides fighters from IV./JG 27, the German command occasionally used Messerschmitts from 2./NAGr 12 for interception and fighter patrols. Luckily, NSGr 7 did not have any aircraft at the airfield the day of the attack, though a Kette or Rotte was often stationed here. The Croatian Air Force, after the reorganization, stationed at least 20 aircraft at this aerodrome, mainly obsolete types used for anti-Partisan tasks, liaison, and transport. There were Breguet XIX and Potez XXV from the 4th Reconnaissance Squadron (4. izvidničko jato); FP-2, PVT, R-100, IK-2, and Avia BH-33Es from the 5th Reconnaissance Squadron (5. izvidničko jato); and several Bücker Bü 131, FP-2, Be-51, Saiman 200, and Avia Fokker from the 20th Liaison Squadron (20. samostalno jato za vezu). All together, more than 50 aircraft were stationed there by the end of 1943. The aerodrome possessed a developed infrastructure for aircraft maintenance consisting of workshops, hangars, fuel and ammunition storage, and army barracks, all built during the time of old Yugoslavia.

The attack was carried out in bright sunlight with 20-kilometer (12-mile) visibility over the target. The formations of American bombers were flying at 6,100 to 6,400m (20,000–21,000 feet). First over Mostar airfield was the 301st BG, followed by the 2nd BG and the 99th BG, while ultimately the 449th BG closed the run over the base. The 2nd BG dropped 54 tons of 9kg (20lb) fragmentation bombs on the airfield. Seven B-24s of the 450th BG, their primary target being the town of Mostar, got lost and instead bombarded the airfield with 225kg (500lb) bombs. Thirty-two aircraft of the 449th BG were over the target in two flights: one flight bombed the target, while the other jettisoned its bombs in the Adriatic after failing to reach the target. Forty-two and a quarter tons of 225-kg (500-lb) GP .1 and .025 fused bombs were dropped on the airfield at 10:50 hours. Thirty-five B-24s of the 450th BG dropped 90½ tons of 225-kg (500-lb) bombs on the town. Three other B-24s of the same group reported hits on the road and a bridge approximately one mile NW of the target. The attack on both targets lasted for about 20 minutes, from 10:35 to 10:55 hours.

Bomber crews reported that flak over the target was heavy and moderate, with good altitude but poor deflection. In total, 33 aircraft of the attacking force were damaged, while 2nd Lt. Edwin Nunnery of the 96th Bomb Squadron of the 2nd BG received a serious flak wound to his left thigh. One of the planes of the 450th BG reported engine failure from the same cause, but it returned safely to its base in Italy. Eight batteries of four AA guns each were seen in the NW section of Mostar. Also, a flak battery was reported West of the town and heavy flak was reported about 27km (16.7 miles) to the SW. The bomber formation was also attacked by Luftwaffe fighters over the target. The first two Bf 109s attacked B-24s and B-17s from behind and closed to 750 meters (2,460 feet) before they were driven off by the P-38 escort and were not seen afterwards. One unidentified aircraft was seen on fire and trailing smoke at 43°23′N–17°45′E; it was falling and disappeared behind a mountain. The 450th BG reported several contacts with the Luftwaffe and aircraft were attacked by seven Bf 109s. The 2nd BG reported passes by four or five Bf 109s from the high rear, but the exact location of this attack was not stated. One bomber crew reported three Bf 109s or Fw 190s (there were no Focke Wulf fighters in Mostar at the time) at 10:50 hours, just beyond the target at 6,100 meters (20,000 feet), coming out of the sun "at 11 o'clock high". On one pass, one enemy aircraft trailed smoke after break-off. No damage resulting from fighter attacks was reported.

USAAF sources identified twenty-four single and two twin-engine airplanes on the ground at the time of the raid. Strike photos showed four of them destroyed, six damaged, and six others probably destroyed. Results of the attack on the town were much more inconclusive, as it was merely stated in the reports that "... much smoke was observed. Bomb strike photos

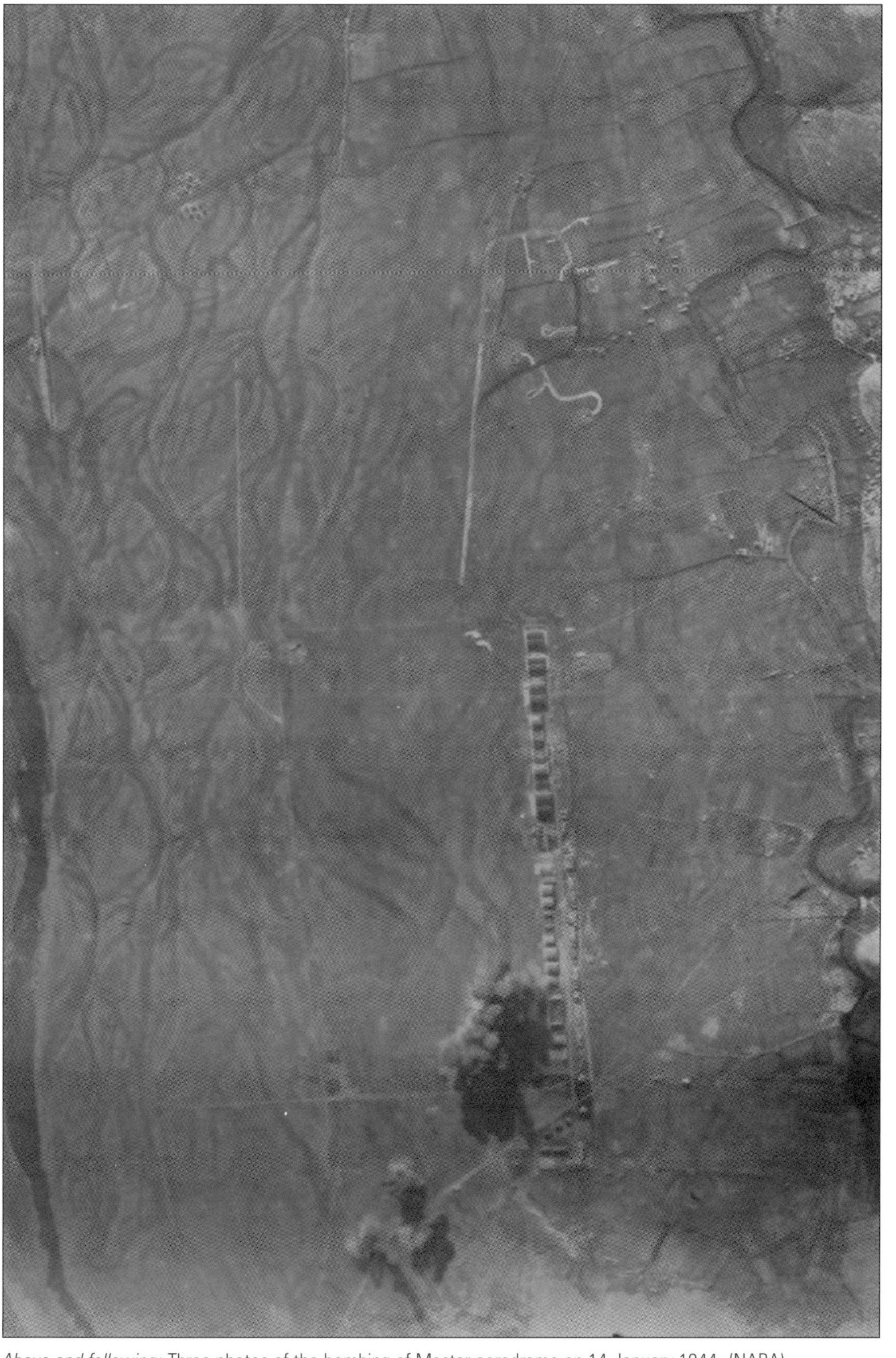

Above and following: Three photos of the bombing of Mostar aerodrome on 14 January 1944. (NARA)

Bombing of Mostar aerodrome (Contined)

disclose many hits." Altogether 68 Liberators and 140 Fortresses dropped 286 tons of high explosive bombs over Mostar that day.

At 10:45, B-24H serial number 41-29243 ("Blind Date") of the 716th BS of the 449th BG, piloted by 1st Lt. Vincent Isgirgg, dropped its bomb load over the target. At the same time, another B-24H (41-28606 "White Fang," of the same group but from the 718th BS) was flying directly under 41-29243. Two bombs penetrated the wing of "White Fang" inboard of number three engine and there was a tremendous explosion and fire that completely destroyed the aircraft with eleven men on board. Just one "White Fang" crew member miraculously survived the inferno, and though seriously injured, became a POW. At the same time, because of the fierceness of the explosion, "Blind Date" went out of control and the pilot warned his crew of the situation. By the time he regained control at an altitude of 6,100 meters (20,000ft), five crew members who could not be contacted by intercom had bailed out. Three crewmen became POWs, while two were picked up by the Partisans after landing 19.5 kilometers (12 miles) South of Mostar around 12:15. One of them, 2nd Lt. Stanley Greszik, stayed with Tito's Partisan forces and became a coordinator.[26] Pilot Vincent Isgirgg and the five other members of the crew successfully returned to their base after an uneventful trip back.

The Group's other casualty from the attack was B-24 serial number 42-07741 "Dumbo," piloted by R.W. Kendall; its engines cut out while on the first leg of its flight to the target. Five crew members bailed out over the Italian coast near Bari, while the others stayed and tried to land the ship with no power at Bari airfield. This is how the crew described their landing in the report: "Landed ship wheels down, rolled about 600 meters (2,000 feet) when left gear gave way gradually. Ship turned on left wing and ball turret, which could not be retracted, dug into ground, ripping fuselage. Bomb bay doors open ripped off. Ship was recovered for salvage."

The Group Report of the 450th BG gives this description of the events: "Encountered Bf 109s in target area and while returning to the Adriatic coast. No damage reported from fighter attacks. Flak was heavy type, intense and accurate over the target. One bomber lost to flak. Twenty aircraft received flak damage. Two crew members wounded by flak." This was the Group's first loss to enemy action. Piloted by Lt. Jack Graham of the 721st Squadron, the B-24 straggled back across the Adriatic and crash landed on the Italian coast near Vieste, East of Foggia. He and copilot Harry Feltenstein were trapped in the gasoline-soaked wreckage for several hours until they were pried out by some Australian troops stationed near the crash site.

Belly landed Messerschmitt Bf 109G-4 Black 4 of 2./NAGr 12 in autumn 1943, near the village of Buna, South of Mostar. (Haraminčić)

During the attack, many German aircraft were damaged. Messerschmitt Bf 109G-8 WNr. 20673 of Stab./NAGr 12 was damaged 25% (fuselage torn by blast, to be replaced), as well as the following aircraft of the 2nd Staffel:
Bf 109G-8, Black 1 of 2./ NAGr 12, WNr. 20675, 60% damage;
Bf 109G-6, Black 2 of 2./ NAGr 12, WNr. 410391, 40% damage, to be replaced;
Bf 109G-8, Black 3 of 2./ NAGr 12, WNr. 20691, 25% damage;
Bf 109G-6, Black 6 of 2./ NAGr 12, WNr. 410095[27], 80% damage;
Bf 109G-6, Black 7 of 2./ NAGr 12, WNr. 410258, unknown damage;
Bf 109G-6, Black 9 of 2./ NAGr 12, WNr. 410094[28], 95% damage;
Bf 109G-8, Black 11 of 2./ NAGr 12, WNr. 20686[29], 10% damage.

On the German side there were several dead and wounded: Ogefr. Walter Möller, wireless mechanic, died; and wounded were Uffz. Bruno Kozlowski, Ogefr. Franz Volmari, and Ogefr. Ernst Schanko. During the attack, several Junkers Ju 87s of 13./SG 15130 were damaged as follows:
Ju 87D-3, WNr. 100044, S7+LU[31], damaged 15% by splinters in fuselage and wings;
Ju 87D-3 WNr. 100426, S7+AU, damaged 7% by splinters in fuselage and wings;
Ju 87D-4 (D-3?), WNr. 110596, S7+KU[32], damaged 75% by a direct hit. Airframe and engine completely destroyed.

A Junkers Ju 87B of StG 151 at Borongaj Airfield on 21 May 1943. At least three later-.model Ju 87Ds were destroyed by bombardment on 14 January 1944 at Mostar and on 12 April 1944 at Zagreb. (Peršen)

Fighters of IV./JG 27 were heavily affected by this attack. No fewer than 13 aircraft were damaged or destroyed, including:
Bf 109G-6, WNr. 160883[33], airframe 15%, engine 1%;
Bf 109G-6, WNr. 160887[34], airframe 5%;
Bf 109G-6, WNr. 140267[35], airframe 50%, engine 2%;
Bf 109G-6, WNr. 160838[36], airframe 1%;
Bf 109G-6, WNr. 161021, airframe 15%, engine very dirty;
Bf 109G-6, WNr. 161018, airframe 30%, engine 1%;
Bf 109G-6, WNr. 160825[37], airframe 90%, engine 1%;
Bf 109G-6, WNr. 140329, airframe 35%, engine 5%.

The same day, two escorting P-38s belonging to the 97th FS of the 82nd FG were downed over Mostar: Second Lt. Robert T. Voelker, flying P-38 G-15, serial 43-2436; and James T. Rogers flying P-38 G-15l, serial 43-2556. The Luftwaffe lost two more fighters in the skirmish with U.S. bombers. Jagdgeschwader 27 lost Bf 109G-6 WNr. 140237, which crashed while attempting an emergency landing after its airframe was shot up. Damage was estimated at 50% and the total loss of Bf 109G-6 WNr. 160834[38] from 2./ NAGr 12 was reported when it failed to return after the dogfight. Its pilot, Oblt. Saar, bailed out, was slightly injured, and spent some time on sick leave.

Ultra reported on 16 January that 2./NSGr 7. was based in Banja Luka, from where it operated C.R. 42 aircraft. Fliegerführer Kroatien reported the loss of one aircraft on 21 January and damage to another one without mentioning any further details. Next day, Sarajevo sought return of the documentation and logs from Banja Luka for two Hs 126 aircraft: CN+MA and DD+RV. Given several earlier similar requests involving the same source and recipient, it is very probable that those two aircraft were in service with 2./NSGr 7 before the latter was equipped with Fiat fighters.

Fliegerführer Kroatien ordered on 18 January that two He 46s of 1./NSGr 7 should be transferred to Zadar, but this was not done due to very bad weather conditions. It seems that

"Kommandeur machine" Heinkel He 111 at Banja Luka aerodrome. (Peršen)

A member of NSGr 7 posing for the camera in an He 46. (Predoević)

only on 28 January did Hptm. Buss manage to ferry He 46 PR+NM from Banja Luka to Zadar, landing in Zemunik at 10:37 after bit more than one hour's flying. As there are no entries in his flying log for a return flight, it is probable that he rejoined his unit by road or as a passenger on another aircraft. The same afternoon, Lt. Gade resumed flying, undertaking a combat sortie from Zalužani for 86 minutes with Heinkel SA+HW.

The same day, Hptm. Buss was awarded a Croatian decoration (Velika srebrna kolajna za hrabrost [Great Silver Medal for Bravery]) for his actions during the fight against the Partisans. Besides the StaKa, Oblt. Rudolf Falke was awarded the same decoration. Oblt. Falke, as well as Hptm. Buss, flew their He 46s and attacked Partisans from the air, despite the fact that fights were raging at the aerodrome itself during the New Year's Eve attack on Banja Luka.

From available sources, it seems that few sorties were flown from Zalužani until 22 January, when the 1st Staffel resumed flying. Routine missions harassing Tito groups were again in the repertoire, involving at least Heinkels 1K+BH on 22 January and DB+ZC on 23 January. Fliegerführer Kroatien requested all three detachments (Zadar, Banja Luka, and Bihać) to estimate their coal needs for heating their barracks due to the very cold winter. On 25 January, at 10:50, three He 46s of 1./NSGr 7 and one Hs 126 (of either 2./NSGr 7 or NASt Kroatien) flew from Banja Luka and attacked Partisans near Orahovica, about 40km (24.85 miles) NNW of Brod, and another sortie was flown by Lt. Gade with He 46 DB+ZC in the afternoon, landing back at Banja Luka at 13:44. After being in Zagreb for a while flying test flights, Buss ferried He 46 1K+GH to Banja Luka on 27 January.

An He 46 of 1./NSGr 7 was destroyed on 29 January, when pilot Fw. Alfred Uhlemann was injured while trying to land his aircraft at Borongaj aerodrome during very bad meteorological conditions and low visibility. During the day, the 1st Staffel had a handful of "jobs" in Bosnia and Herzegovina. Lt. Gade alone flew three missions in He 46 1K+GH, accumulating 4 hours and 32 minutes of combat flying. In the Partisan Navy summary report for the month of February, it is stated that German aircraft intensified their activities over the islands in the Zadar region. It can be assumed that these activities were undertaken by NSGr 7, operating from Zemunik airport, near Zadar.

On 31 January, Buss was airborne again for 13 minutes on a test flight with He 46 1K+HH in Banja Luka, while the other one (NF+NC) was in the air again with Lt. Gade as its pilot. This aircraft was flown twice that day on combat sorties. The detachment in Zadar was still led by Lt. Jessat.

There are three reported losses from the group for January: one on New Year's day and two more on 21 January. The archives do not answer any questions about the first two losses. The aircraft lost on New Year's day might be the same one reported shot down by the Partisans during the fighting in Banja Luka. For the third, it is known that Fw. Alfred Uhlemann was the pilot.

In February, two more aircraft were reported lost or damaged. The first was Macchi M.C. 200 (WNr. 8619), piloted by Uffz. Kaspar Turko of Stab./NSGr 7, which crashed on 3 February. The aircraft was 100% destroyed and the pilot lost his life. This is the first time that a Macchi type is mentioned in the archive materials; it is not known when and how this type came to the unit or if there were more of them with NSGr 7. Next day, an unknown aircraft was reported as damaged in a flying accident. In Banja Luka, few sorties were made by the resident Heinkels. Over these two days Lt. Gade flew his mission numbers 86 to 88 since arriving in Croatia with He 46 NF+NC, in the company of Fw. Hartmann. He added one more sortie with the same aircraft for each consecutive day, his last sorties for two weeks.

Accident of an He 46 at Rajlovac Aerodrome. Note that the aircraft undersides were painted black and for unknown reasons, the area around the fuselage Balkenkreuz has been partly painted over. (Predoević)

On the evening of 6 February, Fliegerführer Kroatien reported NSGr 7's strength as follows:
Stab: four aircraft, of which two were serviceable, with 11 crews, of which three were ready to fly;
1st Staffel: 16 aircraft, of which 10 were serviceable and 20 crews, of which 17 were ready to fly;
2nd Staffel: three serviceable aircraft with 19 crews all ready to fly.

On 8 February, the Partisan navy reported the loss of two ships of the Auxiliary company of the Zadar Partisan Detachment (Dopunska četa zadarskog odreda) at 07:30 hours in the area of Vlašići, on the island of Pag, caused by enemy aircraft. Aircraft were active all day attacking Partisan shipping, and as a result, another ship was damaged and could no longer be used. Again, attacks in this area were a speciality of the Zadar detachment of NSGr 7.

On the evening of 11 February, the strength of the unit was:
Stab: four aircraft, of which two were serviceable, and 13 crews, of which three were ready to fly;
1*st* Staffel: 16 aircraft, of which 10 were serviceable, and 20 crews, of which 17 were ready to fly;
2nd Staffel: 13 aircraft, of which none were serviceable, with 20 crews, of which 18 were ready to fly.

On 13 February, at around 13:00, three Partisan ships were sunk in the Planinski channel (Planinski kanal) between the shore and the island of Rab. Ships named *Mali Ivo*, *Dva brata*, and *Zora* were transporting food for Partisan units. Partisan casualties were one dead and two wounded. Again, this was the hunting ground of NSGr 7 flying from Zemunik.

German reports state that six He 46s of 1./NSGr 7, three Hs 126s of Nahaufklärungsstaffel Kroatien, and three Caproni 311s of an unknown unit were stationed at Zadar on 17 February 1944.[39]

Hauptmann Buss entering his He 46 with aid of ground crew, on the way to a counter-Partisan mission. Note the SD 2 anti-personnel bombs on the rack below the fuselage and the flame damper. (Peršen)

Lt. Gade made his 90th flight with NSGr 7 from Banja Luka on 21 February in Heinkel NF+NC, which he flew for 80 minutes. His 1000th flight of the war took place just one day after, when he took off in Heinkel SA+HW, though this was not a combat sortie. At the Zemunik aerodrome, Partisan intelligence reported five aircraft, which usually operated from 07:00 to 17:00 hours.

The Luftwaffe somehow managed to cover the losses that were mounting as the war was coming to its end. In the report regarding his visit to Trieste dated 21 February 1944, Major Theodor Blaich[40] stated that 14 Fiat biplanes were being overhauled there in the local Caproni factory, a small number of them without bombs and armament. In continuation, he estimated completion of the work on these aircraft within eight days at most, and therefore urgently requested eight pilots be sent to ferry the Fiat fighters. Besides those Falcos, 28 more aircraft were being overhauled there and he was grateful for receiving great assistance from the Caproni factory men and RLM inspectorate.

After a month, on 22 February, 15th Air Force heavies were again attacking Croatian targets during the campaign against the German aircraft industry and Luftwaffe bases. This campaign is known to history as Big Week, and was aimed at destroying the Luftwaffe's planes in the factories and on the ground, its aerodromes, and its facilities and supply chain of spares. Zagreb was attacked because the 2nd BG's primary target, the aerodrome in Graz, Austria, was under solid cloud. Captain Harold Chrismon, Commanding Officer of the 20th BS of the 2nd BG, was leading the attack. Seventeen B-17s departed from their bases in Italy, with 13 aircraft arriving over the target. Heavies dropped 27 tons[41] of 225-kg (500-lb) bombs on the aerodrome. Frozen cameras prevented the 2nd BG from getting a record of the results. Another fifteen or so B-17s from other Bomb Groups dropped their loads over Zagreb, making 81 tons of bombs dropped altogether. Above the target, bombers encountered light and inaccurate flak and no fighters.

Borongaj aerodrome in Zagreb, summer 1943, prior to the attacks of the 15th AF. On the right side of the photo behind the Do 17's tail is a building of the Fligerhorst command. On the left is one Gotha Go 145, possibly of FFS A/B 123 or NSGr 7. (Peršen)

According to the reports of the Civil Protection[42] of the city of Zagreb, most of the bombs fell between the main railway station and Borongaj aerodrome. Railway tracks were heavily damaged in several places. However, some of the bombs fell away from the target, harming the civilian population. A few bombs fell on the Upper Town and Kaptol hills North of the main city square, hitting Tkalčićeva Street and Opatovina. The Dominican monastery on Opatovina was hit by one bomb and eight priests were killed. Near the main railway station, the palace of the Social Security building was hit, as well as an edible oil factory between the main station and Borongaj aerodrome. The Classical High School near the station took a direct hit which killed 50 or so soldiers, as it was used as an army barracks. All together, 36 bombs hit the runway at Borongaj aerodrome; a direct hit on the repair shop totally destroyed it, together with two Croatian Air Force machines inside. The aerodrome was completely out of

The bombing of Zagreb on 22 February, when many bombs hit civilian areas, such as (here) Tkalčićeva street in the old town. (Raguž)

use for several days after the attack. Though it was stationed at Borongaj aerodrome, no losses from NSGr 7 were reported as a result of this attack.

On 23 February, Heinkel NF+NC was ferried to Zadar from Banja Luka—landing at 17:00—by Lt. Gade, who himself returned to Banja Luka by other means of transport to resume his flying only on 6 March. His Flugbuch contains no entries for a flight back. After 12:00 hours, probably two He 46s were flown, as Fw. Hartmann of 1./NSGr 7 reported that the village of Šiprage, SE of Banja Luka, was attacked by eight SD 50 bombs, up to four of which could be carried by a Heinkel. The aircraft landed back in Banja Luka at 13:00 and 13:15, their pilots reporting two mules seen near the village they attacked and three more near Kotor Varoš. They observed that the road from Banja Luka to Kotor Varoš and further on towards Šiprage was badly worn. Some leaflets were dropped in the area during the mission.

Later on another mission was undertaken, taking off from Banja Luka at 14:09. Two Heinkel 46s attacked the village of Jelače, about 3km (1.86 miles) South of Gornji Vakuf, in Bosnia and Herzegovina, with SD 50 bombs. In the area they attacked a Partisan patrol of about 20 men with aircraft armament. The Partisans fled into the wood. In the attack, 300 rounds were used and the aircraft landed back between 14:45 and 15:20.

Lt. Gade resumed flying until his death in Bosnia and Herzegovina, accumulating eight more combat sorties in He 46 DB+ZC with Beobachter Fw. Hartmann.

The detachment in Zemunik reported a stock of 1,285 liters (339.4 gallons) of aircraft fuel on 24 February 1944. They used 1,800 liters (475.5 gallons) of fuel, while 2,000 liters (528.3 gallons) of fuel in total were received during the month. The same day at 10:00 hours, six Spitfires attacked the airfield in Zemunik. At 12:10 hours, the attack was repeated by 12 more British fighters. As a result, several Heinkels of 1./NSGr 7 were completely burnt out, as reported in Ultra CX/MSS/R.106(B)—namely IK+LH (WNr. 35), SA+HW, and MF+NC, which had its oil tank shot to pieces. It is certain that two out of the three markings are wrongly interpreted. Heinkel IK+LH was most probably 1K+LH, while MF+NC was actually NF+NC, which was ferried the day before by Lt. Gade. Nick Beale explains where the mistakes came from: "This was a German mistake; someone wrote down '1', but the cipher clerk read it as 'I'. The enigma machine had no keys for figures, so if the cipher clerk had read a number '1' it would be transmitted as the word 'eins' and the British would understand that was 'one'. You could not mistake the word 'eins' for a letter 'I', so it must have been an error at the German end." Due to years of experience in researching Ultra material, Nick continues: "Before I got into Ultra, I had visited Freiburg and seen a lot of original German signals, so I understood the way they wrote them. If they wanted a Roman number for a Gruppe, it was written: '(ROEM.) DREI' = (römisch) drei = III."

Besides the aircraft of the NSGr 7, several others were destroyed and damaged. Completely destroyed was S.M. 82 (WNr. 61463); Ca. 314, coded NX+ZA, WNr. 12703; one Cant 1007; and a Fiat Br. 20. The detachment reported that the remains of the aircraft would be cannibalized.

From Banja Luka, 1./NSGr 7 was active flying armed recce missions in the area of Našice, in Slavonia, from 13:56 to 14:20 and 15:30 hours, respectively. As landing times are different, most probably this mission was flown by several Heinkel aircraft. A hutted camp was observed West of the village of Kršinci and was engaged with machine guns. Some leaflets were dropped East of Bosanska Gradiška and a message for German troops in Brod.

Taking into consideration successes that the Zadar detachment of NSGr 7 and NASt Kroatien had against shipping and Partisan forces on the islands, the order of the Fliegerführer Kroatien dated 25 February about disbandment of the detachment in Zadar is surprising. The fact is that Allied fighter-bombers were inflicting some casualties on the detachment, but those should not have been a reason for disbandment. Despite this order, the Zadar detachment would continue to exist and operate in this or that form until at least September 1944. An order from

Fliegerführer Kroatien directed the aircraft of 1./NSGr 7 to Banja Luka and the ones of NASt Kroatien to Lučko. The detachment in Zadar can be found in the archive materials under the name Airfield Detachment Storzer.

The same day, 1./NSGr 7 was active from Banja Luka; the weather was fine for flying, cloudless with 8 to 10km (4.97-6.21 mile) visibility. The first sortie was made by one He 46 from 12:41 to 13:31, during which no enemy was observed.

On 26 February, Fliegerführer Kroatien sent a telegram to Hptm. Buss, informing him that Partisans would be using the following fire signals to identify supply drop zones to Allied transport planes near Kovičani village, in the Travnik area: from 1 to 10 March, eight fires in the shape of a letter "F"; from 11 to 21 March, seven fires in the shape of a letter "V"; and for the rest of the month, nine fires in the shape of a letter "Z." Individual fires would be separated by about six meters (19.68ft), and they were to be lit from 20:00 to about 23:00 hours. The Fliegerführer asked him to light fires according to the information supplied, to entice the supply planes to drop their precious cargo to the Germans. After the Allied leaders' Teheran conference, the situation for Tito and his movement changed drastically, both politically and in terms of material aid. One of the outcomes of the conference was to start delivering war materiel and supplies for Partisan forces in sufficient quantities to allow strengthening their movement and therefore enabling them to significantly undermine the German position in Yugoslavia. One of the ways to deliver the aid was by air from Allied bases in Italy.

That same 26 February, the detachment in Zadar had bad luck again: two He 46s were destroyed and one Hs 126 was badly damaged. There is no doubt that the Heinkels in question belonged to 1./NSGr 7. It is assumed that aircraft were destroyed on the ground as a result of yet another Allied air raid. Furthermore, the detachment reported one Heinkel and one Henschel serviceable, while one aircraft of each type could be available for urgent demands. Despite continuous attacks by Allied fighter-bomber aircraft, units stationed on the airfield remained operational, as stated in Ultra CX/MSS/T.108/52: "...owing low-level flight and camouflage in blast bays."

Formation of He 46s of Störkampfstaffel Südost over Bosnia and Herzegovina. (Predoević)

Heinz Buss, commanding officer of 1./NSGr 7, flew his missions between 28 February and 1 March 1944 between Zagreb and Banja Luka and back aboard Heinkel 46s TY+AC and DC+VD. From Zagreb, starting 8 April, he made a series of short test flights until 3 May, when he was back in Banja Luka. German archive materials report two more losses for the Gruppe on 1 and 3 March— one aircraft each day—without further detail.

The Partisan navy reported on the first day of March, again erroneously, that five aircraft of the Storch type were stationed at the Zemunik airdrome and that they operated all day.

On 2 March at 01:00 hours, Uffz. Behrens and Flieger Stadler, both of Stab./NSGr 7, were picked up by German units in the area of Fužine, in Croatia, after their twin-engined aircraft "of rather old type" had been shot up by Partisans at Lič, near Fužine. The right engine failed; they became lost and finally decided to bail out, while the aircraft crashed. They had been ferrying it from Cerklje, in Slovenia, to Zadar a day earlier. Thanks to the research of Radovan Živanović, this machine can be identified as Caproni 309 WNr. 12781. Radovan found few remains of the plane on the spot; according to Ferdinando D'Amico, this Matricola Militare belonged to a Ca. 309 Ghibli of Serie VIII. (German WNr. codes on Italian aircraft corresponded to the original Regia Aeronautica Matricola Militare.)

Crash site of Ca. 309 Ghibli of NSGr 7 in Lič, Fužine, Croatia, as seen in 2012. (Živanović)

Five days later, on 7 March 1944, the third Staffel of NSGr 7 was formed in Zagreb on the Caproni Ca. 314. Hauptmann Willy Rümmelin was transferred from 2./NSGr 7 back to Nahaufklärungsstaffel Kroatien in March 1944 in the position of Technical Officer. On 4 April, he received the highest Croatian military medal, the Vojnički red željeznog trolista (Military Order of the Iron Trefoil).

Several days after the formation of the 3rd Staffel, on 11 March, 1./NSGr 7. attacked Partisans on the Vrbas river with one He 46 from 08:50 to 11:15. Small groups of Partisans were observed in the village of Srbac, and from 10:30 to 11:30, one Hs 126 and three He 46s attacked Srbac, claiming direct hits. In the afternoon, starting at 12:10 and lasting until 13:35, an Hs 126 and an He 46 destroyed a building 13km (8.08 miles) SSW of Bosanski Novi and another Hs 126 made a reconnaissance flight in the area 20km (12.43 miles) South of Banja Luka, where its crew noticed small Partisan groups. Twenty-eight SD 2 bombs were used in the attacks, as well as some 3,000 rounds of ammunition.

In Zadar, one serviceable Hs 126 and an He 46 of NSGr 7 were available. The Partisan navy reported a low level recce mission by two aircraft over the bays of the island Dugi Otok at around 08:00. Not finding anything, the aircraft flew away towards the island of Kornat. Hptm. Storzer, from Zemunik airfield in Zadar, urgently requested 1,000 liters (264 gallons) of fuel. The only identified loss of the day was He 46 WNr.150 (DB+ZC) of 1./NSGr 7, which was shot down during an armed recce mission 500 meters (1,640ft) NW of the village of Drajići, 15km (9.32 miles) WNW of Kolo and in Partisan-held territory; unit veteran Lt. Hermann Gade and Beobachter Fw. Karl-Heinz Hartmann were killed. It was Gade's 98th mission for the Gruppe and his 1,009th of the war. Another plane disappeared and one more was damaged by small arms fire from the ground the same day, but there is no additional information on these incidents.

On 12 March 1944, Major Cuno Wilhelmj (in some literature wrongly interpreted as Kuno Wilhelmy) was transferred to 3./NSGr 7 from II./TG 2, arriving in Zagreb from Wien aboard a Ca. 314. On 15 March, he flew the Caproni to Lučko, where the 3rd Staffel was based. Major Wilhelmj was a pilot and observer, and as such he undertook his first combat flight aboard a Do 17Z coded Z8+EG of the Kroatische Kampfgruppe 1[43], with pilot Hptm. Jarolomitsch. They were in the air for almost two hours over the Drvar area, landing back at Lučko at 16:55. One interesting Partisan report issued on 12 March states that from Pleso aerodrome near Zagreb "60 Stuka and Storch aircraft"[44] were operating. From this, it can be seen that Partisan documents, though rich in data regarding aerial attacks on their forces, are not always a reliable source for historical research. Besides the inaccurate number of aircraft, the Partisans had their own typology for German aircraft. The Storch aircraft they mention certainly refers to high-winged or parasol aircraft, including He 46s and Hs 126s, which were actually the ones attacking them. However, it is certain that some Fi 156 aircraft were also present at the airfields near and in Zagreb, belonging to 32./Fl.VG 2, Stab./Fliegerführer Kroatien, and Verb.St.58.

From left to right: Pilot Obfw. Pink and Technical Officer Obfw. Trusek, Fw. Ratzkow "Spiess" of the Staffel, Hptm. Buss, Fw. Schwope, unknown Fw., pilots Fw. Schmidt and Huber, and unknown Fw. in Rajlovac, 1943. (Peršen)

The loss of an unknown aircraft type was attributed to NSGr 7 on 19 March. Two days later, an He 46 attacked Partisans retreating between the villages of Prpoši and Berići, on the Prijedor—Ivanjska road in Bosnia and Herzegovina. Reports from the German "Tiger Division" state that the Partisans were attacked by bombs and MG fire. At Zemunik, five He 46s were available on 23 March and they flew 46 operations during that month. In the Yugoslav archives, information regarding these operations is well documented. A Partisan Navy report dated 20 March states that in the period from 17 to 20 March, German aircraft of the Storch[45] type were conducting systematic attacks on the island Dugi Otok. In these attacks, small-caliber bombs and machine guns were used in low level flight.

According to the report, the first attacks were conducted from 05:30 to 06:30, while the last ones took place in twilight from 17:30 to 18:30. On 17 and 18 March, attacks were concentrated on the northern part of the island in the area of Veli Rat, targeting the big schooner *Ilirija*; finally, on 19 March, the boat was wrecked by two direct hits to the stern and was no longer usable.

An armed ship of the Partisan Navy, NB-1 (in the back) was armed with 1x40 mm AT, 4x20 mm AA, and 1x15 mm AA guns. She was sunk in Ćuška Duboka bay near Dugi Otok island on 20 March 1944 by the bombs thrown from the parasol aircraft. This photo was taken in January 1944 in the port of Vis. (Čedo Perić family via Raguž)

The same 19 March, the Partisan armed boat (NB-1) was attacked at around 05:00 in Soline bay, Dugi Otok island, by bombs dropped from one aircraft, and in the afternoon, around 18:00 hours, by three aircraft. Bombs hit the NB-1 to the stern, knocking out its engine. Another ship (NB-6) towed the badly damaged NB-1 to Ćuška Duboka bay, near the same island.

Besides the schooner, aircraft were systematically attacking bays, harbors, and installations on the islands. In the afternoon, the aircraft widened their attacks to other parts of Dugi Otok, while Partisan shipping was also attacked in Tajer, as well as the harbors of Sali and Žman. That day, the ship *Zdenka* was slightly damaged by aircraft machine guns. Finally, on 20 March at 06:00, two aircraft[46] (in the Partisan report, Storch type) attacked the armed boats NB-1 and NB-2 *Koča* and the schooners *Dobra obitelj* (Good Family) and *Sv. Nikola* in Ćuška Duboka bay. Already damaged, armed boat NB-1 was sent to the bottom of the bay by two bomb hits, while the schooner *Dobra obitelj* was slightly damaged during the morning attacks of 20 March. The bombs that sunk NB-1 fell very close to her and the ship broke in two and sank. During the attacks, three sailors were wounded, one of whom later died. Several bombs fell on the shore of the bay. Later that afternoon, at 17:30, the schooner *Božje ime* (God's Name) was sunk in Lučice bay, while armed ship NB-6 *Napredak* (Progress) was sunk in Šipnata bay, near Kornat island.

NB-6 *Napredak* was armed with 1x40 mm AT, Breda 2x20 mm AA, and 4x8 mm AA guns. All guns except Breda were out of order after the first attack. Around 17:30, on 20 March 1944, NB-6 was sunk by a direct hit of several incendiaries in the repeated air attack. (Čedo Perić family via Raguž)

Regional Partisan Navy Command requested the Supreme Command of the Partisan navy to demand Allied aircraft attacks on the aerodrome in Zemunik, if possible during the evening when all the German aircraft had landed. A request was also sent to the command to withdraw the shipping from the area and send only the minimum necessary ships with supplies and reinforcements. On 23 March, two German aircraft attacked Patrol boats PČ-5, which was sunk, and PČ-21 *Miran* and PČ-22 *Streljko* (Shooter). Patrol boat PČ-21 was attacked with three bombs which missed, as they were dropped from a great height.

Besides the above mentioned armed ships of the Partisan Navy, German aircraft, most probably from NSGr 7 and NASt Kroatien, sank NB-5 *Ivan* on 27 December 1943 in Mala Grčka bay, near the island of Hvar. At least five smaller boats (with "PČ" markings) were sunk by German aviation during the war on the Adriatic sea. NB-2, mentioned earlier, was armed with 1x40mm AT, 2x20mm AA, and 4x8mm AA guns; it fell victim not to German aviation, but to German S-boats S-36 and S-61, which sank her in the vicinity of the island of Lastovo on 17 March 1944.

Possibly as a result of Partisan Navy requests, Spitfires of the Royal Air Force attacked Zemunik aerodrome on 24 March from 12:30 to 12:35 and from 15:05 to 15:15. The first attack led to fuselage damage for He 46 WNr. 305, which was completely destroyed and left in flames during the second attack. Detachment Zadar reported a strength of two He 46s serviceable and one Falco with tire damage. German archives record the loss of one aircraft on 23 March, and two more were lost on 25 March at Zemunik as a result of Allied strafing and bombing. The identification of these aircraft, apart from the above mentioned WNr. 305,

Armed ship NB-5, sunk by German aircraft in Mala Grčka bay, near the island of Hvar. (Čedo Perić family via Raguž)

remains unclear. It seems that Allied aircraft attacked Zemunik again on 22 March, but no more data is available about this event.

On 24 March, Major Wilhelmj was again in the air over Drvar, this time piloting a Ca. 314 for 100 minutes and 466km (289.5 miles) before landing safely in Lučko at 17:42. This is NSGr 7's first recorded combat sortie with Caproni bombers.

A Caproni Ca. 314 of an unknown Luftwaffe unit at Rajlovac in February 1944. Note the unusual painting of the spinners with one white and the other dark. (Raguž)

Aerial view of Zalužani aerodrome near Banja Luka from an He 46 of NSGr 7 in 1943. Some 18 to 20 aircraft are visible on the ground. (Peršen)

One Heinkel 46 of 1./NSGr 7 was reported at Banja Luka aerodrome on 27 March. The following day, the 3rd Staffel was active from Lučko in the area of Podgarić, in Croatia, where Partisans from Bilogora mountain were active. Major Wilhelmj flew two sorties that day in a Ca. 314 from 10:54 to 11:48 (352km - 218.7 miles), and in the afternoon from 15:22 to 16:30 (340km - 211 miles). On the afternoon flight, he reported problems with the forward firing machine guns. The Caproni was equipped with two forward firing Isotta Fraschini Scotti 12.7mm machine guns mounted in the wing roots with 300 rounds each and two S.A.F.A.T. 7.7 mm machine guns in the ventral (rear downward-firing) and dorsal positions (360 degrees rotatable). Uffz. Wagner, who flew for the 3rd Staffel for a short period in 1944, commented on the quality of the Isotta guns and the Caproni's payload in his interview with Dr. Möller: "... it had only two 50-kg (110-lb) bombs and a fixed front MG firing from the wing root. And it was like this: after every fifth shot it [MG] jammed!" This statement about the payload is in conflict with the Caproni 314 manual and it is not quite clear which bombs were used and in which configuration, so the Caproni could carry only two of them.

On 29 March, an He 46 of 1./NSGr 7's Zadar detachment, piloted by Uffz. Drung, force landed near the village of Tukovi, 1km (.62 miles) South of Prijedor, due to the engine damage. The 373rd Croatian Infantry Division secured the plane and the crew was unhurt. In a separate report, the Zadar detachment stated that it had stocks of 800 liters (211 gallons) of aircraft fuel and about 1,200 liters (317 gallons) of diesel fuel. In North Croatia, the 3rd Staffel, flying from Lučko, was again active in the Podgarić area. Major Wilhelmj flew yet another sortie for 105 minutes, landing back at Lučko at 16:30 for a total flying distance of 490km (304 miles). Calculation from this suggests that his target could have been somewhere in Bosnia and Herzegovina, as the distance flown is very similar to that when the Capronis attacked Drvar several days earlier.

Pilot Uffz. Dietrich Perkuhn and Flg. Helmut Hartwig were captured by Partisans following the crash of their He 46 on 27 March on Motajica mountain, in North Bosnia and Herzegovina. The Heinkel in question (1K+HH, WNr. 871) belonged to the 1st Staffel. According to Partisan reports, Uffz. Perkuhn was captured by the fighters of the 12th Slavonian Brigade, but there is

Butmir aerodrome near Sarajevo. This photo was taken from an He 46 of NSGr 7. (Predoević)

no mention of his Beobachter. It seems that two machine guns were taken out of the wreck, one of which had been synchronized with the propeller. If this is true, it indicates that it was an Hs 126, rather than a Heinkel, and in that case was probably not from the 1st nor any other Staffel, as NSGr 7 had not operated the type since January 1944.

On 4 April, no sorties were possible from Lučko and Borongaj, the ground being too soft due to weather conditions. Mostar, often used by detachments from NSGr 7, was raided by 28 B-24s of the 460th BG and 70.5 tons of bombs were dropped. The same day, a pilot of the 1st Staffel, Unteroffizier Rudolf Ryba, received the Eisernes Kreuz 1st Class for previous actions against the Partisans.

Attack on Partisans by an He 46 in Bosnia and Herzegovina recorded by its photo camera. (Predoević)

The detachment in Zadar reported several sorties for the day. From 04:10 to 04:50 hours, an He 46 made an armed reconnaissance sortie above the islands off Zadar. On the island of Kornat, in Vrulje bay, a single-masted boat of approximately 50 tons was observed. Later on, an He 46 attacked and destroyed a mill used by Partisans SSE of Zadar. On an unnamed island, barracks were heavily damaged by bombs, and cars spotted in the village were machine gunned. A C.R. 42 flew an armed reconnaissance sortie in the area East of Kornat island, observing lively maritime traffic by small vessels, each with two to three men. In both Lokvina and another unidentified bay on the island of Rava, single fishing motorboats were observed, each armed with two machine guns. Both vessels were attacked and damaged. Very strong anti-aircraft defense was noted from both Rava and Mala Rava. In this attack, three SD 50 bombs were used, as well as two Italian 50-kg (110-lb) bombs and 95 rounds of 12.7 mm. The next sortie was undertaken by an He 46 from 16:10 to 16:55 over the Zadar archipelago. East of Kornat island, a small vessel was engaged with 490 rounds from the aircraft's single 7.92mm gun. The day's last sortie was made by another He 46 from 17:15 to 17:50 in the area of Rava island, where a large fishing boat was observed and attacked in Marnica Bay. Despite the very strong anti-aircraft fire, including tracers, from both the boat and from the island, the Heinkel damaged the vessel. After three SD 50 bombs and 310 rounds the vessel was badly damaged but did not sink.

Later in its report, the detachment noted that the C.R. 42, with is heavy machine guns, was well suited to attacks on wooden ships, but was not suitable for reconnaissance missions. Thus, they proposed to have a combination of C.R. 42 and He 46 aircraft in the detachment, since the Heinkel's small-caliber gun could not inflict sufficient damage. The detachment further reported the increased enemy presence on the islands and their superbly organized anti-aircraft defenses. The following day, the Zemunik detachment disposed of just one serviceable Heinkel. Two more planes were on strength but unserviceable: an He 46 requiring a change of the wing and a C.R. 42 grounded by engine wear. The serviceable He 46 made a reconnaissance from Zadar to Starigrad and Ražanac, but made no sightings.

Fliegerführer Kroatien's effort for 5 April included nine sorties by Fiat C.R. 42s from Banja Luka against Podravska Slatina, where German troops were encircled by Tito forces. Aerial attacks were conducted from 09:15 to 10:55 and from 15:20 to 16:45. In the face of strong ground defenses, direct hits were achieved on houses and other Partisan-occupied positions and a factory building was destroyed. Some 2,500 rounds of Italian 12.5mm ammunition were used. A Junkers W. 34 from Zagreb dropped two containers with 10,500 rounds to the surrounded German garrison.

On 6 April 1944, at 09:26, aircraft of No. 2 Squadron SAAF (No. 7 SAAF Wing) attacked Zalužani airfield in Banja Luka, causing devastation among German and Croatian aircraft alike. Besides killing the 2nd ranking Croatian ace of the Second World War and veteran of the Eastern Front Hptm. Cvitan Galić, who tried to engage attackers with an M.S. 406C1, the South Africans destroyed seven Fiat C.R. 42 aircraft of the 2nd Staffel and caused 40% damage to four other Falcos. Hs 126A-1 WNr. 3028 and Hs 126B-1 WNr. 4154 of NASt Kroatien were also destroyed in the attack. All the aircraft were full of fuel, helping fires to spread. Hangars, blast bays, and quarters were hit by bomb splinters and 20mm Hispano cannon shells from the Spitfires; a car and a truck were also destroyed, as well as 20 of the 50-kg (110-lb) bombs and about 13,000 rounds of precious aviation ammunition. German casualties were one dead, one heavily wounded, and six slightly wounded. Four big craters were left on the landing area, but the aerodrome stayed serviceable. The following Falcos of the 2nd Staffel were destroyed: WNr. 9277 black 6, WNr. 9274 black 11, WNr. 9852 black 13, WNr. 4461 black 15, WNr. 9216 black 17, and WNr. 9262 black 18. All these aircraft were Fiat built.

In addition, the destruction of Fiat C.R. 42 WNr. 3990 black 4 is reported in Ultra decrypt CX/MSS.R.151 (B), but no Fiat with this Matricola Militare was produced. The correct Matricola Militare 8990 is given in a later report regarding the losses from the attack (Ultra decrypt CX/MSS/T 152/60). This aircraft too was produced by Fiat. In the war diary of No. 2 Squadron SAAF is written the following:

> Today was one of the best days in the history of the Squadron, and for that matter, in the Wing.
>
> Each carrying 2 x 250lb bombs, 13 Spit. IXs of this Squadron, led by Col. Loftus, D.S.O. D.F.C., took off at 10:05 hours to bomb Banja Luka L.G. No.1 (Yugoslavia). 12 Spit. Vcs of 4 Squadron were in the formation to strafe after we had bombed and six pilots of No. 1 Squadron provided top cover. (Incidentally, it is worth noting that we provided two aircraft for this top cover, thus making our total aircraft in the mission 15.) The mission was a complete success: the take-off was perfect, the form up was perfect, and the results were terrific. Taken completely by surprise, the Jerries put up no defense, except for moderate light M/G fire from the 'drome. The 26 bombs were perfectly placed, all falling on or near hangars and dispersed aircraft. One direct hit was scored on a hangar, setting it on fire, and at least three aircraft exploded or were set on fire by the bombings. Four Squadron then went down to strafe and our boys also climbed in and everyone had a royal time. It

was impossible to assess the damage completely, but after careful comparison between pilots, the following are the claims. They are conservative, but doubtless detailed information will come from Partisans.

Destroyed: two Re 2001, one Ju 87, two Bf 109, six Hs 126, one S.M. 82, ten to fifteen C.R. 42, one He 111, one Bf 210, two MC 202, and one unidentified S/E (Radial). Damaged: one Re 2001, one Fw 190, and four C.R. 42.

Twenty-five to 30 aircraft destroyed and six damaged with no loss to our aircraft.

In addition, three M/G posts were silenced and a terrific explosion (possibly ammo or petrol dump) was observed.

Unfortunately, owing to cloud, subsequent photo coverage was not possible. Col. Loftus, DSO, DFC, estimated, however, that a larger proportion of the Bf 109s were destroyed. It is interesting to note that on the mission 26 Spits used approximately 21,600 rounds of .303" and 4,226 rounds of 20mm with only two stoppages.

Also on 6 April, 38 Flying Fortresses of the 463rd BG and 29 Liberators of the 461st BG bombed Borongaj airfield with, according to the 461st BG's mission report "poor results." German reports do not mention any aircraft of NSGr 7 damaged or destroyed. The same day, one aircraft of the NSGr 7 Zadar detachment flew over Božava, on Dugi Otok island, at a height of 200 meters (656ft). When Partisan units opened fire the aircraft broke off.

Men of NSGr 7 pumping fuel at Banja Luka aerodrome in 1943. (Peršen)

Operations resumed from Banja Luka on 7 April, when a Kette of 2./NSGr 7 led by Ogefr. Basr reconnoitred the area of Banja Luka, the Staffel's only task that day. The Kalnik mountain area was attacked by Capronis of 3rd Staffel the same day, with Major Wilhelmj noting in his Flugbuch a combat sortie of 66 minutes (308km - 191 miles), landing at Lučko at 19:10 and flying Ca. 314 Yellow 2.

Next day, 2./NSGr 7 intensified its activities and the following sorties were recorded: at 05:00, 05:25, 05:50, and 06:15 by four planes in the area of Papuk mountain, where 20 bombs of 12.5kg (27.5lbs) and 2,000 bullets were used against Partisans, hitting a train, Partisan positions on the hills, and weapon pits.

NSGr 7 Heinkels flying on a combat mission in Bosnia and Herzegovina, 1943. (Predoević)

Following up, the next day four more Falcos attacked the Partisans from 11:00 to 11:30 and from 11:50 to 12:20 with bombs and guns. Around 3,000 rounds of 12.7mm ammunition were used, as well as six 50-kg (110-lb) bombs. Hits were observed on the ground, three houses were destroyed and one damaged, and bombs hit the railway tracks. Small arms fire was directed at the attackers from the ground.

Caproni 314 (coded 4X+BL) of 3./NSGr 7 on a combat sortie during operation Rösselsprung. The ventral position of the rear-firing 7.7mm S.A.F.A.T. (with a maximum traverse of +/- 30 degrees and elevation of -3 to -68 degrees) is clearly visible in this photo. (Raguž)

The 1./NSGr 7 detachment at Zadar was also active that day: an He 46 flew a recce mission in the area Novigrad-Obrovac-Karin-Medvide from 08:48 to 10:15 hours on 8 April, but no enemy forces were observed. The Ražanac-Novigrad road had lively traffic, and in the area between Medvide and Ervenik, around 20 small Chetnik groups were observed, each three to five men in strength. The crew also observed one group of about 20 Chetniks and hanged persons (guerrillas, according to their report). The same day, after more than a month off flying, Hptm. Buss was in action with He 46 PR+NM from 10:10 to 12:05, taking off and landing at Zagreb.

Later in the day, the 3rd Staffel recorded a sortie by three Ca. 314 bombers from Lučko airfield against an unidentified target. Major Wilhelmj, however, logged a combat sortie with Yellow 2 from 11:26 to 12:27 hours. He mentions the target's name, but this is illegible (possibly Konjščina in Zagorje). By the number of kilometers flown, the target would have been 100–120km (62-74.5 miles) from Zagreb.

The Fliegerführer Kroatien gave the order for the recce detachment in Rajlovac to be transferred to Banja Luka for a "special undertaking." Upon arrival, they were to report to Oblt. Rudolf Falke of 1./NSGr 7. It is possible that in the preparation for the later Operation Rösselsprung, some Hs 126s of NASt Kroatien were added again to 1./NSGr 7, as had already been the case earlier during the formation of the 2nd Staffel.

Recovery team of NSGr 7 on the way to the emergency landing site of one of their aircraft in Bosnia and Herzegovina. (Peršen)

Total Axis strength at Banja Luka aerodrome for 8 April 1944 was 14 Luftwaffe and 23 Croatian Air Force aircraft. The Luftwaffe had one damaged Ju 87 of a visiting unit; four Hs 126s of NASt Kroatien (of which one was damaged); and nine Falcos of NSGr 7, of which five were in flying condition. The Croatian Air Force disposed of the following: four Caproni (three Ca. 311 and one unknown); one Potez (probably XXV); four ex-French Air Force Morane-Saulnier M.S. 406C1s; one Yugoslav-built Rogožarski PVT trainer; three A.V.I.A. FL. 3s; and four indigenous Fizir N++. But all this mass of machines was out of service; in flying condition there were just three Saiman 200s, two Fizir N++, and one A.V.I.A. FL. 3, while three more FL. 3s and four more Fizir N++ were damaged.

The disastrous month of April continued for the 2nd Staffel, as they lost another C.R. 42 the same day: WNr. 9788, Black 9—this time near Kutina—and its pilot, Oberfeldwebel Walter Bormann, was injured. The aircraft was damaged after returning from a combat sortie and it made an emergency landing due to the bad weather, darkness, and a lack of fuel. This is one of the few times where it is evident that the Nachtschlachtgruppe operated in nocturnal conditions, though not very successfully.

Armorer mounting SD 2 antipersonnel bombs on an He 46 in summer 1943 in Banja Luka. Note that the fez is worn as an everyday part of the uniform. (Peršen)

The 1st Staffel was also active, as Hptm. Buss attacked Partisans with his usual He 46 PR+NM from 10:10 to 12:05, taking off from Zagreb. The aerodrome at Butmir was closed to all aircraft due to bad weather and large-scale works.

The 2nd Staffel reported two Fiat C.R. 42 on strength on 8 April (WNr. 5545 and WNr. 9207), both Fiat-built aircraft and returnees after being repaired.

The 2nd Staffel started attacks on Partisans on 9 April, making early morning sorties at 07:00, 07:30, 07:45, and 08:10. The aircraft used twenty 12.5-kg (27.5-lb) bombs and about 1,000 rounds of ammunition; they faced small arms and machine gun fire from the ground. More assaults were conducted by 2./NSGr 7 from 09:15 to 10:10 and from 09:45 to 10:35, respectively. One C.R. 42 was hit in the engine during the attack in the area of Papuk mountain. At Banja Luka airfield, Falco WNr. 5545 was unserviceable, as mentioned in a letter from the Technical Officer of 2./NSGr 7 dated 9 April to Fliegerführer Kroatien. It seems that this plane was damaged earlier, salvaged, and transported to Banja Luka. Four aircraft attacked the area of Papuk later the same day, using 1,000 rounds of ammunition and six Italian 50-kg (110-lb) bombs. The target of the attacks was Partisan ammunition depots, but the results were not seen by the crews. A report of 9 April mentions the salvage of a crashed aircraft of 2./NSGr 7 which had not yet been recovered (probably referring to WNr. 9788).

The summary report of the Headquarters of the 6th Corps of Tito's Army (6. Korpus) dated 20 May gives insight into the results of the bombing in the Papuk mountain area: "Besides the fact that situation in the commands is better each day, many defects are detected in their work. Those defects were especially evident during the heavy enemy bombardment of our territory, when, for example, chiefs of certain workshops left their working places together with their men and ran around the woods, and nobody knew their whereabouts throughout the day."[47]

Unknown member of NSGr 7 posing in front of an He 46 at Rajlovac. (Predoević)

The Staffel's strength after the above losses was reported as seven C.R. 42s in total, of which only one was serviceable in Banja Luka and one with the detachment at Zadar. Conditionally, two more aircraft were serviceable in Banja Luka and one more in Zagreb. Unserviceable C.R. 42s were WNr. 9816 and 5545, which had problems with their compressed air installations. (On Fiats, this system was used to operate the two 12.7mm SAFAT machine guns in the engine cowling, synchronized to fire through the propeller. To eliminate, for the most part, violent vibration on the structure of the fuselage arising from their recoil, the guns were equipped with a shock absorber between the weapon and the crossbar. Each gun had a box for 500 rounds of ammunition accessible through hatches on either side of the fuselage.)

Fiat WNr. 9169 was supposed to be sent to Stab./NSGr 7 as a reinforcement, but due to 50% crash damage it was put in reserve. Nominally, the Staffel had 22 crews on strength, of which seven were ready: two were on leave in Banja Luka itself and 13 were detached to other units. Next day, only three planes were serviceable at Banja Luka and one at Zadar. Both conditionally serviceable planes in Zagreb and Banja Luka lacked bomb racks and the one at Zagreb had no guns. In the same report, Falco WNr. 5545 is mentioned as unserviceable after a forced landing due to enemy action 20km (12.42 miles) NE of Banja Luka.

On 10 April, nine C.R. 42s made ground support sorties against Partisans encircling Croatian and German troops in Podravska Slatina. In two waves from 9:15 to 10:55 and 15:20 to 16:55, they attacked Partisan positions with a total of 20 Italian 12.5-kg (27.5-lb) bombs, continuing with 12.7mm guns and using a total of around 2,500 rounds. Pilots reported one factory destroyed and direct hits on houses and enemy positions in front of Axis defense lines. During the day, a Junkers W 34 from Zagreb dropped two containers of ammunition to encircled troops with 10,500 rounds. Down South, one He 46 of 1./NSGr 7's detachment in Zadar made a recce in the Starigrad-Ražanac area without spotting any enemy. Ultra reports that "operations detachment Butmir" (a translation of the German "Einsatzkommando"—in other words, the detachment of 1./NSGr 7) resumed its operations from Butmir near Sarajevo. For some reason, later the same day, both "Operations Detachment Butmir" (1./NSGr 7) and "Recce Detachment Butmir" (NAST Kroatien) were temporarily transferred to the aerodrome of Sarajevo-Rajlovac.

At Rajlovac, Stab./NSGr 7 had three Ju 87D-3s (according to Ultra decrypt Ju 87D-4s, but series 110 was D-3 and D-4 was planned as a torpedo bomber) stationed, but Stukas WNr. 110462, 100420, and 110499 did not fly any sorties due to bad weather. In fact, both aerodromes near Sarajevo were closed due to weather conditions.

It is very curious that Ultra KV831 reports the existence of "Cap 309" serviceable at Zagreb on 10 April 1944 for the 2nd Staffel. This stands for Caproni Ca. 309, and in another decrypt from the day before (CX/MSS/R.150(B)), 2./NSGr 7 reports availability of a Cap 309/VII at Banja Luka. ("VII" was sometimes also added to the designations of Ju 87 aircraft in Nachtschlacht service and may refer to adaptations for operating by night.)

On the evening of 10 April, the 2nd Staffel reported on aircraft joining and leaving its strength since the air raid. Apart from the machines already detailed, WNr. 692 had been damaged 10-15% by enemy action after just two days with the Gruppe. (It is not clear what type this was, but the WNr. is not that of a Fiat). Also damaged by enemy action were WNr. 8943 (unknown percentage) and 7574 (5%).

The same day, 10 April, 2./NSGr 7 reported a strength of seven serviceable C.R. 42s: three at Banja Luka and one at Zadar, with six crews ready for action at Zalužani aerodrome. Since 6 April, the Staffel had lost seven aircraft and sustained damage to five others.

It is very possible that Ca. 314s of 3./NSGr 7 were used the same day North of Novo Mesto, in Slovenia, when five SC 250 bombs and 2,000 rounds of ammunition were used against "bandits." Part of the German signal where the type of plane(s) was given was not decipherable.

According to the technical documentation, the Ca. 314 could carry the following combinations of weapons in its internal bomb bay and on the two racks with a total maximum load of 400kg (882lbs) of ordnance:
8 bombs of 160kg (353lbs) (Ca. 314 C only; versions A and B could not load these bombs in the internal bay);
3[48] bombs of 100kg (220.5lbs) against surface targets;
3 depth charges of 100 kg (220.5lbs) against submarines;
6[49] bombs of 50kg (110lbs) against surface targets;
16 bombs of 15kg (33lbs) in groups of four against surface targets;
32 bombs of 12kg (26.5lbs) in groups of four against surface targets.

The external bomb racks could carry:
1 torpedo Italian type S.I. or German type W.H.;
2 bombs of 500kg (1,102lbs) (version B only);
2 bombs of 250kg (551lbs) (version B only);
2 bombs of 160kg (353lbs) (versions A and C only);
2 bombs of 100kg (220.5lbs) (versions A and C only, both against surface or submerged targets).

The Caproni Ca. 314 was equipped with two Isotta Fraschini DELTA Rc. 35 I inverted V air-cooled engines with a centrifugal compressor. Power was 640hp (at sea level) to 730hp (at 3,500m [11,483ft] and air pressure 880mmHg [17psi]). The engine was fitted with a Alfa Romeo type H.365 variable three-blade metal propeller.

With these engines, the Ca. 314 had the following performance: maximum horizontal speed at low altitude 340km/h (211mph); 417km/h (259mph) at 3,500m (11,483ft). Minimum speed at low altitude: 140km/h (87mph). Climbing rate: 4,000m (13,123ft) in 13′ 30″ for the Ca. 314 B and 12′ 30″ for the Ca. 314 C. Service ceiling was 8,000m (26,246ft) theoretical and 7,300m (23,950ft) practical. Take-off and landing runs were both 380m (1,247ft). Range with a full fuel load, all machine guns, and 400kg (882lbs) of bombs at 4,500m (14,764ft) and a speed of 350km/h (217.5mph): 780km (484.6 miles, or 1,200km [745.6 miles] at the same altitude without the bombs and guns). In contrast, the C.R. 42's performance included: maximum horizontal speed at low altitude 342km/h (212.5mph) at 2,520rpm; 360km/h (223.7mph) at 1,000m (3,281ft); and 423km/h (262.8mph) at 7,000m (22,966ft). Minimum speed at low altitude: 128km/h (79.5mph). Climb rate at a weight of 2,295kg (5,060lbs): 1,000m (3,281ft) in 1′ 25″; 6,000m (19,685ft) in 9′. Service ceiling 10,500m (34,448ft) theoretical and 10,200m (33,465ft) practical. Take-off run: 210m (689ft); landing run with brakes: 340m (1,115.5ft). Range with the payload specified above at 5,500m (18,045ft) and a speed of 380km/h (236mph) was 775km (481.6 miles). In practice, with a bomb load these figures were much lower.

Uffz. Wagner remembers his missions in the Caproni bomber, comparing it with the small Italian fighter that replaced it: "Nominally, the plane had the same speed as the Ju 88, but in reality it was just a little bit faster than the Fw 58. It also had opposing motors, and the frames had been drilled from time to time. So we did not fly the Ca. 314 for long. One time, the Technical Officer came along and drilled the main spar, and when water came out it was announced: 'The Caproni can go!' Then we got the Fiat fighter plane, the Fiat C.R. 42. That was a nice plane! You could do aerobatics and such with it. That was nice."

Italian-built Savoia-Marchetti SM. 82 in Luftwaffe markings taking off from Banja Luka in autumn 1943. Note the bad state of the landing ground. (Peršen)

Next day, 11 April, in front of 1st Staffel staff, an Italian-built SM. 82 coded 1K+ZZ of IV./TG 1 crashed and caught fire at Zemunik aerodrome due to pilot error, killing five, including pilot Fw. Tristov. Two more occupants of the Savoia were severely and nine persons slightly wounded. Meanwhile, 3./NSGr 7 was active over Grabovac in today's Plitvice Lakes National Park in Croatia; Major Wilhelmj reported a sortie from Lučko from 13:27 to 14:50 in Ca. 314 Yellow 2, with a total flying distance of 387km (240.5 miles). Apart from that disaster with the SM. 82, Zemunik aerodrome was attacked by eight Spitfires of No. 2 Squadron SAAF led by the notorious—for NSGr 7—Colonel Loftus. Each aircraft was loaded with two 250-lb bombs and six of these fell in the target area, where a hangar was set ablaze. After strafing, the South Africans claimed one Ca 310, one Bf 210 destroyed, and five M/G posts silenced. They reported that the aerodrome was defended by just five machine gun posts.

On 12 April, 2./NSGr 7 had seven crews operational in Banja Luka, two on leave, and 13 detached out of 22 available on strength. The Zadar Detachment of 1./NSGr 7 was not flying that day, although it had two He 46s serviceable out of four on strength; both unserviceable aircraft had suffered wing damage.

15th Air Force heavy bombers damaged this Do 17K of the Croatian Air Force in the hangar at Borongaj aerodrome on 12 April 1944. (Raguž)

That day, the 460th and 461st BG bombed the marshalling yard and Borongaj aerodrome, Zagreb. The 34 B-24s and 32 B-17s over the target dropped 143.5 tons[50] of GP bombs. In the mission summary is written: "Despite a four-tenths undercast and much flak, the crews did an excellent job. 16 aircraft slightly damaged by flak." The mission summary of the 765th BS of the 461st BG mentions 150 hits on the target. The B-24s of the 449th and 451st BG also bombed Borongaj in a cataclysm for the already badly-equipped Croatian Air Force. Bombs heavily damaged the hangar of the 19th Squadron (19. Jato ZNDH) and created huge craters in the tarmac and runway. More disastrous were losses among the already insufficient aircraft: the one and only Avia Fokker F. 39; a Morane-Saulnier M.S. 406C1; two Fiat G. 50Bis; two Dornier Do 17K; two Potez XXV; two Saiman 200; one Bücker Bü 131 Jungmanan; FL. 3; and one Puss Moth were completely destroyed. According to German reports, seventeen Luftwaffe planes were destroyed or damaged. Three Junkers Ju 87s of SG 151 were destroyed, while among the damaged aircraft were one Junkers W34, one Fi 156, one C.R. 42, one Klemm Kl 35, one Bf 110 "Zerstörer," and seven small machines. Also among the total of 17 German aircraft were two He 46s of the 1st Staffel that were heavily damaged and later scrapped, while another of the Staffel's He 46s suffered minor damage.

By 14 April, the number of serviceable aircraft in the 2nd Staffel had fallen to four: one at Zadar and three at Banja Luka. Fiat-built Falco WNr. 5655 needed a new carburetor and WNr. 9816 was still not repaired. Of 22 crews on strength, six were ready and three were on leave.

Remains of several aircraft at Borongaj after the bombing of 12 April 1944. (Raguž)

From left to right: Hptm. Buss, Fw. Ratzkow, Fw. Knimann, Obfw. Trusek, and Fw. Deppe in Rajlovac, 1943. (Peršen)

Major Wilhelmj logged an operation against Partisan forces on Papuk mountain in Western Slavonia, attacking targets in the Dobro area. He flew Ca. 314 Yellow 2 from 11:05 to 12:30 from Lučko; he and his crew covered a total distance of 396km (246 miles).

Next day, there were still only four Fiats serviceable (marked 2, 7, and 10, plus 14 in Zagreb), and six more were "conditionally serviceable" in Banja Luka. That day, a ferry flight was organized to bring in new Falcos from Italy, but C.R. 42 WNr. 9888 crashed on take-off from Cameri and was damaged 100%. Its pilot, Uffz. Alfred Schoenemann, was injured and died later that day (Cameri airfield was home to a major repair facility for several types of aircraft operated by the Luftwaffe).

Hauptmann Buss had flown no ground attack missions since

his last flight on 8 April, only short training flights in Zagreb. His flights 152 to 157 cover the period prior to his departure for Banja Luka, in which he accumulated a total of 85 minutes of flight time in the following He 46s: TY+NC; 1K+KH; 1K+BH (flown twice); CQ+HP; and DC+VD.

Partisans reported that enemy airpower was very active during the first 15 days of April, especially in Central Bosnia and Herzegovina around Kotor Varoš, Skender Vakuf, Maslovara, and Šipraga, where they also supported Chetnik units in their fight against the Partisans. Effects of the Allied bombardment of Banja Luka aerodrome were apparent, as Axis aircraft were not present in the numbers seen prior to bombardment. This is one of the rare testimonies in the Partisan documentation to the effects that Allied bombing had on the battlefield in Bosnia and Herzegovina itself.

On 13 April, the Zadar detachment's strength was four He 46s, of which two were serviceable, one ready for non-armed reconnaissance missions, and one unserviceable. Fliegerführer Kroatien ordered Bihać aerodrome to send two truckloads of B4 aircraft fuel and four barrels of oil to Zemunik airfield with the next army convoy, to be led by "an energetic non-commissioned officer."

In their reports throughout the war, Partisans state that they have been attacked by Storch aircraft with bombs and gun fire. One has to bear in mind that Partisan forces were composed mostly of badly-educated peasants and that many of them saw the aircraft for the first time in their lives when they were being bombed by them. The report of the attack by a Storch-type aircraft on the Srebrenica Partisan Detachment can be seen in that context. They were attacked near the village of Sokolovići, in Eastern Bosnia and Herzegovina, on 16 April, when one man of the detachment was wounded. On the 17th of the month, 3rd Staffel Capronis were attacking Partisans in the Zagorje area in Croatia. Major Wilhelmj reported an attack on Gornje Jesenje, near Krapina, from 13:55 to 14:38 (mission of 200km [124.3 miles]). Next day, he was again in the air, bombing Mrkopalj, in the Gorski Kotar area. This mission of 241km (150 miles) was flown from 09:35 to 10:27 in Ca. 314 Yellow 2. Strength of the Zadar detachment of 1./NSGr 7 on 18 April was four He 46s.

The Luftwaffe was very active on 20 April 1944, with a total of 117 sorties, of which 13 were bomber missions, 79 ground attack, and 25 reconnaissance. Stab./NSGr 7 informed Zadar that at the earliest possible convenience, Oblt. Buchheim would fly to Zemunik and take over the detachment from Lt. Jessat. Six Ca. 314 bombers of "Experimental Detachment Lučko" bombed Partisans in Čabuna, near Virovitica, with 1,020 Italian 2-kg (4.4-lb) fragmentation bombs and 120 Italian incendiaries, also of 2kg (4.4lbs). This "Detachment" was actually 3./NSGr 7, whose first aircraft took off from Lučko at 08:25 and landed back at 09:45 (373 km [232 miles]), while a second attack took place from 11:05 to 12:20 hours (350km [217.5 miles]). Major Wilhelmj flew both missions in Ca. 314 Yellow 2, his Flugbuch naming the target as Suhopolje. However, Suhopolje and Čabuna are neighboring villages on the Virovitica—Slatina road, Čabuna being more easterly and closer to Slatina. This was Major Cuno Wilhelmj's last flight with 3./NSGr 7, as he left Croatia for Germany aboard Ca. 314 Yellow 5 the next day as observer, while another pilot of the Staffel, Obfw. Schniffer, was at the controls. This might also mean that C.R. 42s had begun arriving in the 3rd Staffel and that pilots experienced on multi-engine aircraft were being withdrawn from the unit. After he finished his service with NSGr 7, Wilhelmj was transferred to SG 111 in Stubendorf for Nachtschlacht training, after which he became Staffelkapitän of 3./NSGr. 1 in Idriza, on the Eastern Front, at the end of June 1944. For a short period from the end of August to the beginning of September, he was Staffelkapitän of 1./NSGr. 1. From this assignment he finished his career at Frontfliegersammelgruppe Quedlinburg, a depot unit that gathered flying personnel awaiting new assignments.

The second Staffel was active in the same area that day, attacking Partisan positions with 13 C.R. 42s, which dropped 36 x 12.5kg (2705-lb) bombs and six 50-kg (110-lb) Italian bombs. Three more C.R. 42 sorties were carried out against Partisan positions around the city of Prijedor with six 50-kg (110-lb) Italian bombs. Many Hs 126 armed recce sorties were recorded that day, but these were probably NASt Kroatien missions. The Henschels dropped SD 50 bombs as follows:

Aircraft No.	Target	Bombs	Remarks
6	Čabuna	20	1 broke off, oil leak
2	Prijedor area	8	
1	Višegrad	4	
1	Vlasenica	4	
1	Mrkonjićgrad area	1	
1	Zvornik area	4	
1	Kotor Varoš	4	

Two more Hs 126 sorties over Podravska Slatina and Bijelo Polje were uneventful, with no sightings. One other Hs 126 abandoned its mission to the Prijedor area due to engine trouble. A Falco was lost on 20 April: a second Staffel Fiat, WNr. 9207 piloted by Uffz. Max Ortmann, which crashed and burned in the vicinity of Banja Luka. Otmann was injured and the cause of the accident was reported as "strong downdraughts."[51] Fliegerführer Kroatien reported strong Flak and MG anti-aircraft fire in the areas of Čabuna, Drvar, and Tičevo.

The strongest attacks that day were on Tičevo, when numerous Ju 87s, as well as Kroat Kampfgruppe 1, attacked the locality, the seven Do 17s dropping 75 SC 50 bombs and 900 incendiaries of 2kg (4.4lbs). The Stukas that attacked Tičevo were comprised of 16 from 2./LLG. 1 and 13 of 13./SG 151, dropping a total of 13 SC 250 and 68 SD 50 bombs. It seems that Fliegerführer Kroatien had observed the village for a long time, as he reported to the German XV. Mountain Corps that Tičevo served as a convalescent center for injured Partisans, but that it had become their main depot in the area too. As proof, the airmen cited numerous fires after the attack and very strong anti-aircraft fire during.

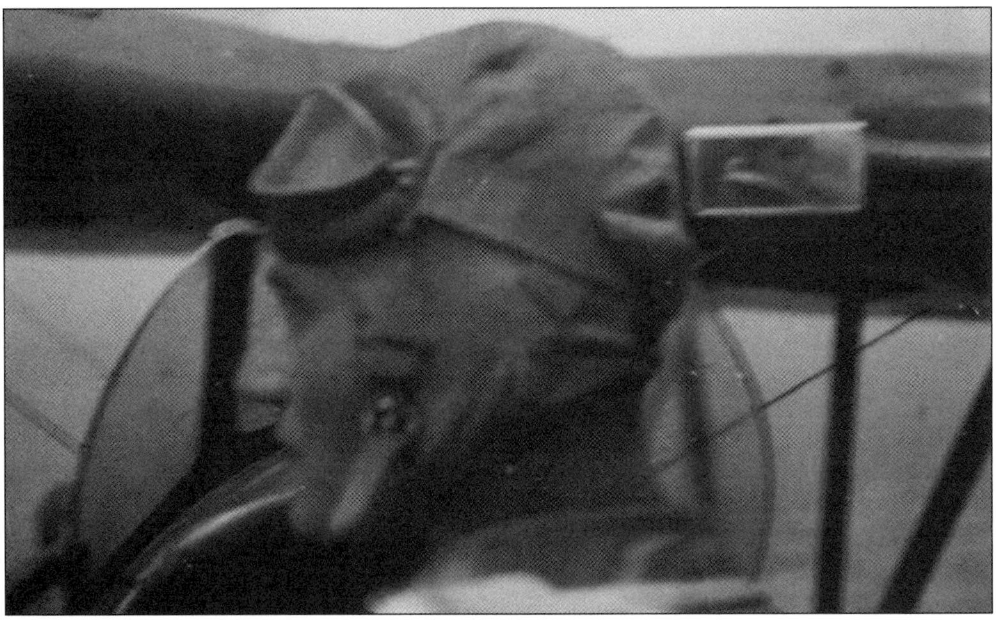

Pilot of the Gruppe in an He 46. (Predoević)

On 21 April, the Zadar detachment of 1st Staffel was active with two He 46s over the islands SSW of Zadar but spotted no targets.

Next day, the situation started to improve for the 2nd Staffel in Banja Luka, where six Falcos (markings: Black 4, 5, 6, 10, 11, and 12) were serviceable. Under repair were: the Fiat-built WNr. 7172, which needed a change of compressor, carried out in the workshops at Banja Luka; WNr. 9170 needed replacement of its machine guns; and finally, WNr. 9816 was repaired and made its long-awaited test flight. Eleven sorties were reported by 2./NSGr 7 that day: in the first wave, six Falcos attacked Partisan positions with 12.5-kilo (27.5-lb) bombs, targeting some houses NE of Banja Luka; and later on, another five planes flew a sortie NNW of Banja Luka without spotting any targets. In the first attack, several direct hits were observed and Fliegerführer Kroatien reported machine guns and small arm anti-aircraft defenses in the areas of Bosanski Petrovac, Drvar, Otočac, Kutina, and NE of Banja Luka.

Luftwaffenkommando Südost reported bombing by Ca. 314s and C.R. 42s on 23 April; the former probably belonged to the 3rd Staffel, while the latter were part of the 2nd Staffel.

Two more aircraft were reported lost on 22 and 23 April, respectively. Though further details were not reported on these losses, it is known that they were not due to any enemy action. Both 1./LLG 1 and 13./SG 151 (the latter from Gorica) were ordered to transfer to Sarajevo as part of the preparations for Operation Rösselsprung (Knight's Move).

During Operation "Ungewitter" (Violent Storm), from 28 April to 11 May 1944, the Wehrmacht's 42nd Jäger Division reported many actions by bombers and ground attack aircraft in the Slavonska Požega—Našice—Podravska Slatina areas. Targets for these air raids were Partisan warehouses, supplies, and "destruction of the gangs," as the Germans called Tito's Partisan movement (and likewise resistance forces in other occupied countries). Aircraft made morning and evening reconnaissance flights every day of the operation. On 30 April, 2./NSGr 7 was reported to be at Banja Luka.

On 1 May 1944, Lt. Gerhard Filges became Offz. z.b.V. of the 3rd Staffel. He served as Staffelführer from 7 June 1944, until the nomination of a new Staffelkapitän in October. Also that day, another crew and Caproni bomber started their journey from Göttingen, via Nürburg-Roth and Wien-Aspern, arriving at Pleso aerodrome three days later. Flying Ca. 314C Yellow 12, WNr. 12206, originally built at Taliedo, near Milan, was pilot Odilo Hübel, Kampfbeobachter Unteroffizier Anton Pauli, and Bordschütze Ogefr. Horst Abramowski landed at their destination on 3 May at 12:20, after flying 350km (217 miles) from Wien.

Next day, 1./NSGr 7's detachment in Zadar was flying combat sorties again. From 03:15 to 03:55, an He 46 made an armed recce in the Starigrad-Seline-Karlobag area, spotting friendly forces and two burnt-out trucks, but did not find any targets to attack. Later that day, another sortie was made from 17:20 to 18:10 along the coastal road Starigrad-Seline. More German troops were observed and a strong motorized column spearheaded by armored cars was spotted 6km (3.73 miles) NW of Starigrad; 1km (.62 miles) NNW of the road, a camouflaged observation post was spotted. Increasingly, the Germans were transferring their own troops by night due to Allied air supremacy over Croatia and the Adriatic in general. Though it is not clear on what, 300 rounds were used during this sortie.

On 3 May, another Taliedo-built Ca. 314C (WNr. 12225) of the 3rd Staffel was lost at Pleso aerodrome, near Zagreb, in a Bruchlandung (crash landing) during a non-combat flight. Flg. Heinz Wagner, crew chief (ground crew), was the only person injured. Next day, another unknown aircraft of NSGr 7 was lost, again on a non-combat flight.

Uffz. Wagner, a 3rd Staffel pilot, told Dr. Möller about landing the Caproni that: "...[on the ground] it also behaved like it had only one wheel. If some little thing happened while landing, one could easily crash!" Nick Beale, in his book *Ghost Bombers*, includes many testimonials from German pilots of NSGr. 9 about how unhappy they were flying Capronis.

Two days later, on 5 May, an He 46 took off from Zadar at 17:20 to perform reconnaissance in the area of Dugi Otok island. Around Lavsa island, in the Kornati archipelago, it attacked a ship and sank it with bombs. Four SD 50 bombs and about 450 rounds of ammunition were used in these attacks. The ridges of Lavsa island were heavily defended by four 20mm AA guns and about ten machine guns, according to the pilot's report, whose aircraft landed in Zadar at 18:25. The same detachment informed the command in Zagreb that only one He 46 was serviceable (conditionally two) and one other was out of action due to damage sustained to its wings. The same day, Luftwaffe command in Sarajevo reported one He 46 sortie from Mostar and five from Butmir had operated against Tito's forces.

At 6 May 1944, the Zadar detachment flew an armed recce, taking off at 17:25 and landing at 18:05 hours. The goal of the mission was again searching for enemy shipping in the area of the Kornati archipelago, between the islands Dugi Otok—Mala Lavsa—Kornat, but none was spotted. In continuation, one of their planes was flown towards Rava island, where two fishing boats were seen and one of them was heavily damaged with bombs, the pilot reporting AA fire from the ground. In the Žman area on Dugi Otok island, the crew attacked Partisan positions with bombs and guns, and again machine gun fire was exerienced from the ground. The Heinkel used six bombs[52] and 250 rounds of ammunition. One has to understand that the Partisan "Navy" made extensive use of traditional fishing and small transport boats to move their men and supplies between the mainland and the islands. Often those vessels were armed with a machine gun, but there was no way to differentiate a Partisan "Navy" boat from a real fisherman's boat. Most probably that is why the 1./NSGr 7 detachment in Zadar urgently requested a hand-held camera to record the ships from Fliegerführer Kroatien the same day.

The next day, 1./NSGr 7 disposed of three He 46s in the detachment, one of which was unserviceable. On 9 May, it reported more activity from Zadar airfield when the He 46 aircraft and their crews attacked an anti-aircraft schooner with bombs 46km (28.6 miles) SSE of Zadar. This vessel opposed the attack with lively 20mm cannon fire. The next attack occurred in the Božava area, 26km (16.16 miles) NNW of Zadar, where three or four machine guns were noticed defending a three-masted vessel. In the area of Verunić, 28km (17.4 miles) WNW of Zadar, two loaded fishing boats and a freight cutter were attacked by a Heinkel. Later on, one

Heinkel He 46 in flight over Bosnia and Herzegovina. (Predoević)

Heinkel bombed and destroyed five fishing vessels in Tri Luke bay, 20km (12.43 miles) NNW of Zadar. In the last reported attack, one He 46 was damaged by ground fire, receiving a hit to its oil installation while attacking the single-masted vessel 19km (11.8 miles) NNW of Zadar, again in the area of Božava.

In these attacks, seven SD 50 semi-armor piercing bombs and 600 rounds of 7.62mm ammunition were used; one bomb was jettisoned. The detachment reported a strength of four He 46s, of which one was fully serviceable, one was able to fly, one was unserviceable after being shot up, and one was completely unserviceable.

On 10 May, aerodrome detachment Zadar asked Luftwaffe command in Lučko to take the mail for Feldpost L 55418 from the main office in Zagreb and bring it over, as men had gone three weeks without any mail. Ultra decrypts also show that during May, the Germans conducted major works on Zemunik aerodrome, building servicing facilities, foundations for radar, etc.

On 11 May, two He 46s from the Zadar detachment made an armed reconnaissance in the area Benkovac-Ervenik-Kistanje-Gradsko, in the Zadar hinterlands, from 17:30 to 18:18. The detachment also requested rations on scale "II" because of the special duties and conditions in which up to 10 aerial attack alarms were given daily. The men were obviously unhappy and had been on a meager diet for a long time, with no fresh food available. The detachment added that they were aware of the conditions, presumably supply problems due to Partisan activity and Allied air raids. Next day, the detachment reported to Fliegerführer Kroatien that its stock of bombs was as follows: 25 pieces of SD 50; 420 pieces of SD 250; and 97 pieces of SD 500.

Two days later, the detachment reported the same quantity of bombs in Zadar, with the addition of three AB 36 three-sided containers.

Several Fiesler Fi 156 Storch of Sanitäter Flugzeugstaffel 5 at Rajlovac aerodrome. This unit was deployed in the NDH throughout the war, taking part in Operation Rösselsprung. One Storch was shot down on 22 May 1944 by No. 249 Squadron RAF. (Peršen)

On 14 May, the loss was reported of one unknown aircraft of the Gruppe during a combat flight. This may have been the same machine that, according to the 369th (Kroatische) Infanterie-Division "Teufels-Division," crashed on Jahorina mountain. The crew was saved and was reported as being in the village of Prača with German forces. The same Division reported an attack by "small plane(s)" on Partisan concentrations near Foča the next day.

The same day, the 3rd Staffel was active from Pleso, attacking Mrkopalj, in Croatia, with incendiaries and general purpose bombs. Aircraft took off from Pleso between 14:00 and 14:05, landing back in Pleso between 14:55 and 15:00. Several crews are known to have participated in this attack, including pilot Fw. Wilhelm Pollak with Kampfbeobachter Uffz. Kurt Gelinek in Ca. 314 (4X+ML), and pilot Uffz. Hübel with Uffz. Pauli and Ogefr. Abramowski flying Yellow 12 (WNr. 12206). This was the first combat sortie by Yellow 12's crew against Partisans since their arrival; the distance flown to the target and back was 225km (140 miles).

Next day, 15 May, Yellow 12 received its unit code, becoming 4X+HL. Nick Beale comments on the discrepancy between the tail number and aircraft letter: "This is interesting; it suggests that the number was applied before a code was allocated. Also H is the eight letter, so the number and the code do not match." The same crews were again in the air that day, but Fw. Pollak's crew was flying a different Caproni (4X+AL). Capronis loaded with incendiaries and general purpose bombs took off from Pleso between 18:20 and 18:30 to attack Široka Rijeka, in Croatia. After a 355-km (220.6-mile) flight, they landed between 19:30 and 19:40 and Ogefr. Abramowski wrote in his flying log that "fires were observed on target."

The 3rd Staffel raided Široka Rijeka again the next day, and that was the last flight for Fw. Pollak's crew, as the four men and their machine disappeared during this sortie: Caproni 314 WNr. 12716, 4X+CL, took off from Pleso at 16:43 and was shot down by enemy ground fire. Its crew—Pilot Fw. Wilhelm Pollak, Uffz. Kurt Gelinek (Kampfbeobachter), Ogefr. Paul-Heinz Rath (Bordschütze), and Ogefr. Walter Burmester (Bordschütze)—burned together with their plane near the village of Široka Rijeka, 30km (18.64 miles) SSE of Karlovac.[53] A search flight took off from Pleso at 16:43, but had no success. Another unknown loss was reported that day, as well. Oblt. Friedrich Haar was named Technical Officer of the 2nd Staffel the same day, a position that he held until 31 December that year.

An He 46 aircraft in flight over Sarajevo. (Predoević)

On 17 May 1944, NSGr 7 was reported using Italian 50-kg (110-lb) bombs on the C.R. 42 and having 4,456 such bombs in stock. The Heinkel 46s were using AB 36 three-sided containers with SD 2 bombs, but there is no information about the quantity held. The later report refers specifically to the Zadar detachment, equipped with the He 46. The 2./NSGr 7. moved to Zalužani, where the first Staffel was already stationed in preparation for Operation Rösselsprung. The total number of serviceable NSGr 7 aircraft assigned to the operation was two Ju 87Ds with two crews from the Stab; nine He 46s with nine crews from the first Staffel; 15 C.R. 42s with 13 pilots from the second Staffel; and 12 Caproni Ca. 314s with 11 crews at Pleso aerodrome from the third Staffel. The Capronis were again active in the morning, attacking Partisans in Burč Selo with GP bombs and incendiaries. Uffz. Abramowski reported "hits on target" after landing his 4X+HL in Pleso at 10:51 after a flight of 310km (192.7 miles).

On 18 May 1944, the 1./NSGr 7 detachment in Zadar had two He 46 aircraft, of which only one was serviceable. That day, the third Staffel attacked Partisan positions at Vukova Gorica with Italian 50-kg (110-lb) bombs, the crew of 4X+HL starting on a 62-minute sortie from Pleso at 14:14 and flying 280km (174 miles) in all.

Bombs at Zalužani aerodrome on the eve of Operation Rösselsprung. (Raguž)

On 19 May 1944, the 3rd Staffel's C.A.B.-built Caproni Ca. 314C (4X+NL, WNr. 12634) was damaged 40% at Pleso, flipping over while taking off on an anti-Partisan operation. Beobachter Uffz. Paul Betz was injured in the accident, while the rest of the Staffel attacked Tito's forces around Donja Dobra with a mixture of general purpose and incendiary bombs. Uffz. Hübel's crew took off at 10:34 and landed at Pleso at 12:10 after a flight of 440km (273.4 miles) to the target and back, reporting "one direct hit on the target with general purpose bomb." An unknown number of NSGr. aircraft attacked Partisan warehouses 14km (8.7 miles) SW of Karlovac, with many explosions and fires observed. Next day, Fliegerführer Kroatien ordered his subordinated units to direct their efforts to the area of Petrova Gora, Banovina, and Kordun in Croatia. At the same time, orders were issued for reconnaissance in the area East of Karlovac and up to 10km (6.2 miles) West of Petrinja, as well as the roads Slunj - Tounj, Otoka-Vrnogač - Velika Kladuša, and Bosanski Novi - Glina. Aufklärung (recce) units received orders for aerial photography of Petrova Gora mountain.

Next day, the Commander of the 1st Proletarian Corps (1. Proleterski korpus), Colonel K. Lalić, reported bombardment of the town of Livno, in Herzegovina, by four Italian-type aircraft around 14:00. At that time in the former Yugoslavia, the only Luftwaffe unit using Italian types was NSGr 7. In the order of the Commander of the 1st Proletarian Division to the 13th Proletarian Brigade "Rade Končar"[54] dated 20 May, a warning was given that enemy aircraft were mostly active from 04:00 to 08:00 and from 19:00 to 21:15 in the Vrbas river valley, and during that time special attention had to be paid to camouflage and no fires should be lit, in order not to attract enemy aviation.

On 21 May, subordinated units were making attacks in the zone Vrnogač, Cetingrad, Velika Kladuša, and Slunj, while next day, efforts were again dispatched to the area of Petrova Gora. From Oberbefehlshaber Südost's daily report for 22 May, it can be seen that ground attacks were especially strong around Slunj, in Croatia.

Tito and his HQ in front of the cave in Drvar in May 1944. (Raguž)

Hptm. Buss ordered Uffz. Wittan to ferry the last He 46 from Zagreb to Banja Luka. The technical officer of 2./NSGr 7 reported a strength of 20 C.R. 42s to Fliegerführer Kroatien and Stab./NSGr 7. Those serviceable were: 4X+AK, WNr. 914; BK, CK, DK, EK, and GK, WNr. 7172; IK, WNr. 9199; MK, NK, and OK; Fiat-built 4X+PK, WNr. 8494; and QK, RK, SK, and UK. The unserviceable aircraft Werk Nummern were given as follows:

> X785[55] in flyable condition, to be ferried to the workshop;
> 9182, change of engine in the light field workshop;
> 5655, (4X+VK) change of the wings in the light field workshop;
> 5545, unserviceable.

The Technical Officer also advised that the Staffel's transport aircraft was serviceable and that there were no changes (in/out) of aircraft. The Staffel disposed of 23 crews (pilots): six crews ready, four sick, four on leave, ten detached, and six on operations. For some reason, the detailed overview of the crews does not correspond to the given total.

On 24 May, Flughafenbereich (Aerodrome Regional Command) Zagreb 6/XVII informed Bihać's airfield commander that the commanding officer of the Luftwaffe in the SE and of the X. Fliegerkorps, General der Flieger Martin Fiebig, was to land there on 25 May 1944, travelling in a Ju 87 with fighter protection. He was to be properly received by the airfield commander, duty officer, and flying control officer. General Fiebig, holder of the Ritterkrutz mit Eichenlaub, was a former commander of KG 4 and during the attack on Yugoslavia back in 1941 he was in a high command post with IV. Fliegerkorps, which was in action during the April war. After the war, he was captured by the British and handed over to the Yugoslav communist authorities, who put him on trial for war crimes. Found guilty, he was executed by hanging in Beograd (Belgrade) on 24 October 1947. Tito never forgave his enemies, no matter if they were "internal" or external ones.

The paras of SS-Fallschirmjägerbataillon 500 are landing at Drvar. (Raguž)

Also on 24 May, Major Benesch of the Brandenburg Division notified Fliegerführer Kroatien that Tito was at his headquarters in a house in Uvala, about 2km (1.24 miles) from Potoci railway station in the Drvar region, guarded by 500 men. It was also reported that he had landed in Drvar in an aircraft that was still on the Partisan airstrip near the town. Major Benesch also gave the best possible location for the paratroop landing that would occur the next day. However, he proposed direct discussion with Gruppenkommandeur Major Theodor Blaich about the methods of bombing and ground attack on 25 May in direct support of the airborne operations, and to ensure that the bombardments were concentrated on the Uvala and the heights around it on 26 May. The 25 May attacks should be carried out from the West and the SW against Drvar and the Bosanski Petrovac area, while on 26 May they should come from the East and the NE. Uvala was the field near Drvar used by Partisan liaison planes as an auxiliary airstrip and after works were done early in May, it could receive two to four small liaison aircraft. Nearby woods were used to camouflage the planes and as a "hangar."

Ju 87, probably LLG 1, towing DFS 230 Gliders with SS-Fallschirmjägerbataillon 500. (Raguž)

On 25 May, the German Heer and Luftwaffe, together with the Croatian army, Ustasha, and some Chetnik units started Operation Rösselsprung, with the aim of destroying or capturing Tito and his HQ, together with the Allied military missions in the town of Drvar, Western Bosnia and Herzegovina. The operation was conceived as an airborne one, in which elite SS paratroopers would jump and land in gliders in Drvar, supported by a large number of ground attack aircraft, fighters, and other auxiliary units. Land units of the Axis armies would simultaneously attack the town's defenses from outside the perimeter.

Mario Raguž has undertaken detailed research on the operation, and in his works he states the following:

> The operational section of the Headquarters of the German 2nd Armoured Army headed by Colonel von Varnbuller made a study how to employ SS-Fallschirmjägerbataillon 500. This study, after its acceptance by higher authority, specified the allocation of the battalion's parachutists and gliders according to their objectives.
>
> Parachutists (485 men in total) were divided in four battle groups: "Blau" (Blue), "Grün" (Green), "Rot" (Red) and the paratroopers of the second wave. The first wave was transported by Ju 52/3m from the airfield of Ečka, near Zrenjanin in Vojvodina while the second wave was transported into the "crater" of Drvar from Zalužani near Banja Luka. This was the same aerodrome on which Stab. 1. and 2./NSGr 7 were based for this operation.
>
> **DFS 230C-1 gliders took off from Cerklje and Lučko aerodromes and were divided into six combat groups:**
>
> 1. "Panther" (Panther), the strongest group which comprised 110 men and whose task was to capture and/or destroy the Supreme Command of the NLAYPD and Tito himself;
> 2. "Stürmer" (Striker), which consisted of 50 men whose main task was the capture of the Soviet military mission (code name "Moskau") to the Supreme Command of the NLAYPD.

3. Draufgänger (Daredevil), had 70 men and its task was to capture and hold the main crossroads in Drvar and main roads leading in and out of the town;
4. "Greifer" (Grabber), had 40 men and the task of capturing the British military mission (code name "London") to the Supreme Command of the NLAPDY;
5. "Beisser" (Biter), a group of 20 men which was to capture a village not far from Drvar in order to complete the encirclement of Partisan forces;
6. "Brecher" (Crusher), consisted of 50 men and its task was to the capture U.S. military mission (code name "Amerika") to the Supreme Command of the NLAPDY.

It is interesting to mention that the gliders also carried six members of the Abwehr's FAT (Frontaufklärungstrupp = Front Reconnaissance Troop) 216, who had the task of capturing the radio station, codes and the archives of the NLAPDY Supreme Command.

Another special unit of 40 men was carried to Drvar with the gliders. It belonged to the 4th and 5th battalions of the "Verband Wildschutz" and was headed by Major Benesch. The Group, formally belonging to the Panzergrenadier Division "Brandenburg" (Mechanized Infantry Division "Brandenburg"), was also known under the ad-hoc name "Benesch Group." This group was composed of Yugoslav ethnic Germans (known in Nazi terminology as Volksdeutsche), Muslims, Croatians, Serbs and Germans and had tasks of a reconnaissance, diversionary and intelligence nature.

The German plan envisaged the following tasks for the aviation component of the assault: "The commander of the Fliegerführer Kroatien must assure the strong engagement of his forces immediately before launching SS-Fallschirmjägerbataillon 500's comprehensive attack on targets to break the enemy gangs, the HQ's security, and anti-aircraft positions, as well as to confine the enemy to the air raid shelters. During the Batallion's descent, the aviation commander had at all times to prevent intervention against it, especially by those enemy forces on the heights on both sides of Drvar. In the further course of the action it had to suppress those Partisan units in immediate contact with SS-Fallschirmjägerbataillon 500."

According to German sources, total losses of SS-Fallschirmjägerbataillon 500 by the end of the operation were 61 dead, 205 wounded, and 11 missing. Partisan sources for their part reported 145 dead and 384 wounded members of the battalion.

DFS 230 gliders and descending paratroops at Drvar. The total number of men landing here by parachute or glider was 825. (Raguž)

Engagement of Luftwaffe units in this operation was very high: 13./SG 151 was transferred to Bihać from Gorica with 17 Ju 87s, and 3./SG 151 and 4./SG 151 were operating from Zagreb and Velika Gorica with around 36 Ju 87s. In Bihać, Nahaufklärungsstaffel Kroatien was stationed with 24 of its Hs 126A-1 and B-1 aircraft and three Do 17P and Z. Fighter support for the operation consisted of three Staffeln of IV./JG 27 based in Lučko and Borongaj; three Staffeln from II./JG 51 based in Cerklje (Zierkle in German), Slovenia; and parts of the Italian-based II./JG 77, whose main task was to assure air superiority over the Lika and Gorski Kotar areas. In Mostar, Stab and 2./NAGr 12 were stationed with around 10 Bf 109G-6 and G-8. The II. and III./LLG 1 with Ju 87 and Hs 126 from Cerklje and Lučko, of which Stukas of II./LLG 1 were used later for ground support in Drvar area and 1. and 2.(DFS)/Schleppgruppe 1 from Cerklje. The Fi 156 planes of the 32./FlVG 2 were also engaged on recce missions around Drvar between 25 and 28 May, as both NASt and NSGr 7 were fully engaged in combat sorties. Various other transport and medical units were added to assure adequate aerial support for the operation. The estimated total of engaged forces was more than 340 aircraft in a relatively small area, of which at least 201 were from the armed recce and ground attack capable units. According to the research of Mario Raguž, 222 Luftwaffe ground support capable and armed recce aircraft participated in the attack on Drvar. This does not take into account aircraft used to tow the gliders or transport and medevac machines.

For the transport of the airborne troops the following units were assigned: 1.(DFS)/Schleppgruppe 1, with five Hs 126 with so many DFS 230; 2.(DFS)/Schleppgruppe 1, with three Ju 87 and that many DFS 230; II./LLG 1, with around eight Ju 87 and that many DFS 230; III./LLG 1, with 12 Hs 126, five Avia tugs, and 17 DFS 230; and II./TG 4, with around 40 Ju 52. Once the gliders continued their flight alone and all the paras were dropped, Luftwaffe aircraft turned back towards their bases: II./TG 4 (with some 40 Ju 52d) at Zalužani aerodrome to pick up a second wave of paras; Group "Avia"[56] first landed at Bihać Ceravci aerodrome to refuel and from there to an aerodrome near Beograd; II./LLG 1 to Lucko to load bombs and fuel and back to bomb the Partisans in Drvar; and III./LLG 1 flew from to Sarajevo Butmir and from there to Kruševac, in Serbia.

German paratroopers getting out of a DFS 230C-1. Note the fuselage-mounted MG 34 machine gun, which the pilot could use in flight, operating it through an opening in the fuselage. When on the ground, it could be removed from its pylon and used as an ordinary infantry weapon. (Raguž)

It is not known exactly how many Caproni Ca. 314 bombers were operational at Lučko aerodrome on 25 May, but they certainly took part in the operation; the author estimates their number at eight, based on the documentation in his possession. According to his logbook, Hptm. Buss rejoined his Staffel at Zalužani on 23 May at 10:20 aboard He 46 4X+EH, coming from Zagreb, where he had spent almost two months and saw very little action.

1. and 2./NSGr 7 attacked Partisan forces in Drvar from 06:35 to 06:40. Buss flew three sorties that day aboard Heinkel 46 4X+AH with Uffz. Karl Nemitz as observer: from 05:45 to 07:20; from 11:25 to 12:55; and his final flight of the day was from 17:05 to 18:30, taking off and landing at Banja Luka. From 06:55 to 07:00, eight or so Ca. 314s of 3./NSGr 7 attacked the Partisan positions in the town; they had taken off from Pleso between 06:10 and 06:15. A big formation of Ju 87s from II. and 13./SG 151 attacked the defenders' positions, then the first paratroops were dropped between 07:00 and 07:10. The gliders, towed to the drop zone by Stukas and Hs 126s of LLG 1, began landing some time after the paratroops. The Stukas of 6./LLG 1 took off from Cerklje with gliders between 05:50 and 06:05 hours, detached towed gliders, and set course for Gorica airfield, where they landed around 07:55 after roughly 415km (257.9 miles) in the air. For their part, 12./LLG 1, flying Hs 126s, took off from Lučko aerodrome with their gliders around 06:05, and after letting the gliders go over Drvar they continued to Butmir, landing there around 07:40 after flying around 360km (223.7 miles). Afterwards, around 08:55, the Henschels of 12./LLG 1 flew from Butmir to Krusevac, in Serbia. In the operational plan, it was envisaged that the first gliders should land at 07:00 and the last at 07:15. As with any plan, unforeseen circumstances caused delay, so the first gliders were ten minutes behind schedule and the last ones were significantly later than planned. Some unconfirmed sources state that Czech-built Avia B. 534s also towed gliders,[56] but this cannot be confirmed from archival sources.

Fighter support for the operation was provided by IV./JG 27. As the glider-towing Stukas arrived, NSGr 7 secured the airspace above the landing zone itself and continued to suppress Partisan positions on the hills around Drvar with SD 2 bombs and gunfire.

An Hs 126 over the Drvar drop zone on 25 May 1944 during Operation Rösselsprung. In the foreground are the remains of the DFS 230 glider that transported ammunition for the SS troops. On landing it hit the wall. (Raguž) on the ground, it could be removed from its pylon and used as an ordinary infantry weapon. (Raguž)

As SS paratroops got blocked fighting with Tito's forces, the second wave of 171 more men of the unit was dropped on Drvar. These men had been waiting at Zalužani aerodrome. Prior to their landing, the remaining Ju 87s of SG 151 and II./LLG 1 and the C.R. 42s and He 46s of 1. and 2./NSGr 7 attacked the vicinity of the landing zone at around 11:30. The unit's last raid was at around 17:30, defending paratroopers withdrawing towards the graveyard, where they established an all-round defense. After NSGr 7's last pass, a formation of Ju 87s of 6./LLG 1 bombed Partisan positions in Drvar; they took off from Gorica at around 18:30, landing back around 20:10.

This second wave was lucky not be completely annihilated by four Spitfire Vcs of No. 73 Squadron RAF piloted by S/Ldr. J.H. Chase, F/Lt. R. Kirker, W/O. E.H. Baker, and F/Sgt. A.D. Rowe. These Spitfires had taken off from Vis at 10:40 and used all their ammunition attacking a convoy of approximately 100 vehicles near Bihac. When they broke off, they popped up on a large formation of Ju 52s, but without ammo they could only sit and look at them. The Spitfires landed at Vis at 12:30 to refuel and rearm.

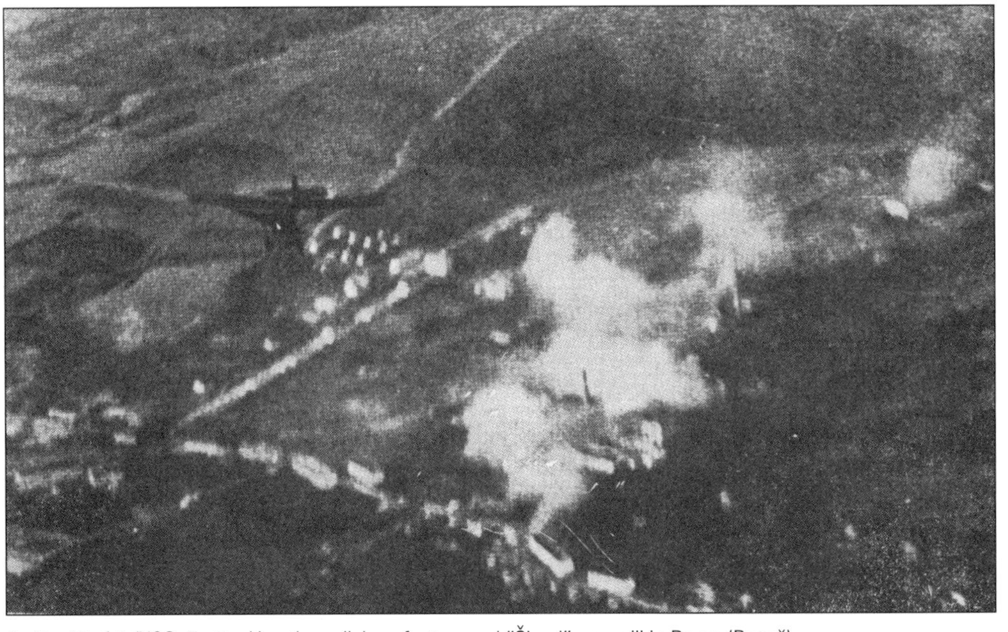

An He 46 of 1./NSGr 7 attacking the cellulose factory and "Šipad" sawmill in Drvar. (Raguž)

As far as NSGr 7 is concerned, two losses were reported on 25 May. During the mission over Drvar, Caproni 314 WNr. 12206 (4X+HL, Yellow 12) was shot down by enemy anti-aircraft fire and crashed around 65km (40 miles) SW of Bihać, killing all aboard: pilot Uffz. Odilo Hübel,[57] Kampfbeobachter Unteroffizier Anton Pauli, Ogefr. Horst Abramowski (Bordschütze), and Lt. Valentin Krempl (war reporter).[58] Hübel's crew took off from Pleso at 6:13. Another war reporter, Lt. Herbert Karnath, was wounded during ground combat at approximately the same location. He was treated for his wounds in German hospital Nr. 690 in Zagreb. Like Lt. Krempl, he was assigned to the 3rd Staffel from Luftwaffenkommando Südost for this operation. Another unknown plane was reported lost the same day.

The 373rd Legionnaire Division, composed of Croatian "volunteers," were attacked erroneously by planes of NSGr 7, resulting in two dead and two wounded, together with the destruction of a few of the Division's trucks. In their report, they mentioned "Italian aircraft with German markings" (Fiat or Caproni) and also Hs 126s, obviously mistaken for He 46s.

Formation of Ca. 314 of the 3rd Staffel on their way to Drvar on 25 May 1944. The dorsal turret—a Caproni-Lanciani type E with a S.A.F.A.T. 7.7mm machine gun—is clearly visible. The turret was operated mechanically and turned 360 degrees horizontally and 0-70 degrees vertically. (Raguž)

Paratroopers with captured British and American flags in Drvar. (Raguž)

On the evening of 25 May, NSGr 7 reported its strength as follows:
Stab./NSGr 7 with two Ju 87s and two crews;
1./NSGr 7 with nine He 46s and nine crews;
2./NSGr 7 with fifteen C.R. 42s and 13 pilots.

From the same report, it is clear that under NSGr 7's command were two Henschel Hs 126s from NASt Kroatien with two crews, as well as five Ju 52s of II./TG 4 with five crews.

Members of the Anglo-American Allied liaison mission to Tito's HQ surrendered and were made prisoners by German paratroopers. The Russian component, on the contrary, managed to withdraw after heavy fighting. (Raguž)

Although Tito managed to escape during the German raid, it is intriguing that Allied forces did not adequately react on Tito's request for air raids on the German attackers, though on the other side of the Adriatic, in Italy, it was pretty hot in the air at the same time. The very same day, 25 May, the Allies received a request for air support, but the first large-scale bombing with four-engined aircraft only started on 29 May, with limited forces. The first real air raids began on 29 May, when the operation was defacto over. Groups of Allied single-engine fighter-bombers attacked aerodromes in the Independent State of Croatia between 25 and 29 May.

Allied attacks on airbases started at noon on 25 May, when 13 Spitfires of No. 249 Squadron RAF made a sweep over Bihać Ceravci aerodrome, claiming destruction on the ground of four Stukas and damage to another 11, besides direct hits on the barracks; they also reported an He 126 and two Macchis present at the airfield. The Germans reported the loss of one Hs 126 down in flight, probably a victim of No. 73 Squadron; and in the dispersals one Ju 87 was completely destroyed and another burnt out, while three other aircraft of the same type received numerous hits.

After being refuelled and rearmed at Vis, a section of No. 73 Squadron composed of F/O G.A. Martin, F.Lt. F.C. Bremner, Sgt. Micklethwaite, and Lt. T.S. Harper was sent against the previously mentioned convoy near Bihać, but they spotted enemy aircraft and broke off that attack. F/O Martin, of B flight, claimed one Hs 126 about two miles west of the town, which was taking off from the aerodrome. He reports about the attack:

> As No. 3 of a section of four Spitfires, I was airborne from Vis at 13:30. The section proceeded to Knin, then followed the road to Bihać. There the four aircraft attacked a large

German elite force members with Tito's Marshal uniform in Drvar. (Raguž)

> M.T. convoy. Whilst doing so, No. 4 reported a suspected aerodrome or landing ground to the West of Bihać. The section leader ordered the attack against the M.T., to be broken off to investigate the reported aerodrome. We sighted the aerodrome about two miles to the West of Bihać and I estimated that there were approximately 20 aircraft on the ground. One aircraft, which I identified as a Henschel Hs 126, was taking off. I was about 100 degrees from the H.S., approaching low on the deck to the starboard of the E/A. The aircraft was about ten feet off the ground when I opened up from quarter astern position from 400 yards with a one second burst. I saw my shots strike the ground under the raising aircraft. Then, from 170 degrees at 200 yards I fired another one-second burst and I saw a few strikes on the tail unit. I closed to 50 yards line astern, slightly below, and gave it a 3-second burst, then breaking off over the top of the E/A skidding to port. I saw numerous strikes all along the fuselage to the engine, and the E/A pitched several times, losing height, then crashed from 20 feet, nose first, completely wrecking the aircraft. The engine was ripped off, the wings and undercarriage were torn off, and the aircraft was a complete wreck. From the pitching of the E/A, I suspected the pilot had been hit."

No. 4 of the section witnessed the attack and the destruction of the E/A. They also claimed three Ju 87 badly damaged on the ground, as well as two strafing attacks against "approximately 20 other aircraft at the 'drome, which included Ju 87s, Hs 126s, and Fieseler-Storchs."

Later on, four Spitfires strafed Bihać airfield at around 15:00 after being refuelled and rearmed at Vis. Five Hs 126s were claimed destroyed and three more damaged. Four Spitfire Vcs of No. 73 Squadron RAF piloted by S/Ldr. J.H. Chase, F/Lt. R. Kirker, W/D. E.H. Baker, and F/Sgt. A.D. Rowe conducted this attack. Sqn. Ldr. John H. Chase, flying Spitfire "E" (serial number JG800), was hit by flak, and his aircraft caught fire and crashed; he was captured by German forces.

During the day, more attacks were recorded when a total of 18 Spitfires claimed the destruction of eight Hs 126s: five on the ground and three in the air.

German paras near a DFS 230 glider in Drvar; it carries the H4 code LLG 1. During the landing, three gliders were shot down by Partisan forces. (Raguž)

On the second day of fighting, MAAF attacked Zadar airfield with fourteen P-38 Lightning fighters, while Bihać was strafed three times during the day and bombed once by the 15th AF. These attacks had little impact on Rösselsprung: Bihać was home to Nahaufklärungsstaffel Kroatien, which had lost 13 Hs 126s to enemy action during May, and Zadar was almost free of aircraft. Around noon, six Spitfire Mk.Vs took off from the island of Vis to patrol the Ripac area. F/O Joe H. Hingston saw two "Hs 126" and the whole flight of Spifires gave chase. Hingston, flying Spitfire JK450, shot down one Henschel, which crashed in the woods on a hillside; the second Luftwaffe aircraft was attacked by Sqn. Ldr. D.A.S. "Jock" Colvin (EF720), with no visible results after a first pass. For around ten minutes, all six Spitfires chased the remaining Henschel until Lt. Rick T. Whittingham, SAAF (flying JK678), shot it down; no one was seen to escape. Subsequently, Flg. Off. D. "Red" Sinclair, RCAF (GN-U, JK101), saw three more Hs 126s and attacked the last in the formation, which was last seen at a height of 50 meters (164ft) heading straight towards earth. Although the crash itself was not observed, Sinclair's victory was recognized. Again, the flight went on to chase the two remaining Henschels, one of which escaped, while the other one was shot down jointly by W/O A.G. Bowman (in JL220), Colvin, Whittingham, and F/Lt. P. Quine (ES299). However, Georg Schlaug, in his article "Der Luftwaffen-Einsatz beim Unternehmen Rösselsprung," states that: "On 26 May 1944, 1./NSGr 7 lost two He 46 aircraft" in encounters with enemy planes between 12:00 and 13:45. They were probably the victims of F/O Sinclair and W/O Bowman, the pilots simply mistaking the high-winged He 46 for the Hs 126 when reporting their victories. In the Operations Record Book of No. 249 Squadron, the following description of events is given:

> Airborne Vis; landed Vis. Patrol in aid of Partisan operations 6 Spitfire of 249 Squadron on patrol crossed (shore) at Rogoznica, round back of Sibenik to near Obrovac and then to Ripac, where they patrolled East to West. Red IV F/O Hingston sighted two Henschel 126s airborne. Whole formation gave chase, but Red IV was only one [illegible] aircraft which Red 1 saw crash into trees on a hillside, nobody bailing out. The second Henschel

> 126 turned back and was chased by Red 1, who gave him long burst. Hits seen on [illegible], all round the enemy, but no direct hits observed. The whole formation now chased the Henschel for about ten minutes, making many attacks and scoring many bursts. Eventually, Red II [Lt. Whittington] fired a final burst and the Henschel crashed, nobody bailing out. Red III [F/O Sinclair] saw 3 more Henschel 126s airborne and fired at rear aircraft. When last seen by Red I, this Henschel was on its back in a nose down attitude about 100 feet from the ground. Red I saw no actual crash, but reports that the enemy could not have pulled out. This aircraft is therefore claimed destroyed. The remaining 2 Henschels were chased by whole formation. Red VI [W/O Bowman] fired at one and was followed by Red I, II, and V. Red VI then closed to 50 yards, firing and still closing. One airman was seen to bail out, then the wing broke away from the aircraft, which was falling to the ground. All enemy aircraft were flying [close] to the hillsides.

Italian-built Savoia-Marchetti SM. 82 dropping bombs and leaflets over the town of Bosanski Petrovac. This was a raid that was intended to divert attention from Drvar and was conducted from 06:40 to 06:50 on 25 May. (Raguž)

In continuation the same day, Hptm. Buss's first mission to the Drvar area was at 04:40 for one hour and 20 minutes, with Uffz. Karl Nemitz aboard 4X+AH. His second mission started at 08:57, landing at 10:25 back at Banja Luka in Heinkel WNr. 1248 (4X+EH). At 12:37, Hptm. Buss took off for his third mission of the day, again flying 4X+EH. En route they were attacked by the Spitfires of No. 249 Squadron SAAF near Banja Luka, and his observer, Uffz. Karl Nemitz, bailed out with severe injuries 11km (6.84 miles) SE of Bosanski Petrovac, while Buss made an emergency landing in the Banja Luka area uninjured at 13:40. Spitfires shot down another of the unit's Heinkels (WNr. 310), which crash landed SE of Bosanski Petrovac. The pilot's fate is not known, but observer Uffz. Leo Weidhaus was injured. Another 1./NSGr 7 loss that day was He 46 WNr. 156 (4X+IH), shot down during a sortie against Partisan-held positions in Drvar. Pilot Ogefr. Shmidt and his observer, Uffz. Breuer, took off from Banja Luka and were the victims of flak or small arms ground fire. The pilot managed to crash land near Drvar; his aircraft was damaged 80-85%, while both crew members were slightly injured and picked up by friendly forces. From a letter of Koča Popović, commander of the 1st Proletarian Corps (1. Proleterski korpus), to Aleksandar Ranković dated 26 May 1944, it is seen that the first "Pikavac" aircraft were already over the town at 05:00, supporting the last 300 paras' defense of the Drvar graveyard. This is further proof that Partisans did not distinguish between Henschels and Heinkels. It is possible that some Henschel aircraft were over the town at that time, but it is definite that Heinkels of Buss's 1st Staffel were there around 05:00 or 05:10, after 20 to 30 minutes of flight from Banja Luka. Stukas of 6./LLG 1 were over Drvar three times that day, taking off from Cerklje the first time round at 6:05. In the morning, their targets were the town and the Uvala area. The attackers landed in Cerklje around 08:05, and after a short break they were in the air again at 12:55 against Drvar, landing back at their airfield of origin at 14:35. The last attack by 6./LLG 1 was in the afternoon, taking off at 17:15 and landing back in Cerklje around 19:20.

On 27 May, there were no reported attacks on Bihać airfield, although from 05:00–05:10 and 05:30–05:40, six Spitfires were observed to the East and one was shot down by anti-aircraft fire during an attack on the railway station. After a belly landing, its pilot was captured unharmed. The Zadar detachment reported stocks of 1,880 liters (496.7 gallons) of B4 fuel, 20,410 liters (5,392 gallons) of diesel, and 141 aircraft bombs.

DFS 230 graveyard near Drvar. In total, 45 of these gliders took part in Rösselsprung. By the number of paratroopers, it can be concluded that 39 gliders contained men of the battalion and adhered units, while six brought in equipment and supplies. (Raguž)

Hptm. Buss was back in the air that day, ferrying He 46 4X+MH from Banja Luka to Zagreb. He landed at 18:15 after 45 minutes in the air; this was his last flight for NSGr 7. After leaving Croatia and a period of rest, Buss joined SG 111 in Stubendorf for instrument flying training and conversion to the Ju 87 from 10 July to 15 September 1944. After that, he went to SG 151 in Lüben from 6 to 17 October for advanced Ju 87 training, finally joining NSGr. 9 in Villafranca, Italy, on 22 November 1944, with which he flew until the end of the war in Stukas as Staffelkapitän of 3./NSGr. 9. He died in 1985 in Göttingen, Germany. Hptm. Buss was replaced by Oblt. (later Hpt.) Rolf Buchheim on 27 May as Staffelführer until his definitive appointment as StaKa of 1./NSGr 7 on 24 July 1944. Buchheim led the Staffel until the very end—20 April 1945.

One of the gliders upside down; it was probably shot down by the NLAPDY HQ's Support Battalion (Prateći bataljon Vrhovnog Štaba NOV i POJ). Three paratroopers survived the crash, but were subsequently killed in an exchange of fire with Partisans. (Raguž)

On 28 May, the auxiliary airstrip in the village of Aleksandrovac, in Bosnia and Herzegovina—about 3.5km (2.17 miles) from Zalužani—was attacked by Allied twin-engine fighter-bombers. 1./NSGr 7 lost six He 46s, while three more Hs 126s of NASt Kroatien were added to the total when around thirty P-38 Lightnings of the USAAF attacked Banja Luka, the airport, and aircraft dispersals from 13:55 to 14:30. Also at Zalužani, 2./NSGr 7 lost three Fiat C.R. 42s. Aleksandrovac was known to the occupying Germans as Adolfstal and/or Rudolfstal, and was populated by a German minority that had come to Bosnia and Herzegovina in the middle ages; in 1944, more than 600 people of German descent were living there. In 1991, the village had approximately the same population, but not one ethnic German still lived there.

Other victims of the Lightnings' attack were a motorized SS column on the road Okučani - Banja Luka, from which 20 trucks, three trailers, and two motor cars were lost; minor damage was also caused to buildings in the town of Banja Luka.

The same 28 May, the 82nd FG attacked Zalužani and its surroundings, reporting destruction of 15-20 aircraft and 35 open railroad wagons. German reports confirm that in the American attacks from 15:20 to 17:43, 13 Luftwaffe aircraft were destroyed or damaged. The second Staffel reported the following Fiat-built C.R. 42s as 100% damaged: WNr. 9140, 4X+AK; WNr. 7172, 4X+GK; and WNr. 8494, 4X+PK. One unknown C.R. 42 of the unit was damaged 60% and a replacement was requested, as well as the replacement of WNr. 5655 (4X+VK), damaged 30%. The smallest damage (20%) was to Falco WNr. 90804, built by Aeritalia. In another report, the following WNr. are listed as damaged or destroyed: 4X+BK, 30% damaged; WNr. 7142, 4X+GK, 100%; WNr. 4494, 4X+PK, 100%; and another Fiat C.R. 42 destroyed.

WNr. 4494 must be a mistake in the German signal, as the last serial number built by Fiat in the February–December, 1939, batch was MM. 4464, and the next batch started with MM. 4967. On the other hand, 4X+PK was certainly MM. 8494, so "4494" was probably a transcription error. Another doubtful entry is 4X+GK, described in different messages as WNr. 7172 and 7142, either of which might be correct, as both aircraft were produced by Fiat.

NSGr 7 ground staff on the way to Banja Luka from Zaluzani aerodrome. (Peršen)

The very same day, Lučko aerodrome, near Zagreb, was under attack by Allied fighters and one He 46D of 1./NSGr 7 (WNr. 312, 4X+NH) was destroyed, as well as an unserviceable Heinkel He 111 H-5 (WNr. 3672, CM+KJ) of Verb. St.58 (Liaison Staffel 58), which burned out. In addition, several P-38s strafed Kurilovec aerodrome, also near Zagreb. Finally, Luftwaffe Command SE issued an order to Fliegerführer Kroatien to organize the evacuation of all serviceable aircraft from airfields in the area of Operation Rösselsprung at dawn on 29 May, as systematic and successful MAAF attacks were causing unacceptable losses. With this in mind, Fliegerführer Kroatien ordered all available aircraft of Stab and 1./NSGr 7 to transfer to Ilandža auxiliary airfield, where they arrived the next day at 06:20 hours (Ilandža is a small village East of Beograd, in Serbia). The ground personnel were ordered to fly to the new location whenever the situation allowed. If space was available in any of the Staffel's aircraft, ground crew should fill those free seats. An order was issued to remove all other personnel and equipment from the airfields around Banja Luka by road; transfer back would be ordered subsequently.

The Fifteenth Air Force was in action over Drvar and the surrounding area on 29 May, the 456th BG twice hitting targets in the Independent State of Croatia. First, they bombed Drvar itself with 35 aircraft and then troop concentrations in Žegar, near Obrovac; another raid targeted Bihać aerodrome with 36 aircraft in two flights. The Luftwaffe had already started to transfer their fighter cover of the operation from Cerklje to Niš, in Serbia. In the morning, at 07:05, II./JG 51's first 16 Bf 109s landed in Niš, followed by three more at around 13:30, leaving the sky free for Allied planes. The 455th BG also bombed the targets twice that day: during the first run forty B-24s attacked Bosanska Krupa with 45-kg (100-lb) GP bombs, and on the second mission of the day, thirty-nine B-24s attacked Banja Luka airfield with the same ordnance. There was no flak, no sign of Luftwaffe fighters, and no casualties. Total damage to Axis air power amounted to around 26 planes on the ground, of which half belonged to the Croatian Air Force; five machines were shot down, one of them a Croatian Do 17. Six C.R. 42s of 2./ NSGr 7 were completely destroyed on the ground at Zalužani and six more heavily damaged, while whatever was left moved to Ilandža auxiliary airfield. Dr. Christian Möller, in his research into the German military, found that NSGr 7 reported 13 aircraft destroyed on

28 May and another nine on the 29th as a result of Allied air raids; all these losses were reported reported from Zalužani. The 459th BG, for their part, bombed troop concentrations around the cities of Prijedor and Livno.

Around 45 USAAF Lightnings from Italy again raided Zalužani and Adolfstal (Aleksandrovac) aerodromes from 14:30–14:50; one unserviceable C.R. 42 was destroyed and another was damaged 50%. Two Lightnings were shot down, killing one U.S. airman, while a 1st Lieutenant was taken prisoner. Motorized Flak Regiment 38 of the 20. Flak Division, deployed in the area of Banja Luka during Operation Rösselsprung, reported that another Allied aircraft had been shot down that day in the Banja Luka area; according to their report it exploded in mid-air, and parts of the wings and fuel tank were recognized at the crash site. At 15:20, Bihać was again strafed and bombed by a low flying aircraft, and in Zagreb, two Ju 87s of 13./SG 151 were destroyed in a separate raid. The same day, Lučko advised IV./TG 1 in Athens that one of their Ju 52s (1Z+SN) had been lost in a raid on the airfield.

Fliegerführer Kroatien ordered the transfer of the 3./NSGr 7 and elements of the Kroat Kampfgruppe from Franzfeld (Kačarevo), eight kilometers (5 miles) North of Pančevo, to Veliki Bečkerek in Vojvodina, where they were to join NASt Kroatien. It seems that 3./NSGr 7 was transferred even before this order came, together with the Stab and 1st Staffel.

Luftgaukommando XXX issued an order for aerodromes in Northern Croatia to disperse all remaining aircraft as widely as possible, including those under repair in the workshops, after transferring flyable aircraft to other non-targeted bases in the region. The order called for maximum attention to be paid to aircraft camouflage. It went on to demand that all personnel and important equipment not essential for maintaining operational readiness and flying activities should be removed from the airfields in question.

On 31 May, the Luftwaffe command in Banja Luka summarized losses from the attacks on Banja Luka on 28 and 29 May for Fliegerführer Kroatien as follows:
Total loss:
Six He 46s
Six C.R. 42s
Three Hs 126s
One Ca. 309s.

Severely damaged and could be used as a source of spare parts:
Six C.R. 42s
Two He 46s
Several[59] Ju 87s.

On 30 May, the 15th AF dropped more bombs on the Independent State of Croatia. Twenty-eight B-17s from the 463rd BG and a few dozen (according to German sources 32) B-17s of the 301st BG bombarded Zagreb's marshalling yards and Borongaj aerodrome in two waves. This was yet another diversionary raid to stretch the Luftwaffe fighter arm to the maximum while the main force attacked targets in Austria, tactics which had proved fruitful during "Big Week." According to German sources, damage to the aerodrome was serious: the Headquarters building, Hangars 1 and 2, and the reception and dispatch buildings received a direct hit each out of 300 bombs that were dropped on the town. Three small Croatian Air Force planes were set on fire in Hangar 1 and five more Croatian aircraft were damaged. German losses were lighter: one Ju 87 was damaged in Hangar 2, one person wounded, and one killed. It seems that this Ju 87 belonged to Stab./NSGr 7, as separate reports mention the type with the Stab, although the report of the raid does not specify the machine's unit. Most of the bombs fell on nearby marshalling yards, destroying rails and locomotives. NSGr 7 was unable to use Borongaj aerodrome til the next afternoon.

Flughafenbereich (Aerodrome Regional Command) Zagreb 6/XVII reported to Lufgaukommando XXX in Beograd that Bihać was again subjected to an attack by 12 Lightnings from 08:55–09:06, and that some new material damage was caused at the aerodrome and some personnel were injured. In the town itself, a fuel depot was blown up by the raiders.

The Zadar detachment reported an attack by six Lightnings which broke off from the bomber formation and strafed the aerodrome from 10:05–10:22. One cannibalized He 46 of the 1st Staffel was burnt out; hits were recorded on the aircraft blast bays, but with no details as to the extent of the damage. There were no casualties among the airfield's personnel and it remained fully serviceable after the attackers departed. The air raid warning was given at 09:45 and all was clear at 10:40.

Pleso aerodrome after liberation. Note the personal inscription "Irmgard" on this C.R. 42. (Jelušić)

That afternoon, four serviceable C.R. 42s of the 2nd Staffel were still at Zalužani, together with two more which were unserviceable. The same report mentions that some Croatian Air Force planes were sharing the aerodrome with the Luftwaffe units. There were no raids on Banja Luka and its surrounding airfields on 30 May, and the Germans reported that all flyable aircraft were cleared from Zalužani by 16:00. It seems that those Fiats and possibly parts of Stab and 1./NSGr 7 came back to Banja Luka in the afternoon of 29 May, flying out again the following afternoon.

Another German report in Ultra decrypt T201/99 brought information about unknown aircraft types WNr. 3194 and 4336 destroyed, in addition to two Ju 87s, one of which was coded 6Q+GX (6Q was the unit code of SG 151). In the same report, reference is made to the attack on 27 May, when seven drums of German 84 octane fuel and two barrels of lubricant were destroyed. It appears likely that the aircraft in question were destroyed at either Bihać, Zadar, or Banja Luka.

The same day, Lt. Werner Goetschke replaced Oblt. Schrenz as adjutant to Kommandeur Blaich, and he was in this position until at least 21 September the same year, but possibly to 10 November, when adjutant duty was confided to Oblt. Kurt Jacobs. Lt. Goetschke was later an adjutant in I./SG 101. On the last day of May 1944, another Allied fighter-bomber raid was reported by Germans on Banja Luka aerodrome at 16:30.

On 31 May 1944, Fliegerführer Kroatien ordered the removal from all subordinated aircraft[60] of the white fuselage band and yellow paint under the cowling, explaining that experience had shown that during low-level flying in valleys and ravines and with cliffs as background, the brightness of white and yellow paint destroyed the otherwise satisfactory camouflage effect.

This order replaced instructions from November 1943 about painting captured and Italian aircraft, as well as orders from December 1941 about painting German and Italian planes cooperating in the Mediterranean; as received by Fliegerführer Kroatien from higher authority, these older painting directions had stated:

- The under parts of the engine cowlings will be painted a bright yellow;
- Round the fuselage there will be a ... white ring about 50cm (19.69in) wide, behind the cross;
- Captured aircraft wing tips are to be painted a bright yellow [for] 1.5 meters (4.92ft) in accordance with No. 3800 of 15/10/42 from OKL.

The first day of June did not bring any amelioration in the air. Bihać was again the target of an attack, this time by four Spitfires from 09:20 to 09:40. No aircraft of NSGr 7 were lost, but the Germans reported the loss of two Hs 126s of NASt Kroatien (coded DF+GF and WNr. 2977, 9X+HL) and a Ju 87D-3 of 13./SG 151 (coded 6Q+DX, WNr. 110483, and not as given in Ultra QS+DX).

After suffering heavy losses in Operation Rösselsprung, 2./NSGr 7 started its movement to Pleso on 2 June, joining the third Staffel, which was already there. The 2nd Staffel reported six combat sorties, in the course of which C.R. 42 WNr. 7514 (4X+YK) was lost. Obfw. Kuehn force landed his Fiat-built biplane in Partisan-held territory due to lack of fuel, destroyed the aircraft, and regained German lines the following day.

The third day of the month, Major Blaich ordered a complete transfer of 1./NSGr 7 and the remains of 2./NSGr 7 to Gorica. Personal belongings and vehicles were to be forwarded by train as soon as possible, while a small rear detachment of personnel was to remain in Banja Luka to cater for intermediate landings during future operations. (This order was sent to Banja Luka in the name of Ltn. Harr.) Later the same day, the Stab told the two Staffeln that ferrying was not possible due to the bad weather, but pilots were to take off as soon as the weather cleared if no orders arrived to the contrary.

It is known that during 3 June 1944, the following Fiat C.R. 42s managed to reach Pleso between 09:10 and 09:40: 4X+KK, 4X+JK, 4X+SK, and 4X+VK. Six operations were reported that day and one loss, but there are no further details. That evening, 2./NSGr 7 reported a total strength of 22 crews, of which seven were ready in Gorica; two were ready in Pleso; five were ready in Banja Luka; three were on leave and another three sick; and two were detached.

Yet another summary report with the same date states that at the beginning of May, 2./NSGr 7 had 12 C.R. 42s and one Ca. 309, and that total losses for the month had been ten aircraft. Six Fiats were lost through Allied attacks and three more through operational damage, while just five replacement aircraft were received. The Caproni was the one lost on 29 May in Banja Luka and no replacement for it was received.

At the same time, the 1st Staffel was ordered to Gorica, but the details of their transfer are not known. A few days later they were transferred again to Borongaj, retaining a detachment of three aircraft in Zadar until September 1944, as well as an unknown but certainly small number of machines detached in Banja Luka.

Wreckage of a Fiat C.R. 42 of NSGr 7 at Pleso airfield. (Jelušić)

Stab./NSGr 7 ordered the 2. Staffel to complete the transfer in the time given without fail. This seems to be a good indicator that ferrying had not been completed on 3 June as ordered by Major Blaich, but was extended to at least 7 June.

During a non-combat flight on 10 June, another aircraft was lost; next day, C.R. 42 WNr. 6289 of the 2nd Staffel crashed and was written off at Banja Luka aerodrome and its pilot, Ofw. Helmut Rauer, was injured. On 17 June, Partisan positions in the area of Sunja were attacked with eight SC 50 by two He 46s of 1./NSGr 7. Around Sunja, anti-aircraft fire from machine guns was encountered.

Three aircraft of NSGr 7 were reported damaged at Borongaj aerodrome when three Spitfire Vcs of No. 73 Squadron RAF attacked on 26 June 1944, having taken off from Vis at 15:00. Besides the above-mentioned casualties, NSGr 7 reported eight more planes set on fire (five Ju 87s, a Do 217, a Macchi Mc. 202, and an Fw 190). Southeast of Zagreb, the Spitfires attacked and destroyed a locomotive, while another was damaged in the station in Karlovac. This mission was the last for F/Lt. Frank G. Bremner, whose Spitfire (ER914) was last seen in the vicinity of Zagreb. One of the remaining Spits landed at Vis at 17:20, while the other flew on to Italy.

Bihać-Ceravci was subjected to Allied air raids again and again. This time, on 26 June, Spitfires used guns and bombs to destroy five planes, a truck, and a small fuel depot, as well as to kill two German soldiers. After this low-level attack, the aerodrome was attacked by four-engine bombers at 08:15, the Germans reporting 40 aircraft over the target. The initial report of the attack, sent at 09:00, claimed only slight casualties among the personnel, but warned that details could not yet be established. They also reported heavy damage to buildings, barracks partially destroyed, and all phone communication with the outside world cut. Later during the day, a section of four Spitfires of No. 73 Squadron took off from Vis at 13:05 and attacked NSGr 7 aerodromes in Zagreb, namely Borongaj and Lučko. At Borongaj, they claimed eight aircraft destroyed and two damaged, among them Fw 190s, Do 215s, and Ju 87s. At Lučko they claimed two more Do 215s destroyed and one damaged. There are no reports from either side about the eventual losses of NSGr 7. On that occasion, F/Lt. F.C.

Technical personnel of NSGr 7 at Rajlovac aerodrome. (Peršen)

Bremner did not appear after the attack on Lučko airfield, while three other Spits landed at Vis at 17:30.

Later the same day, another Hs 126, probably of NASt Kroatien, was shot down near Kralje, on the Una river, when six Spitfires patrolled an area North of Bihać. The Henschel's pilot was rescued unharmed, but no information was given about the observer.

On 29 June, again a section of four Spitfires of No. 73 Squadron attacked one of the airports from which NSGr 7 operated. At Banja Luka they claimed at least one Ju 87 aircraft. South African pilot 2/Lt. R.H. Van Den Bergh's Spitfire was shot down by intensive flak and crashed into the side of a hill, killing the pilot.

In the morning on 30 June, a section of four Spitfires of the same RAF unit led by F/O. G.A. Martin attacked Rajlovac aerodrome, where at least 15 aircraft were reported in line. Two Spitfires attacked hangars and buildings with bombs and guns, while the other two used the same lethal combination to attack the aircraft. On this occasion, Sgt. Woodruff's aircraft was hit by flak and crashed and burned on the ground.

On the last day of June 1944, several targets in the Independent State of Croatia were raided again. The targets were aerodromes used by the Luftwaffe and Croatian Air Force in Banja Luka and Zagreb (Borongaj). In Split, the targets of the attack were the harbor and marshalling yards. After the disaster on 12 April 1944, the commanders of the Croatian Air Force and Luftwaffe dispersed their aircraft on auxiliary fields so bombardment of the two airfields did not cause greater damage in Banja Luka or Zagreb. Banja Luka was attacked by 25 B-17s of the 463rd BG, and though Allied reports claim excellent results, most of the bombs missed the target and the city. Borongaj aerodrome in Zagreb was attacked by 40 B-24s of the 449th BG and 38 B-24s of the 450th BG, but due to weather conditions only 12 aircraft of the former dropped 21.5 tons of fragmentation cluster bombs between 09:38 and 09:40.

Six Croatian Macchi Mc. 202 fighters (possibly Mc. 205s) tried to intercept—most probably, the 449th BG—but they hit the escort from the 52nd FG instead. Escorting fighters quickly shot down five Croatian fighters. Though the patrol was led by Eastern Front veterans of 15. (kroat)/ JG 52—Major Helebrant, Captain Bencetić, and Officer Bartulović—the Croatian 11th Fighter

Squadron's Macchis were no match for Mustangs. All the Croatian pilots survived the encounter to fight and fly another day, but only Bencetić came back to base the way he left it, in the cockpit of his now badly damaged Macchi.

During a practice flight on 3 July, one C.R. 42 was lost in Ljubljana, Slovenia; Falco WNr. 7126 suffered an engine failure on approach to the tarmac and crashed and burned out. Its pilot, Fw. Heinz Drunk of the 2nd Staffel, was injured. On 6 July, five Falcos (E8+WK, DK, RK, OK, and FK) of NSGr. 9 flew from two aerodromes in Italy on a ferry flight. The destination of these aircraft may have possibly been NSGr 7.

On 7 July, more than 560 U.S. bombers attacked oil production facilities in Blechhammer and Odertal in Germany, as well as Zagreb's marshalling yards and Borongaj aerodrome. During the raid by 15th Air Force bombers, eight more Falcos were destroyed at Borongaj. Flying in the formation at 6,100–6,700m (20,000–22,000ft), the 51 four-engine bombers of the 449th and 450th BG dropped 126 tons of 225-kg (500-lb) GP bombs on the marshalling yards and aerodrome. A concentration of bursts on the Northeast end of the aerodrome and a direct hit on a hangar on the eastern side were observed by the photo reconnaissance cover. This was the last attack by U.S. strategic forces on Croatia for more than three weeks. German reports describe the destruction of several buildings: the compressed air plant, a hangar (90%), three ammunition dumps (60%), and about 30 direct hits on the runway, putting the aerodrome completely out of use for several days. Besides Falcos, seven other aircraft were reported destroyed in the bombardment.

Four days later, seven Spitfire Vcs of No. 73 Squadron RAF were sent on an offensive sweep to Zemunik aerodrome, taking off from Vis at 6:10. During the flight, one section was diverted to assist a rescue mission. No reports survive about the eventual results of this attack.

On 20 July 1944, in order to assure direct support to the 369. (Kroatische) Infanterie-Division "Teufels-Division" (369th Croatian Infantry Division, "Devils Division"), fighting in Bosnia and Herzegovina, Fliegerführer Kroatien ordered II./LLG 1 to detach six of its Ju 87s and NSGr 7 to detach four of its C.R. 42s to Mostar. They were to be subordinated to Nahaufklärungsgruppe 12, whose commander would control operations in direct collaboration with the 369th Division. Instructions from Fliegerführer Kroatien were clear that these aircraft must be used only when enemy air activity was weak, and again, special attention was drawn to aircraft dispersal and camouflage. The detachment's return to Zagreb was scheduled for 22 or 23 July, according to circumstances on the battlefield. On 22 July, these aircraft were heavily engaged against the Partisans in Bosnia and Herzegovina, with five Ju 87s and the four Falcos from NSGr 7 bombing Partisan strongholds in Novo Selo with five SD 250 and 19 SD 50 bombs. In the monthly summary report of the 13th Herzegovina Brigade (13. Hercegovačka brigada) for July 1944 dated 3 August, another attack by nine aircraft was mentioned for 23 July. The Brigade was attacked by five Stukas and four other aircraft near the village of Studenci during the day. No doubt the other four aircraft were Falcos of NSGr 7.

The 2nd German Panzer Army advised Fliegerführer Kroatien of their interception of Tito's order dated 26 August, intending to engage his own Air Force in all forthcoming battles. His aircraft markings would be a five-pointed red star with and without the tricolored round marking (blue, white, red).

On 28 August, Fliegerführer Kroatien was renamed to Fliegerführer Nordbalkan, a name it retained until 1 February 1945, when it was renamed yet again to 17. Flieger-Division. Generalmajor Walter Hagen was the first and last Fliegerführer Nordbalkan. Bearer of the Knight's Cross with Oak Leaves and a Stuka veteran, Hagen had been with Fliegerführer Kroatien since 14 June 1944. With the re-designation, higher command widened Hagen's area of responsibility. The first known mention of the new organization comes in a German communiqué of 10 September 1944. This message related to the shooting down of a Croatian Government Savioa aircraft by German fighters near Udine, in Italy.

Out of historical curiosity, it should be mentioned that another Nachtschlachtgruppe operated in the territory of Yugoslavia during the war. On 9 September, the II./LLG 1 was renamed to NSGr. 10. Gruppekommandeur was Maj. Jahnke Eberhard, who held this position until 13 March 1945. Stab./NSGr. 10 was formed from Stab II./LLG1, its 1. Staffel from 5./LLG1, and its 2. Staffel from 6./LLG 1. The unit started its operations in Ju 87 aircraft from Kacarevo (Franzfeld) airfield in Vojvodina the next day. Many of its Stukas wore the H4 (LLG 1) unit code and it operated mostly on the Romanian front, Vojvodina, and Serbia. During October (18 October for 2./NSGr. 10), NSGr. 10 flew away from the Yugoslavian front and via Hungary (Pecs) and Slovenia (Cerklje) they went further inland.

In September, the detachment of Fiat C.R. 42s from Zadar rejoined the rest of the Staffel at Pleso. On 11 September, Major Klaus Ostermann was posted as NSGr 7's new commanding officer, holding this position until the end of the war. Four days later, on 14 September, Falcos of 2./NSGr 7 were sent to Kraljevo, Serbia, while the 3. Staffel was moved to Graz Thalerhof, in Austria, where it would stay for the rest of the war.

The decision to remove NSGr 7 from Banja Luka to Zagreb and its surroundings proved very wise, as during the night of 21 to 22 September, the former town fell into Partisan hands. On 21 September, the 5th Assault Corps (5. Udarni korpus) of Tito's army occupied the town and managed to hold it for a week. At the aerodrome they captured 11 Croatian Air Force aircraft, of which five were serviceable; they also found some 17,500 aircraft bombs of diverse caliber, ranging from 12kg (26lb) Italian to 500kg (1,102lb) German, together with more than 400 tons of aircraft fuel. After the town was recaptured, Fliegerführer Nordbalkan inspected Zalužani and Adolfstal (Aleksandrovac) on 29 September and discovered about 30-40 wrecked aircraft, but much of the equipment was still in place. Aircraft that were captured in a flyable state were deployed by the Partisans against their previous owners immediately. Besides the ground attacks against German and Croatian forces that were still resisting in the Trappist monastery in Banja Luka, one aerial battle was recorded. On 27 September, Partisan pilot Sulejman "Suljo" Selimbegović, flying captured ex-ZNDH Morane-Saulnier 406C1 (coded 2332), popped up on two Fiat C.R. 42s belonging to NSGr.7 above the village Bronzani Majdan.

Ex-ZNDH Morane-Saulnier 406C1 coded 2332 in Partisan markings on the airstrip at Sanski Most. (Dragan Savić via Ciglić)

After a short exchange of fire the Morane started to overheat and Suljo broke off, landing on the Partisan airstrip at Prijedor. No victories were claimed after the skirmish.

During the German and Croatian counterattack to recapture Banja Luka, air power was widely used. Partisan reports of the 4th Corps (4. Korpus) mention especially strong aerial attacks on the 27th by 11 aircraft around 07:00. That afternoon, around 14:00, Partisan positions were again attacked by seven aircraft. Reports mention combined aerial and artillery attacks as direct support to the infantry, so it can be concluded that NSGr 7 took part in these attacks. Around 18:00, Partisans were again attacked by seven aircraft. Overall, the aerodrome was badly damaged, an inspection concluding that dispatch of salvage teams with adequate equipment and transport was needed, as the forces on the spot were insufficient to salvage this many aircraft. The airport was guarded by only a small force of German soldiers and in response Zagreb informed the Luftwaffe in Banja Luka that it would dispatch 15 trucks with 10 trailers the next morning to save whatever could be saved. Orders were given to evacuate first Zalužani and then Aleksandrovac airfields.

At the end of September, all three Staffeln of the Gruppe introduced a white spiral on their spinner covers in conformity with the orders from the end of June, but yellow markings were not reintroduced. From 2 August to 18 September, NSGr 7 reported the damage or loss of 14 of its aircraft, the archives offering no further details. According to Dr. Möller's research:

02.08.1944—1 aircraft;
03.08.1944—1 aircraft;
09.08.1944—5 aircraft,
14.08.1944—1 aircraft;
17.08.1944—1 aircraft (100 %);
30.08.1944—1 aircraft;
01.09.1944—1 aircraft;
16.09.1944—1 aircraft;
17.09.1944—2 aircraft and
18.09.1944—1 aircraft (100 %).

On 21 September, during a practice flight over Kragujevac, Serbia, friendly aerodrome flak defenses fired on a 1./NSGr 7 Falco piloted by Ofw. Anton Huberth. Aircraft WNr. 5623 (White 12) was damaged and a less-than-successful emergency landing caused further damage finally estimated at 50%.

By the end of September, six more planes were lost or damaged, according to Dr. Möller:

21.09.1944—2 aircraft;
24.09.1944—1 aircraft;
27.09.1944—2 aircraft (of which one 100 %) and
28.09.1944—1 aircraft

Transport of the 2nd Staffel back to Zagreb started on 5 October, and the unit was back at full strength at Pleso from mid-October, staying there til the end of the war. It seems that during the first week of October, 2./NSGr 7 operated 10-12 aircraft against Partisans in the area of Zaječar, while the 1st Staffel operated against Tito's forces in the zone Sunja-Kostajnica.

Six Partisans posing in front of the wrecks of two C.R. 42s in German markings. This photo was probably taken in Kraljevo and the aircraft belong to 2./NSGr 7. Note the "white outline only" type of Hakenkreuz on both machines, which was very unusual for the aircraft of NSGr 7. The camouflage pattern can clearly be seen on the elevators of the second aircraft. (Peršen)

On the evening of 9 October, Luftwaffenkommando Südost reported that 1./NSGr 7 was to transfer to Graz, in Austria, and would be operationally subordinated to Luftflotte Reich, but for administration and supplies it would continue to rely on Fliegerführer Nordbalkan. The Staffel was to be employed against guerrillas only in urgent cases and on patrol duties over defensive positions in Lower Styria. They were informed that "some" Arado Ar 66 and Gotha Go 145 were to be supplied, as well as some hand cameras. Bombs, spare parts, and engines for the C.R. 42s were all on the way from Italy.

On 10 October, the second Staffel reported a strength of nine C.R. 42s, of which five were operational, with 10 crews. The same day they reported the loss of two C.R. 42s and another three damaged. During an attack on Partisan units from Kraljevo, Serbia, C.R. 42 WNr. 9221 (tail number Black 20) was shot down by small arms fire near the village of Kalinovac. Pilot Ofw. Helmuth Rauer was mortally wounded and died five days later in a German field hospital. The pilot of the second Falco (WNr. 9199, Black 9), Ofw. Walter Bormann, was killed instantly when his plane was hit by Partisan ground fire and his Black 9 crashed 20km (12.43 miles) south of the village of Lapovo, in central Serbia. Three more unidentified aircraft of the Group were damaged the same day: one in a dogfight and another by small arms fire, while the last was damaged during a non-combat sortie. By the end of the first week of October at the latest, all NSGr 7 components (the Stab and three Staffeln) were fully equipped with the Falco, operating no fewer than 51 aircraft of the type on 10 October. Thirty-seven planes were serviceable, nine of them in the 2nd Staffel with ten pilots available.

Uffz. Wagner remembered his days in Serbia: "... But there [in Kraljevo] we flew only day missions, avoiding nocturnal ones"; and he proceeds with his story: "In Kragujevac, the Allies were bombing the airfield. We had just landed and had to take off immediately. Our Staffel landed in Novi Sad instead. Later we returned to Kragujevac."

Several destroyed C.R. 42s of NSGr 7 at Pleso airfield in 1945. (Jelušić)

For all high-winged aircraft, Partisans were using the name Storch. Here one Fi 156 at Borovo airfield has Croatian pilot Zvonimir Planinc in front of it. How similar are the Storch and Heinkel really? (Raguž)

On 11 October, Oblt. Rolf Bucheim informed Stab./NSGr 7 that the 1st Staffel did not need winter equipment, as they already possessed it.

One more of the Gruppe's planes was reported damaged on 12 October, during a combat sortie, and the day after another two were damaged on the ground by Allied bombers. The source gives no further details for these events.

October 14th was disastrous for the first Staffel, which lost no fewer than seven planes. Two Falcos were destroyed at Graz-Thalerhof during Allied bombing and mechanical failure was the probable cause of the crash of a third Fiat in the vicinity of Marija Bistrica, in the Hrvatsko Zagorje region. Jože Vedrina, a member of 2nd Platoon of the 1st company of the Zagreb Partisan Detachment (2. vod, 1. četa, Zagrebački Partizanski Odred), was brave and lucky at the same time. He managed to shoot down a fourth C. R. in the area of Konjščina, close to the village of Prepolno. Vedrina fired some 75 bullets from his MG 34, downing the Fiat which he reported as a "reconnaissance plane Storch." The pilot was reported dead.

Another pilot, Uffz. Ewald Jost, died on 14 October around 15:30, when his C.R. 42 WNr. 9768, tail number White 8, was shot down during take-off from Varaždin aerodrome by what the Germans reported as Mustangs. The Staffel reported another loss from the same Mustangs, but without further details. All these supposed "Mustangs" were in fact four Spitfire Mk.IXs of No. 73 Squadron RAF "A" flight which, after destroying a locomotive near Zagreb and one MT, surprised five C.R. 42s escorting a transport plane over Medvednica mountain, North of Zagreb. F/O George Andrew Martin, flying serial number MA484, shot down one, while F/O W. Chumack (MK444) and W/O F.F. Potvin (NH271) shared another. The fourth member of the patrol was Sgt. F.G. Parker, who flew serial number PT681. Croatian reports mention that another C.R. 42 was damaged during the dogfight. F/O Martin describes his fight with Falcos 15 miles north of Zagreb in the report:

> I was airborne from Canne at 14:00, leading a section of four aircraft on an offensive sweep of the Zagreb area. Patrolling just North of Zagreb, I saw one enemy aircraft at A.4 to the North, three miles ahead climbing slightly on a Northerly course. I pursued and saw that there were five enemy aircraft: three scattered line abreast and two line abreast further ahead. On overtaking the three enemy aircraft I identified them as C.R. 42s. The two further North appeared to be transport aircraft, one a low-winged monoplane. I attacked one C.R. 42 from line astern at A.5, giving a one second burst at 400 yards. The enemy aircraft immediately rolled on its back and dived for the ground. I followed down and E/A commenced hedge hopping and evasive actions, during which I was able to fire one two-second burst from 200 yards from an angle of 45 degrees. I did not observe any strikes. Closed to 100 yards and the E/A did a steep turn to the left, then changed to a right turn. I skidded to line astern and as he came to level position I fired a two-second burst from 100 down to 50 yards and saw numerous strikes along the fuselage. Pilot was probably hit. E/A caught fire and I saw flames along the engine cowling. The E/A then pulled up slightly, rolled on its back, and went into an inverted dive, crashing into the ground and exploding violently in flames at position approximately five miles due North of Zagreb. The E/A was green mottled with plain green band around the fuselage on which was the usual black cross marking.

The other two pilots mention that "their" Falco crashed down into some trees and exploded, while they did not observe the pilot leaving the plane. W/O F.F. Potvin went down over the treetops and saw the plane "completely disintegrated." Another German report mentions two more Falcos probably destroyed in Kragujevac that day by ground fire.

The description of the shot-down Fiat's camouflage is the only one that might help us in a reconstruction of the "native" pattern used on C.R. 42 aircraft, as almost all available photos of those aircraft show them in a pitiful state from which clear conclusions about their camouflage cannot be drawn with certainty. Though surprising, the description of the green band has a logical explanation. Nick Beale suggests this: "You begin with an aircraft that is dark green on the top and sides and with crosses in the normal places, then you apply a mottle camouflage, but avoid the area around the fuselage cross, leaving a cross on a plain green background.". Also it seems that the order to abandon the white fuselage band and yellow wing tips and the lower part of the cowling had been respected.

The Germans and the Partisans were engaged in heavy fighting in Serbia during the Partisan push towards Beograd. 2./NSGr 7 was stationed in Kragujevac, where it had operated in direct collaboration with the commander of the troops in the town since 3 October. The German command advised 2./NSGr 7 that due to heavy fighting in the areas of Ćićevac and Paraćin, close to the Staffel's aerodrome, and advancing enemy tanks near Obrež, all available aircraft should transfer to Kraljevo immediately. All remaining bombs were to be ferried there by road. On the same day at 15:00, the flying control officer in Kraljevo reported that 2./NSGr 7's transfer was complete.

From a report to the Wehrmacht command in Beograd, it can be seen that Germans threw a great number of aircraft into the battle in an effort to stop the Partisan advance on the city from the South. During the day, besides reconnaissance operations South of Beograd and the bridge over the Morava near Plana, numerous Luftwaffe aircraft were engaged in ground attacks and troop support sorties in the area of Stari Bečej: one Hs 126, one Bf 110, three Fw 190s, six Bf 109s, two Ju 88s, sixteen Ju 87s, and 31 C.R. 42s. These last undoubtedly belonged to 2./NSGr 7. The report mentions heavy aircraft losses at the hands of enemy fighters, but it is not clear whether these were Russian or long-range fighters from MAAF. Operations continued as before on 15 October, with more casualties: four of the Gruppe's planes were damaged in different accidents, while two were lost. One of the lost Falcos was that destroyed in the vicinity of Zagreb, probably by a P-51 of the 213th FS.

The 2./NSGr 7 transferred to Vukovar from Kraljevo and continued their transfer to airfields still functioning around Zagreb. Tragedies for the Gruppe continued when a Junkers Ju 52 of III./TG 3 (WNr. 3050, ST+GT) crash landed about 15km (9.32 miles) SW of Gorica, near Kravarsko.[61] This "Tante Ju" was transporting the equipment of 2./NSGr 7 and men from all three Staffeln. It had taken off from Borovo airfield near Vukovar, where it had landed as a stopover from Kraljevo. The intention was to land and unload at Pleso. As it had crash landed in enemy-held territory, the crew fled the aircraft after a short shoot-out with Partisans in a forested area. The Oberwerkmeister[62] of the 2nd Staffel, Ofw. Gerhard Paulik, was killed during the clash with the Partisans. Other Germans were taken prisoner and sometime later exchanged for captured Tito fighters:

- 1st Staffel: Aircraft mechanics[63] Uffz. Alois Hollesch and Ogefr. Johann Weber;
- 2nd Staffel: Pilot Ofw. Erwin Kühn and 1st mechanic Fw. Frieder Hellmuth;
- 3rd Staffel: Pilots Ofw. Willi Schiffner and Uffz. Günther Christophe, and 1st mechanics Ogefr. Jakob Strixner, Fw. Hans Walter, and Fw. Rudolf Isringhaus.

According to Partisan documents, Vlado Matijašić from the 1st Batallion of the Žumberak Brigade fired at a low-flying Ju 52 that was already having technical difficulties and looking for a suitable place to land. After being damaged further, the aircraft made an emergency landing in a vineyard and plum plantation near Kravarsko. A small group of Partisans saw the landing and headed towards the aircraft, from which MG fire opened. Once the Luftwaffe men had fled, the Partisans found a large quantity of food and material in the aircraft. It seems the plane was 50% damaged and was salvaged later by German troops and incorporated in TG 2 after repairs.

Uffz. Wagner of 3rd Staffel offers his distorted version of what is probably the same story: "And in Amstar [probably Kraljevo], a few aircraft [of the Staffel] were in pieces, and the boys then had to fly home aboard a Ju 52. I still had my plane [a C.R. 42]. The Junkers was shot down and all the comrades were lynched!"

While retreating from Greece and Albania, German commanders in the Kosovo area asked on 17 October to be sent a Staffel from NSGr 7, as they were "blind," but this request was denied. On the 18th of the same month, Beobachter Oblt. (later on Hptm.) Ernst Wiemann was named Offz. z.b.V. of 1./NSGr 7, in which position he served until 13 March 1945.

A Ju 52/3m and a Fiesler Fi 156 at Borovo aerodrome near Vukovar on 12 July 1943. Last three numbers of the WNr. of the Ju 52 are 158. (Raguž)

On 21 October, Fliegerführer Nordbalkan reported an average availability for the month of 15 serviceable C.R. 42s with NSGr 7 in Agram-Lučko, their range limited to 150km (93 miles) due to fuel shortage. The same day, Partisans occupied Kragujevac aerodrome, at which they reported capturing no fewer than eight damaged C.R. 42s of 2./NSGr 7. Three days later, Fliegerführer Nordbalkan was disbanded and the command of NSGr 7 was taken over by Luftflotte 4. Major Schneider became the new Kapitän of the third Staffel in October, remaining in this position until 13 March 1945.

On 31 October, Zadar was liberated by the Partisans, and a few days later Zemunik aerodrome. The first day of November brought the first loss of the month, when an unknown Fiat was totally destroyed due to an accident. During the heavy fighting in Eastern Slavonia and Vojvodina, the 118. Jäger-Division had the task of holding the defenses on the line Šid—Ilok against the Russian and Partisan advance. It requested aerial support from Fliegerführer Nordbalkan on 3 October, but was refused, as the only unit in the area with ground attack capability was 2./NSGr 7, stationed in Lučko, whose aircraft were obsolete and likely to suffer high losses.

On 3 November, Uffz. Wagner was on his way to Italy to pick up a new C.R. 42 for the unit and was wounded during an Allied air raid on the railway station. Here is his account of that day: "I was wounded on 3 November 1944. I had my parachute with me and was at the railway station on my way to Udine to pick up a Fiat C.R. 42. While sitting on the train, we were surprised by British planes." Uffz. Wagner continues: "... and then aircraft came using the longitudinal approach and I thought: 'I have to get out of the train.' So I ran out of the train straight to the railway embankment. I laid down, but was hit in my arm by a bullet. I couldn't fly anymore and never returned to my unit."

One Do 17, a W 34, a Ju 52, and a Bf 110 at Borongaj aerodrome in January 1944. These aircraft are parked on the "German" part of the aerodrome, so this is probably the Gruppenkommandeur's Bf 110. (Raguž)

During the morning of the same day, a Spitfire with a Partisan pilot (Mileta Protić of No. 352 (Y.) Squadron, RAF) flew a recce over Zemunik airport but did not notice any activity there.

Two days later, on 5 November 1944, 1./NSGr 7, stationed in Graz, reported aircraft movements for October as follows: in total, 11 Fiat C.R. 42s were serviceable; six had come to strength, of which five were from repair and one from another unit. Eight aircraft went off strength, three of them due to Allied action and one to other causes; and two had gone for overhaul and two to other units. Dr. Möller, in his research, discovered the presence of a Messerschmitt Bf 110 in NSGr 7, which was shot down by over-efficient German Flak and its pilot, Fw. Willi Uhl,[64] was killed in the crash. According to what is typed on the source document, the aircraft belonged to 2./NSGr 7, but the word "Stab" was added by hand. Dr. Möller also states that: "A Bf 110 belonged to the group commander, Major Blaich. Its existence was revealed by the 'newspaper' which the 1./NSGr 7 compiled for Christmas 1944." He adds: "I've learned that Major Blaich was said to have belly landed his Bf 110 once due to engine trouble. Later he used a Bf 108 and then a Saiman (202 or 204) from the 1st Staffel."

On 18 November, Fliegerführer Nordbalkan reported to Luftflotte 4 with a summary of its operations for the day, mentioning aerial attacks aimed at destroying the railway system serving the advancing enemy. It was reported that 18 sorties had been flown, with the result of eight locomotives destroyed and several more trains shot up. Ground attack operations were conducted with 28 aircraft in support of German troops preventing the Partisan army from forcing the Danube river and establishing a bridgehead on the present-day border of Croatia and Vojvodina near Batina. In this report, Luftflotte 4 stated that no fewer than 37 trucks had been destroyed and 30 more effectively shot up; five barges on the Danube had been sunk or damaged; and one enemy aircraft was shot down "in flames." Though no individual units are mentioned, it is credible that whatever was flyable of the NSGr 7 Fiats in Croatia were engaged in these battles.

1./NSGr 7 men at the end of 1944 in Graz. Note the fez is no longer part of the uniform. (Möller)

The Heinkel aircraft were used against Partisans in Bosnia and Herzegovina at least until the end of November 1944. (Predoević)

On 22 November, many aerodromes in Croatia and Bosnia and Herzegovina were having problems and were partially or completely closed for operations due to weather. NSGr 7 was affected, as Gorica and Pleso, near Zagreb, were closed for all aircraft types due to the soft ground and there were no operations from either. Lučko airfield was fully serviceable and Butmir and Rajlovac likewise, except for the Bf 109. On 25 November, a report from Kraljevo brought information that one unserviceable Fiat was still there. The same aircraft had been

Aerial view of Rajlovac aerodrome from an He 46. (Peršen)

mentioned in a report dated 9 November, and was probably from the 2nd Staffel that had operated from Kraljevo in October. Fliegerführer Nordbalkan reported 57 operations for the day without precise information on which units he was referring to. On the last day of November 1944, three He 46s were stationed at Butmir, near Sarajevo, operating under the name "Nachtschlachtstaffel Butmir" (revealed by Ultra decrypts), which was probably an ad hoc unit composed of worn-out Henkels of the 1st Staffel. The same day, the unknown Lieutenant (his name is not visible on the original document), commander of the 3.(F)/33 advance party, reported that at Borongaj, the remaining elements of 3./NSGr 7 were occupying one of the barracks intended for accommodation of the technical staff of 3.(F)/33 and his unit still could not take it over. In continuation, he reported that he had an unpleasant surprise when he discovered a day earlier that NSGr 7's men took away all the furniture from the accommodation they were using and which was intended to host the Staka and the z.b.V. officer of 3.(F)/33.

Unknown member of NSGr 7. The photo was taken in Sarajevo. (Predoević)

At the end of November, the Luftwaffe command in the area informed their station in Sarajevo that the provisional date for the demolition of installations at Butmir aerodrome, prior to its abandonment, was 3 December.

Next day, on 4 December, the first certain loss of a Gruppe-owned Ju 87 was recorded when, during a ferry flight, a pilot of Stab./NSGr 7 (Fw. Bernhard Wortmann and his Bordfunker, Fhj.Fw. Rolf Schlieder) crashed in Hungary. Both men were buried in Zamoly cemetery. Five days later, on 9 December, two Fiat biplanes were damaged in accidents; on 11 December, Fliegerkorps II sent a telegram to Fliegerführer Nordbalkan that the demarcation line between them for reconnaissance and bombing sorties was set by the rivers Drava, Dunav,[65] and Tisa.

The Fliegerführer reported that a recce mission over Zemunik aerodrome, Zadar, on 12 December, had found it unoccupied by enemy aviation, and apart from spotting two destroyed Bf 109s there was nothing else to report. Furthermore, Luftflotte 4 issued an order that its branch commanding the SE had been disbanded and that the Fliegerführer and his Stab were directly subordinated to the Luftflotte in every respect. The control of all flying units operating in Croatia and the North Balkan area were the responsibility of Fliegerführer Nordbalkan, who was instructed to support the war effort of Army Group F by every possible means through the Luftwaffe liaison officer in HQ SE. Fliegerführer Nordbalkan (person) represented "all Croatian flying units" with the Oberkommando der Luftwaffe and his status was that of a divisional commander.

On 18 December, C.R. 42 tail number Yellow 17 was shot down near Pitomača by anti-aircraft fire; its pilot from the 3rd Staffel, Fhj. Fw. Hans Kruschel, lost his life.

A few days after, on 24 December, the third Staffel moved to Varaždin, in NE Croatia, where it stayed until 1 April 1945, when it came back to Gorica. Just two days later, Flying Officer Henry E. Simpson, Jr., in his P-51 of the 4th FS, 52nd FG, shot down and killed Uffz. Harald Arlt of the 3rd Staffel while he was taking off on a harassment mission with his Fiat WNr. 9906, Yellow 4. The Falco was shot down eight kilometers (5 miles) West of Varaždin, reportedly "near village Cianic" (actually Šijanec). According to recent research by Mario Raguž, the aircraft fell into the garden of the Zagorec family and burned out completely; its pilot was buried in Varaždin cemetery.

On 27 December 1944, Stab./NSGr 7 (still stationed in Velika Gorica) ordered 3./NSGr 7 (operating from Varaždin) to report on its consumption of "O" fuel and Diesel. The same day, Luftflotte IV ordered Fliegerführer Nordbalkan to perform vital armed recce "at any cost," with emphasis on finding adequate targets, such as enemy troop concentrations, for German bombers.

During December, the loss of a plane piloted by Fw. Adolf-Gerhard Peche was recorded, but without further details, except that it had happened in Bosnia and Herzegovina.

On the last day of a bloody 1944, a Schwarm of C.R. 42s from 3./NSGr 7 was performing armed reconnaissance in Croatia in support of the German army on the Drave (river Drava) front. Also that day, the 3rd Staffel was active in the area of Barcs, in Hungary, 40km (25 miles) WSW of Pecs (known in German as Fünfkirchen). At the end of 1944, Oblt. Rolf Bucheim became StaKa of 1./NSGr 7 and he commanded first Staffel until the end of the war.

During November and December 1944, German forces were in full withdrawal from Greece, Albania, and Montenegro. The aggravated situation on the Hungarian and Srijem fronts endangered this withdrawal, threatening complete German armies with outflanking with no possibility of withdrawal. Due to intense Allied bomber and fighter-bomber activities, as well as increased Partisan forces that were constantly on the offensive, this retreat was more than complicated. Constant disruption of railway and road traffic by Allied aircraft and diversions by Partisans forces, especially in Bosnia and Herzegovina, required desperate measures in order to save whatever could be saved. For this purpose, the Luftwaffe threw all available Ju 52/3ms into the area, from schools (C4, BFS5, etc.) and transport groups (TG 2 and TG 3), as well as Deutsche Lufthansa aircraft. It was of the utmost importance to keep the aerodromes around Sarajevo at maximum operational readiness. The route for evacuation and supplies was from Kraljevo, Kragujevac, Podgorica, and Durazzo via and from Sarajevo to Slavonski Brod and Zagreb, and further on to Wiener Neustadt. Exhausted troops were often disembarked at Slavonski Brod and Zagreb and incorporated into the German 2nd Panzer Army, which was collapsing under Russian pressure on the Drave front. It was no matter whether these troops belonged to Navy, Air Force, or Army; they all continued to fight and live the miserable life of German infantrymen with little chance of seeing the end of the war. No doubt, amongst those men there were some from NSGr 7, withdrawn from Sarajevo.

Chapter 5: Epilogue

A change took place on the first day of the final year of the war, when Oblt. Friedrich Haar was named Technical Officer of the 1st Staffel. Originally, he was a pilot and Technical Officer of the 2nd Staffel. Two days later, two Falco aircraft were lost and two others damaged during a combat mission. In January 1945, NSGr 7 had 37 serviceable aircraft out of 51 in the unit. January's armed recce missions were conducted in the areas of Zadar and Virovitica in Croatia, Zvornik and Bihać in Bosnia and Herzegovina, and Černomelj in Slovenia, and losses were increasing. The 3./NSGr 7 was still operating on the Drave (river Drava) front in the first week of 1945. On 17 and 18 January, one unidentified Falco of NSGr 7 was lost each day in an accident. On the 20th, the Gruppe reported the loss of yet another Falco and damage to one more, neither as a result of enemy action. Dr. Möller has identified two more losses from the unit during January but with unknown dates: Fw. Gerhard Beier went missing near Wien (Vienna) and Ogefr. Rudolf Miosga was missing somewhere in the "Balkans." The 3./NSGr 7 was stationed at Gorica on 22 January, and received orders to be at one hour's readiness for operations from 08:00 the next day.

Badly damaged Falco at Kurilovec aerodrome in 1945. (Aralica)

February 1945 was catastrophic for the unit. On its second day, 34 P-51s of the 31st Fighter Group (17 each from the 308th and 309th FS), with top cover from another 14 (307th FS), strafed the airstrip in Kurilovec, SW of Zagreb. The American fighters took off from their base at San Severo, Italy, around 13:15. After an hour and a half of uneventful flight, the attack started at 14:42, led by the aircraft of the 308th FS which, after setting ablaze two Falcos in their first pass, called the 309th FS to attack. When the 309th approached the target from the East, intense and accurate Flak (mostly 20 and 30mm guns) and small arms fire transformed the sky into hell. Flak was concentrated on the SE and NW sides of the airfield and near the road on the West.

The scene was apocalyptic: on the snow-covered airfield NSGr 7 planes were burning and Flak was pumping its deadly load into the sky, where P-51s were flying in all directions, firing at ground targets. Glycol traces from damaged Mustangs were visible in the sky, and with each succeeding pass the Flak became deadlier and more accurate.

Nine of the Gruppe's C.R. 42s were destroyed, while five more were damaged from 15-20%. The Werk Nummern of the completely destroyed Falcos were 7206, 9168, 9224, 9776, 9885, 9828, 9896, 90804, and 90886. Those damaged were WNr. 5655 (20%), 7151 (20%), 8524 (20%), 8975 (15%), and 90887.[66] Lt. Anderson of the 309th FS claimed one Hs 126, but no confirmation for this can be found in the archive materials.

The Americans, in their turn, lost a total of six Mustangs to Flak. The 308th FS lost five aircraft, namely:

- P-51D-15-NA (S/N 44-15447), piloted by Commanding Officer Major Frank Wagner, who was hit in the right side of the engine and bailed out at 14:55, ten miles SE of Kurilovec;
- P-51B-10-NA (S/N 43-7161), piloted by 2nd Lt. Alton L. Hall and part of Green flight, was hit in the engine and belly landed at 15:15, five miles West of Sisak;
- P-51D-15-NA (S/N 44-15215), flown by 308th Yellow flight leader 1st Lt. Ralph D. Lockney and named "Alabama Gal," around 15:10 hours;
- P-51[67] of 1st Lt. Luther W. Martin (S/N 44-14483) was hit in the engine, which immediately started to loose glycol. He opened his canopy and bailed out at 14:55, landing five miles East of Kurilovec airfield.
- P-51D-5-NA (S/N 44-13278) of 2nd Lt. Harry S. Carlton (named "Weary Willie") was part of Yellow flight. He crash landed at 15:15 in a snow-covered field about two miles NE of Sisak. The tail of 2nd Lt. Carlton's Mustang is exhibited in the Museum of Yugoslavian Aviation in Beograd.

View of Kurilovec aerodrome with the wreckage of C.R. 42s of NSGr 7. (Aralica)

For its part, the 309th FS lost one P-51C-10-NT piloted by 1st Lt. George W. Gibson (S/N 43-25126). Six more Mustangs of the 31st FG were badly damaged by flak.

Six days later, 10 Falcos of Stab and 2./NSGr 7 took off from Gorica to attack what was thought to be a Partisan airstrip at Grabovica. On their way to the target they were jumped by P-38s of the 14th Fighter Group. In the ensuing battle, four biplanes were shot down, with 1st Lieutenant Lawrence V. Bach, Jr. of the 37th FS alone claiming two destroyed, one probable, and one damaged. Four of NSGr 7's pilots were killed: Hptm. Eduard Jacob of Stab./NSGr 7, flying Aeritalia-built Falco WNr. 90897 (90% damage); Hptm. Kurt Jacobs Staffelführer of 2./NSGr 7, flying Aeritalia-built Falco WNr. 90841, Black 1 (100% damage); Ofw. Wolfgang Harnack, flying Aeritalia-built Falco WNr. 9832, White 2 (100% damage); and Gefr. Hans-Heinrich Schreiber, flying Fiat-built Falco WNr. 8864, Black 2 (100% damage), all from 2./NSGr 7.[68] There are claims that one of the C.R. 42s shot down a P-38, which would make it the last biplane victory in history, but this is impossible to verify through the available archive materials, since the Americans reported no losses. Also on 8 February, Hptm. Stauf[69] took on the duties of the adjutant of the Group, where he stayed until the end of March 1945.

Next day, Fiat-built C.R. 42 WNr. 9183 of 2./NSGr 7 crash landed after a combat flight, causing 70% damage to the aircraft (a write-off). A week later, another Fiat-built C.R. 42 of the third Staffel (WNr. 9850) suffered a tire failure while taking off from Varaždin and was destroyed (80%) when it flipped over. On 17 February, Fw. Walter Broscheit also overturned on take-off from the same airfield and his Fiat-built Falco (WNr. 9247, Yellow 19) was damaged beyond repair (80%). After these accidents and the unstoppable Partisan advance in the area during March 1945, the Staffel was transferred to Gorica, where it remained until the end of the war. One of the aerodromes frequently used by NSGr 7 near the town of Mostar fell into Partisan hands on 14 February.

From 23 to 25 February, one more C.R. 42 was lost each day. In calendar order these were: Stab./NSGr 7 C.R. 42, WNr. 8992 crashed in Reichenau, Austria, due to pilot error, suffering 30% damage; 2./NSGr 7 (WNr. 9801) crashed with 60% damage in what was reported as "an involuntary contact with the ground" when landing after a combat sortie; and WNr. 9840 crash landed in Aigen, Austria, causing 45% damage to the aircraft.

During the transfer of 3./NSGr 7 from Varaždin to Gorica, seven C.R. 42s bombed Hasan Breg with 14 SD 50 bombs. A hutted camp 1km (.62 miles) from this locality was set afire and the aircraft used their 12.7mm guns against Partisan positions in the village of Velike. Two C.R. 42s attacked Menina Planina with four SD 50 bombs. The pilots reported bombs on target, which was confirmed after a recce mission undertaken by an Hs 126 of an unknown unit. Menina Planina is situated 33km (20.5 miles) West of Celje, Slovenia, and Hasan Breg is 22km (13.7 miles) SSW of Zagreb.

On 13 March, as per Luftflotte 4's orders, the following units were officially disbanded: Nahaufklärungsstaffel Kroatien (Lučko); 1./NSGr 7 (Graz); and Stab 2. and 3./NSGr 7 (Gorica). Despite its official disbandment, NSGr 7 was still operational in Croatia and Slovenia, all within the limits of available fuel, and its name can still be found in the orders and exchanges of information between different Luftwaffe units.

On 19 March, Allied fighter-bombers attacked Borongaj, but there was no damage, as the airfield was practically deserted. From his research, Mario Raguž provides the following description of events on 20 March 1945:

> During mission No. 321, while attacking an Axis motorized column of around 30 vehicles on the road Jahorina—Igman near Sarajevo, Spitfire Mk. Vcs of No. 352 Squadron RAF, flown by Yugoslav pilots, observed a low-flying Hs 126. A section of the Yugoslav squadron headed by Hinko Šoić in Spitfire serial number MH592; first wingman Mehmed Alija Lošić

Luftwaffe graves at Mirogoj cemetery, Zagreb, in 1943. After the war, the Communists completely destroyed (by digging) all the graves of Axis soldiers buried there. Small, almost symbolic graveyards of German soldiers exist today in Zagreb and Split. (Peršen)

Pilots of No. 352 (Y) Squadron on Vis island in January 1945, in front of a Spitfire. Standing from left to right: Šime Fabijanić (Wingman No. 3), Milan Delić, Juraj Tomšić, Nedeljko Pajić, Hinko Šoić (Leader), Đuro Ivanišević, Milan Srdanović, Živojin Gavrilović, Ciril Vrabič, and Mirko Kovačić (Wingman No. 4). Below them: Radovan Radulović, Luigi Rugi, Husein Okanović, and Marijan Semolić. (Raguž)

> in BR130; wingman three Šime Fabijanović in JG871; and Mirko Kovačić in LZ830 as wingman four gave chase to the German aircraft. The Luftwaffe crew spotted their attackers, the German pilot trying to avoid the attacks and save himself by taking his aircraft down to the tree tops. The Henschel was flying from Butmir aerodrome towards Kalinovik and constantly altered its course, trying to avoid the Hispano cannons. The Partisan pilots were ruthless, and after several joint passes the German aircraft was just a burning wreck on the ground. According to some reports, this parasol-winged machine hit a hill while avoiding the Spitfires' attacks, while others say it was a victim of their powerful cannon. Whichever story is true, this was the first and only aerial victory by the Partisan pilots of 352 Squadron in WWII. Because of the insufficient information available, it is impossible to establish which unit this Henschel belonged to, but there are fair indications that it was attached to NSGr 7, probably within "Detachment Butmir."

The victory was attributed to the leader of the formation, Squadron Leader Hinko Šoić. During 28 March, Bihać, another airfield often used by NSGr 7, fell into Partisan hands. Two days later, five Allied fighter-bombers attacked Rajlovac, near Sarajevo.

The last recorded losses which can with certainty be attributed to NSGr 7 were in March (all on unknown dates), as follows:

- In Graz, unknown aircraft, Fw. Hermann Aust missing;
- In Marburg (Maribor, Slovenia), unknown aircraft, Uffz. Kurt Haupt missing; and
- In St. Pölten, unknown aircraft, Uffz. Walter Reiter missing.

On the last day of March, German sources reported that 13 Fiat C.R. 42s took part in bombing operations in Austria.[70] In another Ultra decrypt for the same date, German sources place these attacks in the area of the village of Zalabaksa, in Hungary, near the Slovenian border. The targets of the attacks were columns on the road Zalabaksa—Zalaoevoe.[71]

On the second day of April, Luftflotte 4 signalled to Fliegerdivision 17 to remain in its current battle HQ (Zagreb). Reports dated five days later show an attack by 12 Fiat aircraft West of Graz on enemy troop concentrations; one C.R. 42 was reported shot down on this occasion, probably of NSGr 7, but this cannot be confirmed.

On 9 April 1945, Luftflotte 4 ordered Fliegerdivision 17 to disband Fliegerführer Nordbalkan's staff. The remaining elements of NSGr 7 were to be employed within the limits of the fuel situation until final disbandment. The final disbandment of the Second and Third Staffeln at Gorica aerodrome occurred the same day, together with the disbandment of NASt Kroatien. The 1st Staffel in Graz was also to be disbanded according to Luftflotte 4's orders and all disbanded units were to hand over their personnel to the 10th Para Division being set up in Graz, Austria, to fight as infantry.

Even after their official disbandment, Fliegerdivision 17 reported activities by the night ground attack units. The night of 17 to 18 April, it reported 30 night ground attack aircraft attacking vehicles around St. Pölten in Austria and six night ground attacks on vehicles at Mistelbach and NW of Lundenburg in Austria. These were the last recorded missions of Nachtschlachtgruppe 7 during the largest conflict in human history.

After the liberation of Zagreb and all the aerodromes around the town, the Partisans, now renamed the Yugoslav Army, captured 107 German and Croatian aircraft there, but only six of them were serviceable. By the end of the war, around 20 of the Gruppe's C.R. 42 Falcos were still serviceable.

The wreck of a Falco at Kurilovec aerodrome on 8 May 1945. (Military Museum Belgrade via Dejan Savić)

Zagreb, the capital of the Independent State of Croatia, was liberated by Tito's forces on 8 May 1945, and all operational aerodromes of the Axis forces in Croatia were now in the hands of the Partisans. Several wrecked Fiat C.R. 42s were found at Pleso and Kurilovec aerodromes. The war ended everywhere in Europe the day after the liberation of Zagreb, one of the few exceptions being Yugoslavia, where German and Croatian forces continued their fighting withdrawal towards the British positions in Austria; they were unwilling to surrender to the Yugoslav Army for fear of retaliation for the atrocities committed during the last four years of war. Numerous civilians fled with the defeated armies to find protection with the British Army. A week later, fighting ended and the last Axis forces still fighting in Europe finally surrendered at Bleiburg field, on the Slovenian/Austrian border. The British disarmed and handed over more than 150,000 Ustasha paramilitary, Croatian and Slovenian Home Guard, regular army, and some Cossacks and Chetniks to Tito, aware of what would follow. So-called Head of State Pavelić left his forces and fled initially to Argentina to find permanent residence in Madrid, Spain, where he died in 1959 under Franco's protection.

As far as Nachtschlachtgruppe 7 is concerned, it is likely that the last pilots and mechanics stationed in Croatia found themselves among the Axis columns withdrawing towards Austria after 8 May, and that they shared the fate of the defeated in these last weeks after Germany's capitulation. How many they were, how many lost their lives, and how many actually survived this calvary is impossible to establish after almost 70 years.

From the establishment of the Störkampfstaffel within Fliegerführer Kroatien in 1942, the unit grew and gained significance on this battlefield of secondary importance for the outcome of the war. This fact accounts for the historiographical ignorance of the unit and its members. Most works of aviation history simply ignore the existence of NSGr 7 or accord it marginal importance, even amongst authors from the former Yugoslavia. Besides the Croatian Air Force and NASt Kroatien, this was the longest lasting air force unit permanently fighting Tito and his forces from Serbia and Montenegro in the East to Slovenia in the West. The unit was employed in all the major battles in the area and fought fiercely and bravely using obsolete aircraft, operating in impossible conditions and fighting on foot and in the air until the end (and possibly a bit longer). As we have seen, the Gruppe's first losses were sporadic and often the result of a lucky shot from the ground. With time, the Partisan forces grew and became better equipped with MG and decent AA weaponry and losses from ground fire mounted progressively, with many brave aviators falling victim to the way the unit was employed in the battle—flying low and in daylight in obsolete machines unsuited for the purpose.

An He 46 of the Gruppe in low-level flight below the peaks of Bosnia and Herzegovina. (Predoević)

From January 1944, Allied forces had undisputed command of the air over the Yugoslav battlefield, despite some attempts by Oberkommando der Luftwaffe to establish their defenses beyond the borders of what was seen by them as the 1,000-year Reich. Except over the area of Drvar during a few days in May 1944, where engagement of the Luftwaffe fighter arm assured short-term command of the air over a limited geographical area, all Luftwaffe units in the area suffered heavy losses from Spitfires, Mustangs, and Lightnings of MAAF. Late and inadequate efforts by Germany to strengthen the Croatian Air Force's fighter squadrons did not change this permanent loss of control of the air. The situation for the Gruppe was further aggravated by a systematic bombing campaign by Allied heavy bombers that visited almost each and every aerodrome they used.

The Allies' command of the air, obsolete aircraft, and improvement of the equipment of Tito forces were not the only reasons for high losses, but also the nature of the terrain in which NSGr 7 was used. Examples are numerous, especially in Bosnia and Herzegovina, where they were obliged to fly low and often below the mountain peaks from which the enemy was firing at them.

During the writing of this history, the author exchanged many messages with Nick Beale, and we came to the same conclusion once we saw the photos of the He 46 equipped with SD 2 bombs, with which accurate aiming was impossible: "they didn't bother to aim." Also, due to the type of warfare in which the Partisans were engaged until they gained the strength and organization for a frontal confrontation with Axis forces, any house that was not the Gruppe's own barracks could be occupied by the enemy and one could be shot at from it. A single lucky shot was enough to bring down an He 46 or a Fiat. The Partisans often used human shields to

The winner and the defeated; a Partisan in front of a NSGr 7 Falco at Kurilovec airstrip in May 1945. (Aralica)

protect themselves; not only POWs, but their own people, hiding in villages with no military significance and densely populated by civilians. Official historiography is written by the winner, and in the communist regimes (even as liberal as Tito's) such statements have even heavier weight.

With the renewal of equipment that brought the C.R. 42 and Ca. 314 into the theatre of operations, accuracy was certainly improved due to the provision of proper aiming devices on these aircraft. While the pilots loved the small buzzing Fiats, the "flying coffin" Caproni was widely detested by its crews and therefore quickly replaced by Falcos. Some Capronis were sent back to Germany and some were given to the Croatian Air Force.

Crash of one of the Croatian Capronis probably given to the Croatian Air Force by the Germans. (Raguž)

Scrapyard with at least four C.R. 42s of NSGr 7. The picture was taken somewhere in Serbia in 1944/45, possibly Zemun or Kraljevo. (Baćković)

Although unable to aim with any great precision, no evidence was found, especially in the Yugoslav Partisans' archive, that NSGr 7 was employed purely against civilian targets or for retaliation purposes during its existence. There were, however, inevitable errors, but certainly these were not part of any systematic planning.

The history of Nachtschlachtgruppe 7 is solidly cross-linked with its "sister" unit Nahaufklärungsstaffel Kroatien, the greater part of which became its Second Staffel in autumn 1943. Aircraft of both units often operated jointly from Bihać, Zadar, Banja Luka, Mostar, and Sarajevo, and it was very hard to establish clear boundaries for who did what. Maximum effort was made by the author to make this part clear and the question will remain open until the story of NASt Kroatien is told.

This book is a modest effort to present to a wider public the history of one of the most significant and longest-lasting Luftwaffe units that operated in the territory of former Yugoslavia, and to try to make their story known. NSGr 7 flew and fought a different war, different even from any other Nachtschlachtgruppe in existence in the East or West. All those brave men deserved this dedication, as despite their obsolete equipment they fought heroically and within the context of the battle against Tito until the very end of the war, often causing him nightmares.

Appendices

A. Aircraft availability of Stab./Nachtschlachtgruppe 7

(Courtesy of Dr. Christian Möller)

Date	Target	Actual	Operational	Aircraft Type
20.11.1943	2			
30.11.1943	2			
10.12.1943	2			
20.12.1943	2			
31.12.1943	2			
10.01.1944	2			
20.01.1944	2			
31.01.1944	2	2	2	Ju 87
06.02.1944	2	4	2	Ju 87
10.02.1944	2	2	2	Ju 87
20.02.1944	2	4	3	Ju 87
29.02.1944	2	5	2	Ju 87
10.03.1944	2	4	3	Ju 87
20.03.1944	2	5	5	Ju 87
31.03.1944	2	7	5	Ju 87 (6/5), C.R. 42 (1/0)
10.04.1944	2	7	4	Ju 87 (6/4), C.R. 42 (1/0)
20.04.1944	2	4	2	Ju 87
30.04.1944	2	3	3	Ju 87
10.05.1944	2	3	3	Ju 87
20.05.1944	2	3	2	Ju 87
31.05.1944	2	3	3	Ju 87
10.06.1944	2	6	3	Ju 87
20.06.1944	2	6	3	Ju 87

Date	Target	Actual	Operational	Aircraft Type
30.06.1944	2	6	3	Ju 87
10.07.1944	2	3	2	Ju 87
20.07.1944	2	3	3	Ju 87
31.07.1944	2	3	3	Ju 87
01.08.1944	2	3	?	Ju 87D
10.08.1944	2	3	2	Ju 87
20.08.1944	2	1		Ju 87
31.08.1944	2			
10.09.1944	2			
20.09.1944	2	2	2	
20.10.1944	2	1	0	C.R. 42
31.10.1944	2	1	1	C.R. 42
10.11.1944	2	1	1	C.R. 42
20.11.1944	2	2	2	C.R. 42
23.11.1944	2	2	2	C.R. 42
30.11.1944	2	2	2	C.R. 42
10.12.1944	2	2	2	C.R. 42
20.12.1944	2	2	2	C.R. 42
31.12.1944	2	2	2	C.R. 42
10.01.1945	2	2	2	C.R. 42

B. Aircraft availability of 1./Nachtschlachtgruppe 7

(Courtesy of Dr. Christian Möller)

Date	Target	Actual	Operational	Aircraft Type
10.10.1943	20/25(16)	He 46 (15/10), Hs 126 (10/6)		
20.10.1943	20/25(22)	He 46 (16/13), Hs 126 (9/9)		
31.10.1943	20/19(17)	He 46		
10.11.1943	20/19(16)	He 46		
20.11.1943	20/16(15)	He 46		
30.11.1943	20/17(14)	He 46		
10.12.1943	20/18(16)	He 46		
20.12.1943	20/17(17)	He 46		
31.12.1943	20/19(16)	He 46		
10.01.1944	20/17(14)	He 46		
15.01.1944	20/17(14)	He 46		
20.01.1944	20/17(12)	He 46		
31.01.1944	20/14(12)	He 46		
06.02.1944	20/16(10)	He 46		
10.02.1944	20/16(10)	He 46		
11.02.1944	20/16(10)	He 46		
20.02.1944	20/17(11)	He 46		
29.02.1944	20/13(7)	He 46		
10.03.1944	20/13(0)	He 46		
20.03.1944	20/12(9)	He 46		
31.03.1944	20/10(4)	He 46		
10.04.1944	20/13(9)	He 46		
20.04.1944	20/14(6)	He 46 (9/4), Ju 87 (5/2)		
30.04.1944	20/14(8)	He 46 (10/5), Ju 87 (4/3)		
10.05.1944	20/15(11)	He 46 (11/9), Ju 87 (2/1), C.R. 42 (2/1)		
20.05.1944	20/15(9)	He 46 (12/8), Ju 87 (1/0), C.R. 42 (2/1)		

Date	Target	Actual	Operational	Aircraft Type
31.05.1944	20/4(3)	He 46 (2/1), C.R. 42 (2/2)		
10.06.1944	20/9(2)	He 46 (2/2), C.R. 42 (9/0)		
20.06.1944	20/10(2)	He 46 (2/2), C.R. 42 (8/0)		
30.06.1944	20/10(2)	He 46 (2/2), C.R. 42 (8/0)		
10.07.1944	20/11(7)	He 46 (-/-), C.R. 42		
20.07.1944	20/12(10)	He 46 (-/-), C.R. 42		
31.07.1944	20/12(11)	He 46 (-/-), C.R. 42		
01.08.1944	20/12(?)	C.R. 42		
10.08.1944	20/16(15)	C.R. 42		
20.08.1944	20/16(15)	C.R. 42		
31.08.1944	20/16(15)	C.R. 42		
01.09.1944	20/16(?)	C.R. 42		
10.09.1944	20/15(15)	C.R. 42		
20.09.1944	20/17(15)	C.R. 42		
30.09.1944	20/13(9)	C.R. 42		
01.10.1944	20/13(?)	C.R. 42		
10.10.1944	20/15(9)	C.R. 42		
20.10.1944	20/14(5)	C.R. 42		
31.10.1944	20/13(13)	C.R. 42		
10.11.1944	20/13(11)	C.R. 42 (11/11) Ar 66 (1/0), Go 145 (1/0)		
20.11.1944	20/11(11)	C.R. 42		
30.11.1944	20/11(11)	-		
10.12.1944	20/20(16)	-		
20.12.1944	20/20(17)	C.R. 42 (13/13) Ar 66 (4/4) Go 145 (3/1)		

Date	Target	Actual	Operational	Aircraft Type
31.12.1944	20/15(13)	C.R. 42 (13/13) Hs 126 (1/0) Fw 189 (1/0)		
10.01.1945	20/18(12)	C.R. 42 (16/10) Hs 126 (1/1) Fw 189 (1/1)		

C. Aircraft availability of 2./Nachtschlachtgruppe 7

(Courtesy of Dr. Christian Möller)

Date	Target	Actual	Operational	Aircraft Type
10.10.1943	20/18(14)	Hs 126 (14/11), Do 17 (4/3)	from Nah.Aufkl. Kroatien	
20.10.1943	20/16(10)	Hs 126 (13/8), Do 17 (3/2)	2./NSGr 7, used at Lw.Kdo. Südost; Nah. Aufkl.Kroatien	
31.10.1943	20/11(9)	Hs 126	2./NSGr 7	
	12/14(10)	Hs 126 (12/8), Do 17 (2/2)	Nah.Aufkl. Kroatien	
10.11.1943	20/11(7)	Hs 126	2./NSGr 7	
	12/13(11)	Hs 126 (11/9), Do 17 (2/2)	Nah.Aufkl. Kroatien	
20.11.1943	20/-	-	2./NSGr 7: Order for deployment is to be given.	
	12/18(16)	Hs 126 (16/15), Do 17 (2/1)	Nah.Aufkl. Kroatien	
30.11.1943	20/8(6)	Hs 126	2./NSGr 7	
	12/11(10)	Hs 126 (9/9), Do 17 (2/1)	Nah.Aufkl. Kroatien	
08.12.1943	20/8(7)	Hs 126	2./NSGr 7	
10.12.1943	20/8(8)	Hs 126	2./NSGr 7	
	12/10(8)	Hs 126 (8/7), Do 17 (2/1)	Nah.Aufkl. Kroatien	
20.12.1943	20/-	-	2./NSGr 7: Airplanes taken out of action. Nah.Aufkl. Kroatien	
	12/19(12)	Hs 126 (12/12, plus 5/-), Do 17 (2/-)		
31.12.1943	20/-			
10.01.1944	20/-			
20.01.1944	20/9(8)	C.R. 42		
31.01.1944	20/14(2)	C.R. 42		

Date	Target	Actual	Operational	Aircraft Type
06.02.1944	20/13(3)	C.R. 42		
10.02.1944	20/3(0)	C.R. 42		
11.02.1944	20/3(0)	C.R. 42		
20.02.1944	20/2(0)	C.R. 42		
29.02.1944	20/3(0)	C.R. 42		
10.03.1944	20/7(5)	C.R. 42		
20.03.1944	20/12(8)	C.R. 42		
31.03.1944	20/14(10)	C.R. 42		
10.04.1944	20/7(6)	C.R. 42		
20.04.1944	20/11(7)	C.R. 42		
30.04.1944	20/16(12)	C.R. 42		
10.05.1944	20/18(13)	C.R. 42		
20.05.1944	20/20(15)	C.R. 42		
25.05.1944	20/20(15)	C.R. 42		
31.05.1944	20/12(10)	C.R. 42		
10.06.1944	20/9(7)	C.R. 42		
20.06.1944	20/16(10)	C.R. 42		
30.06.1944	20/20(15)	C.R. 42		
10.07.1944	20/19(16)	C.R. 42		
20.07.1944	20/19(15)	C.R. 42		
31.07.1944	20/19(16)	C.R. 42		
01.08.1944	20/19(?)	C.R. 42		
10.08.1944	20/17(15)	C.R. 42		
20.08.1944	20/17(15)	C.R. 42		
31.08.1944	20/18(17)	C.R. 42		
01.09.1944	20/18(?)	C.R. 42		
10.09.1944	20/15(15)	C.R. 42		
20.09.1944	20/18(12)	C.R. 42		
30.09.1944	20/13(9)	C.R. 42		
01.10.1944	20/13(?)	C.R. 42		
10.10.1944	20/18(12)	C.R. 42		
20.10.1944	20/13(6)	C.R. 42		
31.10.1944	20/18(15)	C.R. 42		
10.11.1944	20/19(19)	C.R. 42		
20.11.1944	20/18(17)	C.R. 42		

Date	Target	Actual	Operational	Aircraft Type
30.11.1944	20/18(18)	C.R. 42		
10.12.1944	20/19(15)	C.R. 42		
20.12.1944	20/18(16)	C.R. 42		
31.12.1944	20/19(13)	C.R. 42		
10.01.1945	20/17(12)	C.R. 42		

D. Aircraft availability of 3./Nachtschlachtgruppe 7

(Courtesy of Dr. Christian Möller)

Date	Target	Actual	Operational	Aircraft Type
xx.02.1944	?	Ca. 314	Aircraft supplied from Hörsching [KBS2]	
01.03.1944	20/12(?)	Ca. 314	preparation	
10.03.1944	20/-		preparation	
20.03.1944	20/-		preparation	
31.03.1944	20/-		preparation	
10.04.1944	20/-		preparation	
20.04.1944	20/12(11)	Ca. 314		
30.04.1944	20/12(11)	Ca. 314		
10.05.1944	20/14(12)	Ca. 314		
20.05.1944	20/14(8)	Ca. 314		
31.05.1944	20/11(10)	Ca. 314		
10.06.1944	20/14(7)	Ca. 314		
20.06.1944	20/10(8)	Ca. 314		
30.06.1944	20/6(6)	Ca. 314		
10.07.1944	20/5(5)	Ca. 314		
20.07.1944	20/5(5)	Ca. 314		
31.07.1944	20/-	C.R. 42	Conversion	
01.08.1944	20/0	C.R. 42	Conversion	
10.08.1944	20/11(7)	C.R. 42	Conversion	
20.08.1944	20/16(14)	C.R. 42	Conversion	
31.08.1944	20/19(17)	C.R. 42		
01.09.1944	20/19(?)	C.R. 42		
10.09.1944	20/19(19)	C.R. 42		
20.09.1944	20/19(19)	C.R. 42		
30.09.1944	20/18(16)	C.R. 42		
01.10.1944	20/18(?)	C.R. 42		
10.10.1944	20/18(16)	C.R. 42		
20.10.1944	20/8(4)	C.R. 42	Luftflotte 4	
31.10.1944	20/8(8)	C.R. 42		
10.11.1944	20/16/16)	C.R. 42		

Date	Target	Actual	Operational	Aircraft Type
20.11.1944	20/17(17)	C.R. 42		
30.11.1944	20/17(17)	C.R. 42		
10.12.1944	20/16(15)	C.R. 42	Refreshment in Wiener Neustadt, Luftflotte 10	
20.12.1944	20/18(16)	C.R. 42	Refreshment in Wiener Neustadt, Luftflotte 10	
31.12.1944	20/18(12)	C.R. 42	Refreshment in Wiener Neustadt, Luftflotte 10	
10.01.1945	20/17(11)	C.R. 42	Luftflotte 4	

E. Aircraft of the Group

Stammkennzeichen, Werknummer, and Verbandskennzeichen table

Plane type	Stammkennzeichen	Werknummer	Verbandskennzeichen and/or fin number	Unit
Caproni Ca. 309				
Ca. 309 Ghibli of Serie VIII		12781		Stab./ NSGr 7 (?)
Caproni Ca. 314				
Ca. 314C		12289[72]		3./NSGr 7
Ca. 314		12301[73]		3./NSGr 7
Ca. 314			Yellow 1	3./NSGr 7
Ca. 314C		12693[74]		3./NSGr 7
Ca. 314			Yellow 6	3./NSGr 7
Ca. 314			Yellow 14	3./NSGr 7
Ca. 314			Yellow 16	3./NSGr 7
Ca. 314			Yellow 15	3./NSGr 7
Ca. 314C		12288[75]		3./NSGr 7
Ca. 314			Yellow 2	3./NSGr 7
Ca. 314			Yellow 5	3./NSGr 7
Ca. 314C		12225		3./NSGr 7
Ca. 314			4X+ML	3./NSGr 7
Ca. 314C		12206	4X+HL, Yellow 12	3./NSGr 7
Ca. 314			4X+BL	3./NSGr 7
Ca. 314B		12176[76]	4X+CL	3./NSGr 7
Ca. 314			Yellow 9	3./NSGr 7
Ca. 314			4X+AL	3./NSGr 7
Ca. 314C		12634	4X+NL	3./NSGr 7
Fiat C.R. 42 Falco				
C.R. 42		9140[77]	4X+AK	2./NSGr 7
C.R. 42			4X+BK	2./NSGr 7
C.R. 42			4X+CK	2./NSGr 7
C.R. 42			4X+DK	2./NSGr 7
C.R. 42			4X+EK	2./NSGr 7

Plane type	Stammkennzeichen	Werknummer	Verbandskennzeichen and/or fin number	Unit
C.R. 42		7172[78] or 7142[79]	4X+GK	2./NSGr 7
C.R. 42			4X+MK	2./NSGr 7
C.R. 42			4X+NK	2./NSGr 7
C.R. 42			4X+OK	2./NSGr 7
C.R. 42		8494[80]	4X+PK	2./NSGr 7
C.R. 42			4X+QK	2./NSGr 7
C.R. 42			4X+SK	2./NSGr 7
C.R. 42			4X+UK	2./NSGr 7
C.R. 42		5655[81]	4X+VK, Black 9	2./NSGr 7
C.R. 42		9182[82]		2./NSGr 7
C.R. 42			4X+KK	2./NSGr 7
C.R. 42			4X+JK	2./NSGr 7
C.R. 42			4X+SK	2./NSGr 7
C.R. 42		7514[83]	4X+YK	2./NSGr 7
C.R. 42			4X+VK	2./NSGr 7
C.R. 42			4X+TH	1./NSGr 7
C.R. 42			(Yellow?) 2	3./NSGr 7
C.R. 42			(Yellow?) 8	3./NSGr 7
C.R. 42			(Yellow?) 17	3./NSGr 7
C.R. 42		7206[84]		2./NSGr 7
C.R. 42		9168[85]		2./NSGr 7
C.R. 42		9224[86]		2./NSGr 7
C.R. 42		9776[87]		2./NSGr 7
C.R. 42		9885[88]		2./NSGr 7
C.R. 42		9828[89]		2./NSGr 7
C.R. 42		90804[90]		2./NSGr 7
C.R. 42		90886[91]		2./NSGr 7
C.R. 42		9896[92]		2./NSGr 7
C.R. 42		7151[93]		2./NSGr 7
C.R. 42		8524[94]		2./NSGr 7
C.R. 42		8975[95]		2./NSGr 7
C.R. 42		90887[96]		2./NSGr 7
C.R. 42		90841[97]	Black 1	2./NSGr 7

Plane type	Stammkennzeichen	Werknummer	Verbandskennzeichen and/or fin number	Unit
C.R. 42		9832[98]	White 1	1./NSGr 7
C.R. 42		90897[99]		Stab./ NSGr 7
C.R. 42		8864[100]	Black 2	2./NSGr 7
C.R. 42		9183[101]		2./NSGr 7
C.R. 42		9850[102]		3./NSGr 7
C.R. 42		9247[103]	Yellow 19	3./NSGr 7
C.R. 42		8992[104]		Stab./ NSGr 7
C.R. 42		9801[105]		2./NSGr 7
C.R. 42		9840[106]		2./NSGr 7
C.R. 42		8990[107]	Black 4	2./NSGr 7
C.R. 42		9277[108]	Black 6	2./NSGr 7
C.R. 42		9274[109]	Black 11	2./NSGr 7
C.R. 42		9852[110]	Black 13	2./NSGr 7
C.R. 42		4461[111]	Black 15	2./NSGr 7
C.R. 42		9216[112]	Black 17	2./NSGr 7
C.R. 42		9262[113]	Black 18	2./NSGr 7
C.R. 42		5545[114]		2./NSGr 7
C.R. 42		9816[115]		2./NSGr 7
C.R. 42		9169[116]		2./NSGr 7
C.R. 42		5664[117]		2./NSGr 7 ?
C.R. 42		9198[118]		2./NSGr 7 ?
C.R. 42		9888[119]		?./NSGr 7
C.R. 42		9207[120]		2./NSGr 7
C.R. 42		9170[121]		2./NSGr 7
C.R. 42		6289[122]		2./NSGr 7
C.R. 42		7126[123]		2./NSGr 7
C.R. 42		5623[124]	White 12	1./NSGr 7
C.R. 42		9221[125]	Black 20	2./NSGr 7
C.R. 42		9199[126]	Black 9	2./NSGr 7
C.R. 42			Yellow 17	3./NSGr 7
C.R. 42		9768[127]	White 8	1./NSGr 7

Plane type	Stammkennzeichen	Werknummer	Verbandskennzeichen and/or fin number	Unit
C.R. 42		8899[128]		2./NSGr 7
C.R. 42		7574[129]		2./NSGr 7
C.R. 42		9788[130]	Black 9	2./NSGr 7
Fi 156 Storch				
Fi 156	PO+AL	601	Stöka.St.Kroatien	
Fi 156	DB+ZY	690	Stöka.St.Kroatien	
Fi 156	GF+YN	5397[131]	Stöka.St.Kroatien	
Gotha Go 145				
Go-145			1K+BK from 2./NSGr. 4	?./NSGr 7
Heinkel He 46				
He.46	VF+UC	403	Stöka.St.Kroatien	
He 46D		312	4X+NH	1.NSGr 7
He 46E-2	BB+CV	1247		1./NSGr 7
He 46C	TP+AC		From 1./NSGr. 4	1./NSGr 7
He 46		339	-	Stöka. St.Kroatien
He 46		331	-	Stöka. St.Kroatien
He 46		394		Stöka. St.Kroatien
He 46		510		Stöka. St.Kroatien
He 46C	DB+AO			1./NSGr 7
He 46	PR+NM		White 1	Stöka. St.Kroatien
He 46D	CW+AW	33	-	Stöka. St.Kroatien
He 46	NL+NY		-	Stöka. St.Kroatien
He 46	SA+HW			Stöka. St.Kroatien and 1./ NSGr 7
He 46	SA+HV			Stöka. St.Kroatien and 1./ NSGr 7

Plane type	Stammkennzeichen	Werknummer	Verbandskennzeichen and/or fin number	Unit
He 46	CA+CI		-	Stöka. St.Kroatien
He 46		732		Stöka. St.Kroatien
He 46E		882		Stöka. St.Kroatien
He 46	CQ+HP		White 2	Stöka. St.Kroatien
He 46		160		1./NSGr 7
He 46	DB+ZC	150	-	Stöka. St.Kroatien and 1./ NSGr 7
He 46		144		1./NSGr 7
He 46	CA+CH[132]			1./NSGr 7
He 46		12		Stöka. St.Kroatien
He 46	DB+AQ	[737 or 237? = He 45]	-	Stöka. St.Kroatien and 1./ NSGr 7
He 46	CN+HJ		-	Stöka. St.Kroatien and 1./ NSGr 7
He 46			1K+CH from 1./NSGr. 4	Stöka. St.Kroatien and 1./ NSGr 7
He 46	PR+NL		-	Stöka. St.Kroatien and 1./ NSGr 7
He 46			1K+EH from 1./NSGr. 4	1./NSGr 7
He 46	VA+AC		-	1./NSGr 7
He 46			1K+JH from 1./NSGr. 4	1./NSGr 7
He 46			1K+BH from 1./NSGr. 4	1./NSGr 7

Plane type	Stammkennzeichen	Werknummer	Verbandskennzeichen and/or fin number	Unit
He 46	PR+NN		-	1./NSGr 7
He 46	TY+NC		-	1./NSGr 7
He 46D	BO+FX	735	-	1./NSGr 7
He 46			1K+FH from 1./NSGr. 4	1./NSGr 7
He 46		871	1K+HH from 1./NSGr. 4	1./NSGr 7
He 46		343		1./NSGr 7
He 46E-2	BB+CI	1234	white 3	1./NSGr 7
He 46			4X+VH White 9	1./NSGr 7
He 46			1K+GH from 1./NSGr. 4	1./NSGr 7
He 46	NF+NC		-	1./NSGr 7
He 46	VH+AC			1./NSGr 7
He 46	TP+BA		-	1./NSGr 7
He 46	DC+VD		-	1./NSGr 7
He 46	TY+AC		-	1./NSGr 7
He 46	TP+BH		-	1./NSGr 7
He 46		305		1./NSGr 7
He 46		310		1./NSGr 7
He 46			1K+NU (NH?) from 1./NSGr. 4	?./NSGr 7
He 46			1K+KH from 1./NSGr. 4	1./NSGr 7
He 46			1K+KU(KH?) from 1./NSGr. 4	?./NSGr 7
He 46			1K+OU (OH?) from 1./NSGr. 4	?./NSGr 7
He 46			1K+BU (BH?) from 1./NSGr. 4	?./NSGr 7
He 46		35	1K+LH from 1./NSGr. 4	1./NSGr 7
He 46			4X+AH	1./NSGr 7
He 46			4X+MH	1./NSGr 7
He 46		156	4X+IH	1./NSGr 7
He 46		1248	4X+EH	1./NSGr 7

Plane type	Stammkennzeichen	Werknummer	Verbandskennzeichen and/or fin number	Unit
He 46			White 11	Stöka. St.Kroatien
Henschel Hs 126				
Hs 126		3371	From NASt Koatien	2./NSGr 7
Hs 126		3297	From NASt Koatien	2./NSGr 7
Hs 126B-1		4297	From NASt Koatien	2./NSGr 7
Hs 126		2928	From NASt Koatien	2./NSGr 7
Hs 126	CY+RB		From NASt Koatien	2./NSGr 7
Hs 126	GE+AR	3038	From NASt Koatien	2./NSGr 7
Junkers Ju 87				
Ju 87D-4		110462		Stab./ NSGr 7
Ju 87D-4		100420		Stab./ NSGr 7
Ju 87D-4		110499		Stab./ NSGr 7
Macchi M.C. 200				
M.C. 200		8619		Stab./ NSGr 7

F. Known Losses of the Störkampfstaffel Kroatien, Störkampfstaffel Südost, and NSGr 7

In this table, all aircraft identified by Stammkennzeichen and/or Werknummer and/or Verbandskennzeichen and/or Fin Number are given. All other losses not precisely identified within criteria, for which only date and/or type is known, are given within the text of the book.

Date	Marking and WNr.	Type	Explanation	Unit
11/04/43	VF+UC, WNr. 403	He 46	Crashed near Bosanski Petrovac. On board the Pilot Ogefr. Heinz Rennberg and Gefr. Josef Hansen observer died.	Stöka. St.Kroatien
22/05/43	WNr. 339	He 46	Crashed in Central Bosnia and Herzegovina on unknown location with damage estimate 80%. Pilot Uffz. Erich Kaldyik and Beobachter Gefr. Edmund Elei were wounded (according to some sources killed).	Stöka. St.Kroatien
22/05/43	WNr. 331	He 46	Damaged (60%) during the landing at Rajlovac aerodrome while returning from the mission when their landing gear collapsed. The crew survived the accident but were hurt. Dr. Möller is mentioning in his research materails that this He 46 was damaged 100%.	Stöka. St.Kroatien
31/05/43	WNr. 12	He 46	Hit by a small arms fire and crashed NW of village Ustikolina. Uffz. Hermann Caspers killed.	Stöka. St.Kroatien
10/06/43	WNr. 394	He 46	Hit by a small arms fire from the ground. Subsequently aircraft crashed and exploded, in vicinity of village Vrbnica near Tjentište on Sutjeska river . Pilot Gefr. Heinrich Fuchs and observer Gefr. Helmut Gödecke were killed.	Stöka. St.Kroatien
Summer 1943	BB+CI WNr. 1234, White 3	He 46E-2	This aircraft made emergency landing near Banja Luka and was recovered. See photos in the book.	1./NSGr 7

Date	Marking and WNr.	Type	Explanation	Unit
27/07/43	CW+AW, WNr. 33	He 46D	Lost during the combat sortie near Podgar in Bosnia and Herzegovina. Engine failed and crew was obliged to make emergency landing. Pilot Ogefr. Kurt Ilker and observer Gefr. Erwin Weiser injured.	Stöka. St.Kroatien
29/08/43	WNr. 732	He 46	Lost near Bihać as the result of a Partisan small arms fire. It seems that observer was from ZNDH and was wounded on that occasion while the plane was damaged 70% during the crash landing.	Stöka. St.Kroatien
31/08/43	WNr. 510	He 46	Force landed after being damaged by AA fire from the ground.	Stöka. St.Kroatien
25/09/43	WNr. 882	He 46E	Lost between Kupinečki Kraljevec and Zdenčina SE of Zagreb around 17.00. Hit by a small arms fire and made force landing, crew was saved, though injured, and Partisans looted the plane and set it ablaze. Pilot Ogefr. Peter Schmidt Injured, while Ogefr. Karl Heinz Lorenz died later from injuries.	Stöka. St.Kroatien
07/11/43	WNr. 3371	Hs 126	Shot down by flak near Trogir on an armed recce mission. Crew set aircraft on fire.	2./NSGr 7
07/11/43	WNr. 2928	Hs 126	Damaged during the strafing and bombardment mission and it made emergency landing on Banja Luka airfield. Aircraft was damaged 50% and Uffz. Rudolf Fuhr, observer, was injured.	2./NSGr 7
09/11/43	WNr. 160	He 46	Crash landed East of Zagreb due to engine problem. Aircraft damage 65%.	1./NSGr 7
12/11/43	WNr. 3297	Hs 126	Around 12:30, ten allied fighter bombers attacked airfield Jasenica near Mostar destroying this aircraft (100%).	2./NSGr 7

Date	Marking and WNr.	Type	Explanation	Unit
13/11/43	WNr. 144	He 46	20% damage during take off when rammed DB+ZC.	1./NSGr 7
21/11/43	WNr. 4297	Hs 126B-1	Crashed in flames near Sisak around 15:00 .	2./NSGr 7
27/11/43	1K+FH	He 46	Hptm. Heinz Buss made an emergency landing behind enemy lines 1 km SW of village Babče; when hit by small arms fire from the ground. Hptm. Buss and observer Fw. Hartmann unharmed.	1./NSGr 7
29/11/43	BB+CV, WNr. 1247	He 46E-2	Emergency landing between Koprivnica and Čazma.	1./NSGr 7
02/12/43	WNr. 343	He 46,	Due to the bad weather made emergency landing to Banja Luka aerodome and was damaged 40%.	1./NSGr 7
03/12/43	GE+AR, WNr. 3038	Hs 126	Staffelkapitän Max Griewatsch with Ofw. Roth as an observer was shot down by the Spitfire of No. 126 Squadron RAF NW of Dubrovnik. Both regained lines without injuries.	2./NSGr 7
03/02/44	WNr. 8619	M.C. 200	Zagreb, aircraft was destroyed 100% in crash and its pilot died.	Stab./ NSGr 7
24/02/44	1K+LH, WNr. 35	He 46	Burnt out on the ground after Spitfires attack on Zemunik	
24/02/44	SA+HW	He 46	Burnt out on the ground after Spitfires attack on Zemunik	
24/02/44	NF+NC	He 46	Damaged, oil tank shot to pieces after Spitfires attack on Zemunik	
02/03/44	WNr. 12781	Ca. 309 Ghibli of Serie VIII	Shot up by Partisans at Lič, near Fužine in Croatia. Uffz. Behrens and Flieger Stadler picked up by German forces.	Stab./ NSGr 7

Date	Marking and WNr.	Type	Explanation	Unit
11/03/44	DB+ZC, WNr.150	He 46	Shot down during armed recce mission 500 meters NW of village Drajići, 15 km WNW of Kolo; on Partisan held territory. Pilot Lt. Hermann Gade and observer Fw. Karl-Heinz Hartmann killed. Earlier on 13/11/43 this plane was damaged on Borongaj 20% when rammed WNr. 144.	Stöka. St.Kroatien and 1./ NSGr 7
24/03/44	WNr. 305	He 46	In two occasions, from 12:30 to 12:35 and from 15:05 to 15:15 Royal Air Force Spitfire(s) attacked the Zemunik aerodrome. First attack led to fuselage damage; the He 46 was completely destroyed and left in flames during the second attack.	1./NSGr 7
27/03/44	1K+HH WNr. 871	He 46	Pilot Uffz. Dietrich Perkuhn and Flg. Helmut Hartwig were captured by Partisans and exchanged when aircraft crashed on Motajica mountain in North Bosnia and Herzegovina.	1./NSGr 7
06/04/44	WNr. 8990, Black 4	C.R. 42	Destroyed by No. 2 Squadron SAAF Spitfires during the attack on Banja Luka aerodrome	2./NSGr 7
06/04/44	WNr. 9277, Black 6	C.R. 42	Destroyed by No. 2 Squadron SAAF Spitfires during the attack on Banja Luka aerodrome	2./NSGr 7
06/04/44	WNr. 9274, Black 11	C.R. 42	Destroyed by No. 2 Squadron SAAF Spitfires during the attack on Banja Luka aerodrome	2./NSGr 7
06/04/44	WNr. 9852, Black 13	C.R. 42	Destroyed by No. 2 Squadron SAAF Spitfires during the attack on Banja Luka aerodrome	2./NSGr 7
06/04/44	WNr. 4461, Black 15	C.R. 42	Destroyed by No. 2 Squadron SAAF Spitfires during the attack on Banja Luka aerodrome	2./NSGr 7
06/04/44	WNr. 9216, Black 17	C.R. 42	Destroyed by No. 2 Squadron SAAF Spitfires during the attack on Banja Luka aerodrome	2./NSGr 7

Date	Marking and WNr.	Type	Explanation	Unit
06/04/44	WNr. 9262, Black 18	C.R. 42	Destroyed by No. 2 Squadron SAAF Spitfires during the attack on Banja Luka aerodrome	2./NSGr 7
April/44	WNr. 5545	C.R. 42	Force landing 20 km NE of Banja Luka. Could be on the 8th or the 9th of April.	2./NSGr 7
April/44	WNr. 9169	C.R. 42	Was to be given to Stab but due to crash landing and 50% damage suffered it was put in reserve. Date is sometime around the 9th of April.	2./NSGr 7
08/04/44	WNr. 8899	C.R. 42	Banja Luka, damaged by enemy action 15-20%	2./NSGr 7
08/04/44	WNr. 7574	C.R. 42	Banja Luka, damaged by enemy action 5%	2./NSGr 7
08/04/44	WNr. 692	Uknown type	Banja Luka, damaged by enemy action 10-15%	2./NSGr 7
08/04/44	WNr. 9788	C.R. 42	Combat damaged a/c did emergency landing due to bad weather, darkness and the lack of fuel in vicinity of Kutina. Pilot Ofwb. Walter Bormann was injured in the process.	2./NSGr 7
15/04/44	WNr. 9888	C.R. 42	During take-off from Cameri in Italy crashed and was damaged 100%, Uffz. Alfred Schoenemann injured.	?./NSGr 7
20/04/44	WNr. 9207	C.R. 42	Uffz. Max Ortmann crashed to the ground and burned in Banja Luka vicinity. Pilot was injured. Cause of the accident was reported as: "strong downwards going airstreams."	2./NSGr 7
03/05/44	WNr.12225	Ca. 314C	Crash landed on Pleso on a non-combat flight. During the accident Flg. Heinz Wagner was the only person injured.	3./NSGr 7

Date	Marking and WNr.	Type	Explanation	Unit
16/05/44	4X+CL, WNr. 12176	Ca. 314B	Pilot Fw. Wilhelm Pollak, Uffz. Kurt Gelinek (KampfBeobachter), Ogefr. Paul- Heinz Rath (Bordschütze) and Ogefr. Walter Burmester (Bordschütze) all killed when shot down by enemy ground fire. Plane caught fire when crashed near village Široka Rijeka, 30 km SSE of Karlovac. They took off from Pleso at 16.43 .	3./NSGr 7
19/05/44	4X+NL, WNr. 12634	Ca. 314C	Damaged 40% on Pleso aerodrome during flip over on a take-off to combat sortie against Partisans. Observer Uffz. Paul Betz was injured.	3./NSGr 7
25/05/44	4X+HL, Yellow 12, WNr. 12206	Ca. 314C	Plane crashed 65 km SW of Bihać killing all aboard: pilot Uffz. Odilo Hübel, Unteroffizier Anton Pauli, Ogefr. Horst Abramowski and Lt. Valentin Krempl (war reporter) from Kriegsberichterzug 19, Luftwaffen Kriegsberichter Abteilung to Luftwaffen-kommando Südost assigned to the 3rd Staffel. Uffz. Hübel crew took off from Pleso at 6:13 .	3./NSGr 7
25/05/44	WNr. 156, 4X+IH	He 46	Shot down during the sortie against Partisan held positions in Drvar by AA fire. Pilot Ogefr. Shmidt and his observer Uffz. Breuer injured. Plane damaged to 80-85%.	1./NSGr 7
26/05/44	WNr. 310	He 46	Attacked by Spitfires of No. 249 Squadron RAF near Banja Luka and shot down SE of Bosanski Petrovac. Uffz. Leo Weidhaus injured.	1./NSGr 7

Date	Marking and WNr.	Type	Explanation	Unit
26/05/44	4X+EH, WNr. 1248	He 46	Attacked by Spitfires of No. 249 Squadron RAF near Banja Luka. Observer Uffz. Karl Nemitz bailed out with severe injuries 11 km SE of Bosanski Petrovac, while pilot Hptm. Buss made emergency landing in Banja Luka area without injuries at 13:40 .	1./NSGr 7
28/05/44	4X+NH, WNr. 312	He 46D	Destroyed on the ground by Allied attack on Lučko airdrome	1./NSGr 7
28/05/44	4X+AK, WNr. 9140	C.R. 42	Destroyed on the ground by Allied attack on Zalužani airdrome (100%)	2./NSGr 7
28/05/44	4X+GK, WNr. 7172 or 7142	C.R. 42	Destroyed on the ground by Allied attack on Zalužani airdrome (100%)	2./NSGr 7
28/05/44	4X+PK, WNr. 8494	C.R. 42	Destroyed on the ground by Allied attack on Zalužani airdrome (100%)	2./NSGr 7
28/05/44	4X+VK, WNr. 5655	C.R. 42	Damaged on the ground by Allied attack on Zalužani airdrome (30%)	2./NSGr 7
28/05/44	WNr. 90804	C.R. 42	Damaged on the ground by Allied attack on Zalužani airdrome (20%)	2./NSGr 7
02/06/44	4X+YK, WNr. 7514	C.R. 42	Obfw. Kuehn force landed on Partisan-held territory due to lack of fuel. Falco was subsequently destroyed by pilot who reach German lines on 03/06/44.	2./NSGr 7
11/06/44	WNr. 6289	C.R. 42	Crashed and was written off on Banja Luka aerodrome. Pilot Ofw. Helmut Rauer was injured.	2./NSGr 7
03/07/44	WNr. 7126	C.R. 42	Ljubljana, Slovenia due to the engine failure, in the approach to landing strip a/c crashed and burned down. Pilot Fw. Heinz Drunk was injured.	2./NSGr 7
21/09/44	WNr. 5623, White 12	C.R. 42	Kragujevac, Serbia Ofw. Anton Huberth shot by friendly flak, crashed. 50% damage. Pilot injured.	1./NSGr 7

Date	Marking and WNr.	Type	Explanation	Unit
10/10/44	WNr. 9199, Black 9	C.R. 42	Ofw. Walter Bormann was killed in his Falco when shot by ground fire 20 km South of village Lapovo, Serbia.	2./NSGr 7
10/10/44	WNr. 9221, Black 20	C.R. 42	Shot down by ground fire and Flak in central Serbia near village Kalinovac. Pilot Ofw. Helmuth Rauer was mortally wounded and he died a few days later on 15 October.	2./NSGr 7
14/10/44	WNr. 9768, White 8	C.R. 42	Uffz. Ewald Jost was shot down around 15:30 during take-off from Varaždin aerodrome by Spitfire Mk. IXs of No. 73 Squadron RAF. Pilot killed.	1./NSGr 7
18/12/44	Yellow 17	C.R. 42	Shot down near Pitomača by anti aircraft fire. Fhj. Fw. Hans Kruschel killed.	3./NSGr 7
02/02/45	WNr. 7206	C.R. 42	31st Fighter Group P-51 strafed airstrip in Kurilovec. Destroyed.	2./NSGr 7
02/02/45	WNr. 9168	C.R. 42	31st Fighter Group P-51 strafed airstrip in Kurilovec. Destroyed.	2./NSGr 7
02/02/45	WNr. 9224	C.R. 42	31st Fighter Group P-51 strafed airstrip in Kurilovec. Destroyed.	2./NSGr 7
02/02/45	WNr. 9776	C.R. 42	31st Fighter Group P-51 strafed airstrip in Kurilovec. Destroyed.	2./NSGr 7
02/02/45	WNr. 9885	C.R. 42	31st Fighter Group P-51 strafed airstrip in Kurilovec. Destroyed.	2./NSGr 7
02/02/45	WNr. 9828	C.R. 42	31st Fighter Group P-51 strafed airstrip in Kurilovec. Destroyed.	2./NSGr 7
02/02/45	WNr. 90804	C.R. 42	31st Fighter Group P-51 strafed airstrip in Kurilovec. Destroyed.	2./NSGr 7
02/02/45	WNr. 90886	C.R. 42	31st Fighter Group P-51 strafed airstrip in Kurilovec. Destroyed.	2./NSGr 7
02/02/45	WNr. 9896	C.R. 42	31st Fighter Group P-51 strafed airstrip in Kurilovec. Destroyed.	2./NSGr 7
02/02/45	4X+VK, WNr. 5655	C.R. 42	31st Fighter Group P-51 strafed airstrip in Kurilovec. Damaged 15-20%.	2./NSGr 7

Date	Marking and WNr.	Type	Explanation	Unit
02/02/05	WNr. 7151	C.R. 42	31st Fighter Group P-51 strafed airstrip in Kurilovec. Damaged 15-20%.	2./NSGr 7
02/02/05	WNr. 8524	C.R. 42	31st Fighter Group P-51 strafed airstrip in Kurilovec. Damaged 15-20%.	2./NSGr 7
02/02/05	WNr. 8975	C.R. 42	31st Fighter Group P-51 strafed airstrip in Kurilovec. Damaged 15-20%.	2./NSGr 7
02/02/05	WNr. 90887	C.R. 42	31st Fighter Group P-51 strafed airstrip in Kurilovec. Damaged 15-20%.	2./NSGr 7
08/02/45	WNr. 90841, Black 1	C.R. 42	Hptm. Kurt Jacobs, Staffelführer, killed in the dogfight with P-38s of the 14th FG. Aircraft 100% damage.	2./NSGr 7
08/02/45	WNr. 9832, White 1	C.R. 42	Ofw. Wolfgang Harnack killed in the dogfight with P-38's of the 14th FG. Aircraft 100% damage.	1./NSGr 7
08/02/45	WNr. 90897	C.R. 42	Hptm. Eduard Jacob, killed in the dogfight with P-38's of the 14th FG. Aircraft 90% damage.	Stab./ NSGr 7
08/02/45	WNr. 8864, Black 2	C.R. 42	Gefr. Hans-Heinrich Schreiber killed in the dogfight with P-38s of the 14th FG. Aircraft 100% damage.	2./NSGr 7
09/02/45	WNr. 9183	C.R. 42	Crash landed after combat flight causing 70% of damage to the aircraft.	2./NSGr 7
16/02/45	WNr. 9850	C.R. 42	Suffered tyre failure in Varaždin, and was destroyed (80%) in flip over.	3./NSGr 7
17/02/45	WNr. 9247, Yellow 19	C.R. 42	Fw. Walter Broscheit overturned on take-off from Varaždin destroying the aircraft beyond repair (80%).	3./NSGr 7
23/02/45	WNr. 8992	C.R. 42	Crashed in Reichenau causing 30% damage.	Stab./ NSGr 7

Date	Marking and WNr.	Type	Explanation	Unit
24/02/45	WNr. 9801	C.R. 42	60% damage in what is called in the report "an involuntary contact with the ground."	2./NSGr 7
25/02/45	WNr. 9840	C.R. 42	45% damage in crash landing in Aigen.	2./NSGr 7

Ranks

Luftwaffe	RAF	USAAF	ZNDH
	Officer Ranks		
Reichsmarschall	—	—	
Generalfeldmarschall	Marshal of the RAF	General (Five Star)	Vojskovođa
Generaloberst	Air Chief Marshal	General (Four Star)	—
General	Air Marshal	Lieutenant-General	General zrakoplovstva
Generalleutnant	Air Vice-Marshal	Major-General	General-poručnik
Generalmajor	Air Commodore	Brigadier-General	General
Oberst	Group Captain	Colonel	Pukovnik
Oberstleutnant	Wing Commander	Lieutenant-Colonel	Podpukovnik
Major	Squadron Leader	Major	Bojnik
Hauptmann	Flight Lieutenant	Captain	Nadsatnik / Satnik
Oberleutnant	Flying Officer	First Lieutenant	Nadporučnik
Leutnant	Pilot Officer	Second Lieutenant	Zastavnik
	NCO Ranks		
Stabsfeldwebel	Warrant Officer	Flight Officer	Častnički namjestnik
Oberfeldwebel	Flight Sergeant	Master Sergeant	Stožerni narednik
Feldwebel	Sergeant	Technical Sergeant	Narednik
Unterfeldwebel	—	Staff Sergeant	—
Unteroffizier	Corporal	Corporal	Vodnik
Hauptgefreiter	—	—	—
Obergefreiter	Leading Aircraftman	—	Razvodnik
Gefreiter	Aircraftman 1st Class	Private First Class	Desetnik
Flieger	Aircraftman 2nd Class	Private Second Class	Zrakoplovac

G. Color Profiles

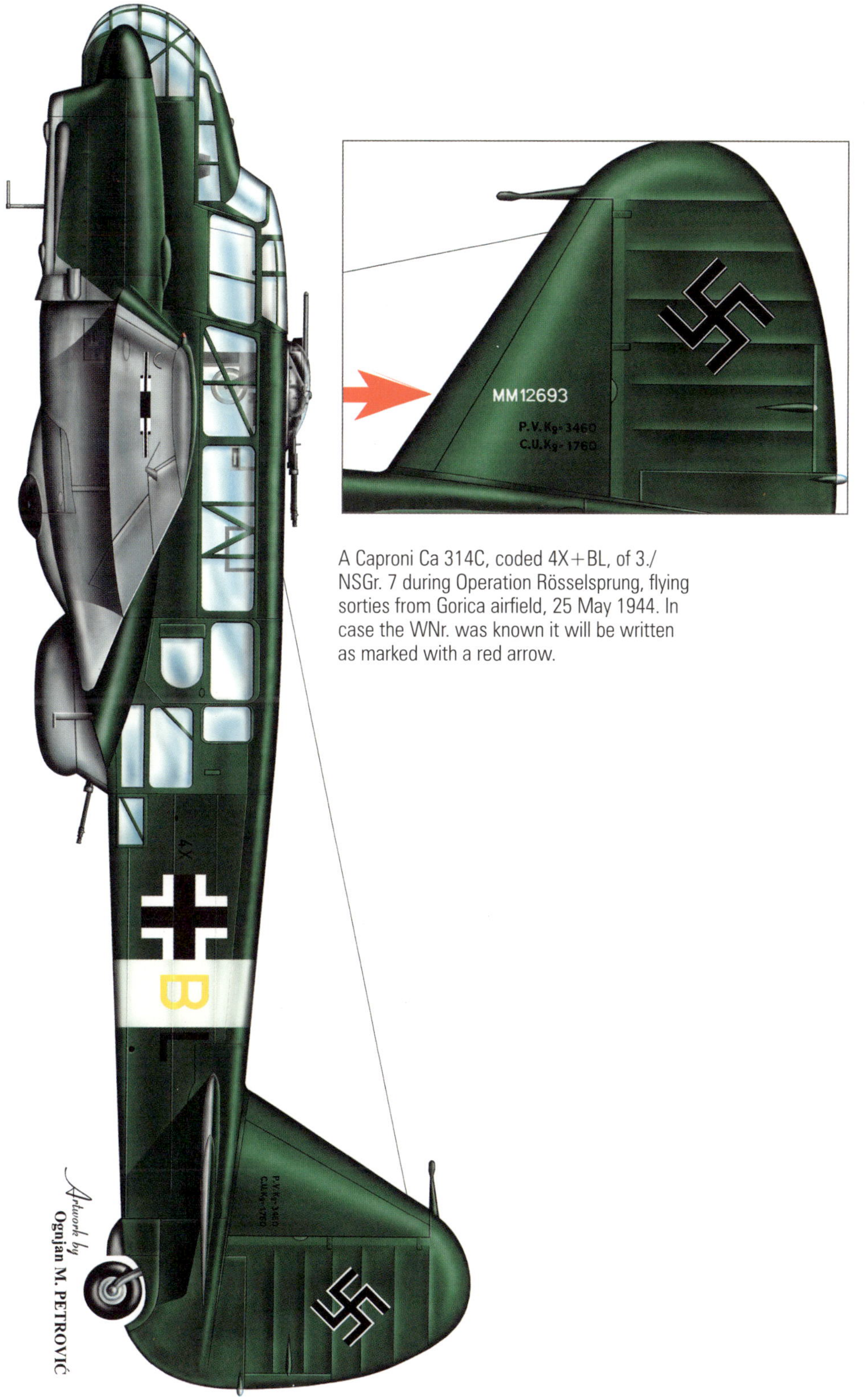

A Caproni Ca 314C, coded 4X+BL, of 3./NSGr. 7 during Operation Rösselsprung, flying sorties from Gorica airfield, 25 May 1944. In case the WNr. was known it will be written as marked with a red arrow.

A Heinkel He 46C, coded BB+CI (WNr. 1234) "Weiss 3" of 1./NSGr. 7 piloted by Ltn. Hermann Gade and observer Fw. Ernst from Borongaj on 12 October 1943.

PI

A Heinkel He 46C, coded PR+NM, "Weiss 1" of Störkampfstaffel Südost piloted by Staffelkapitän Heinz Buss from Rajlovac on 28 June 1943.

Henschel Hs 126B-1 (GE+AR) WNr. 3038, 2./NSGr. 7, (ex-NASt Kroatien machine). This aircraft was shot down by a Spitfire of No. 126 Squadron RAF NW of Dubrovnik on 3 December 1943. Pilot was Staffelkapitän of 2./NSGr. 7 Hptm. Max Griewatsch and observer Ofw. Roth.

Fiat C.R. 42 coded 4X+TH of 1./NSGr. 7. Location and year unknown. Color profile is made on the basis of the photo. Note that on the photo there was no Swastika on the vertical stabilizer.

References

Chapter 1: Störkampfstaffel Kroatien

[1] Of 10kg
[2] Of 2kg
[3] Reports for dates: 31 March 1943; 10 and 20 April 1943.
[4] Damage of 60% meant that the aircraft was considered not to be repairable.

Chapter 2: Störkampfstaffel Südost

[5] 10km SW of Žabljak
[6] Popović, p. 255, 256
[7] Popović, p. 421, 422
[8] Popović, p. 423, 424
[9] Zbornik, tom IV, knjiga 14, p. 236. Comrade Stari is code name for Tito.
[10] Between the peaks of Mala Košuta and Velika Košuta.
[11] For his biography please see http://www.nytimes.com/1990/12/04/obituaries/vladimir-dedijer-tito-biographer-and-Partisan-fighter-dies-at-90.html
[12] Probably Pogar, North of Sarajevo in Bosnia and Herzegovina
[13] Dr. Möller leaves doubt as to the exact post number.
[14] Zbornik, tom V, knjiga 20, p. 175

Chapter 4: Nachtschlagtruppe 7

[15] 1. Kosaken-Division
[16] Zbornik, tom V, knjiga 22, p. 103
[17] Unknown to author
[18] Unknown to author
[19] "Renovo-Dubropolve blown up 3km SSE Renovo" as given in CX/MSS/R.19(B)
[20] CX/MSS/T19/7 identifies the unit
[21] Zbornik, tom IV, knjiga 22, p. 182
[22] Unknown locality as in report, with certainty it refers to Kola near Banja Luka
[23] 36 to some sources, but most probably 34 over the target
[24] Reconnaissance Squadron Zagreb-Zemun
[25] 2./NAGr. 12
[26] S.Sgt. Ottawo F. Tosti was the other member of the crew that evaded.
[27] According to web site http://www.stammkennzeichen.de the Stammkennzeichen of this aircraft was RK+EP
[28] According to the same source the Stammkennzeichen of this aircraft was RK+LO

29 According to the same source the Stammkennzeichen of this aircraft was SL+DT

30 Schlachtgeschwader 151 had been renamed from Sturzkampfgeschwader 151 on 27 December 1943 though general order was given on 18 October 1943. Sven Carlsen explains: "Problem is that for example the Luftwaffenführungsstab said, at 18.10.44 - StG 151 changed name to SG 151. It took a long time before the unit itself knew, that they have a new name. Every organisation downwards (Luftgau - Division - Fliegerführer) wrote an new order. Suddenly two, three weeks or more were off."

31 According to web site http://www.stammkennzeichen.de the Stammkennzeichen of this aircraft was DS+ZR

32 According to web site http://www.stammkennzeichen.de Stammkennzeichen of this aircraft was VC+JP

33 According to web site http://www.stammkennzeichen.de Stammkennzeichen of this aircraft was NT+TI, MTT Regensburg

34 According to web site http://www.stammkennzeichen.de Stammkennzeichen of this aircraft was NT+TM, MTT Regensburg

35 According to web site http://www.stammkennzeichen.de Stammkennzeichen of this aircraft was VO+UQ

36 According to web site http://www.stammkennzeichen.de Stammkennzeichen of this aircraft was PR+GP

37 According to web site http://www.stammkennzeichen.de Stammkennzeichen of this aircraft is PR+GC

38 According to web site http://www.stammkennzeichen.de Stammkennzeichen of this aircraft is PR+GL

39 Research of Nick Beale via Radovan Živanović

40 In the report was stated "Hauptmann"

41 U.S. Tons

42 Narodna Zaštita

43 (kroat)KGr. 1

44 Zbornik, tom V, knjiga 25, p. 616

45 As in original, but it is an obvious error for the parasol He 46 and/or Hs 126 type.

46 In some reports three aircraft.

47 Zbornik, tom V, knjiga27, p. 434. Refers to bombardments of both the 8th and the 9th of April.

48 8 in internal bay for Ca. 314 C

49 16 in internal bay for Ca. 314 C

50 460th 80.5 tons and 461st 63 tons.

51 Fallboe

52 SD is visible while exact type is not visible in the report.

53 The German name for Karlovac is Karlstadt

54 Named in the honor of the Partisan "People's hero" Rade Končar, shot by the Italians in Šibenik on 22 May 1942.

55 "X" stands for the smudged number

56 LLG 1 used the Avia B-534 as a glider tug, so this may be what they are referring to.

57 Dr. Möller noted that name might be Hübl

58 From Kriegsberichterzug 19, Luftwaffen Kriegsberichter Abteilung to Luftwaffenkommando Südost assigned to the 3rd Staffel for this mission.

59 Exact number smudged at source

60 N.Beale, www.ghostbombers.com

61 The exact location is Golo Brdo.

[62] Master craftsman, a technician who oversees all other mechanics
[63] Flugzeugmechaniker
[64] Hand written "Ihl" on source document, notes Dr. C. Möller
[65] Danube river
[66] Luftwaffe Gen.Qu. 6. Abt. loss reports
[67] Author could not find more details on this a/c.
[68] Luftwaffe Gen.Qu. 6. Abt. loss reports
[69] Possibly Stauh
[70] Mur-Raab area
[71] Location unknown

Appendices

Aircraft of the Group, Stammkennzeichen, Werknummer, and Verbandskennzeichen table

[72] Built at Taliedo
[73] Built by A.V.I.S.
[74] Built at Taliedo
[75] Built by C.A.B.
[76] Built at Taliedo
[77] Built by Fiat, July to October 1942
[78] Built by Fiat, February to March 1941
[79] Built by Fiat, February to March 1941
[80] Built by Fiat, September 1941 to January 1942
[81] Built by Fiat, March to August 1940
[82] Built by Fiat, July to October 1942
[83] Built by Fiat, March to September 1941
[84] Built by Fiat, February to March 1941
[85] Built by Fiat, July to October 1942
[86] Built by Fiat, July to October 1942
[87] Built by Fiat, November 1942 to June 1943
[88] Built by Fiat, November 1942 to June 1943
[89] Built by Fiat, November 1942 to June 1943
[90] Built by Aeritalia after June of 1943
[91] Built by Aeritalia after June of 1943
[92] Built by Fiat, November 1942 to June 1943
[93] Built by Fiat, February to March 1941
[94] Built by Fiat, September 1941 to January 1942
[95] Built by Fiat, February to July 1942
[96] Built by Aeritalia after June of 1943
[97] Built by Aeritalia after June of 1943
[98] Built by Aeritalia after June of 1943
[99] Built by Aeritalia after June of 1943
[100] Built by Fiat, February to July 1942
[101] Built by Fiat, July to October 1942
[102] Built by Fiat, November 1942 to June 1943
[103] Built by Fiat, July to October 1942
[104] Built by Fiat, February to July 1942

[105] Built by Fiat, November 1942 to June 1943
[106] Built by Fiat, November 1942 to June 1943
[107] Built by Fiat, February to July 1942
[108] Built by Fiat, July to October 1942
[109] Built by Fiat, July to October 1942
[110] Built by Fiat, November to June 1943
[111] Built by Fiat, February to December 1939
[112] Built by Fiat, July to October 1942
[113] Built by Fiat, July to October 1942
[114] Built by Fiat, March to August 1940
[115] Built by Fiat, July to August 1942
[116] Built by Fiat, July to August 1942
[117] Built by Fiat, March to August 1940
[118] Built by Fiat, July to October 1942
[119] Built by Fiat, November 1942 to June 1943
[120] Built by Fiat, July to October 1942
[121] Built by Fiat, July to October 1942
[122] Built by Fiat, in October 1940
[123] Built by Fiat, February to March 1941
[124] Built by Fiat, March to August 1940
[125] Built by Fiat, July to October 1942
[126] Built by Fiat, July to October 1942
[127] Built by Fiat, November 1942 to June 1943
[128] Built by Fiat, February to July 1942
[129] Built by Fiat, February to March 1941
[130] Built by Fiat, November 1942 to June 1943
[131] Photo at http://www.stammkennzeichen.de/
[132] Photo at http://www.stammkennzeichen.de/

Bibliography

Beale, Nick, personal research materials and notes

Dr. Christian Möller, personal notes, research materials, and information exchange

Boris Ciglić, personal research materials and notes

Mario Raguž, personal research materials and notes

Beale, Nick; Ghost Bombers, Classic publications Ltd., Crowborough, 2001

Mikić, Vojislav V.; Nemačka avijacija u Jugoslaviji 1941-1945, Beograd, Vojno-istorijski institut Vojske Jugoslavije, Target Beograd, 1998

Frka, Danijel; Novak, Josip; Pogačić, Siniša; La forcé aeriene Croate 1941-1945; Outreau; Lela Presse; 2000

Werhas, Mario; Prodor Nijemaca na Područje Dalmacije, Šifra Achse, 4. Dio; Magazin za vojnu Povijest prosinac 2012, Večernji list, Zagreb, 2012

Jelavić, Tino; No. 352 (Y) R.A.F. Squadron; Zagreb; Tino Jelavić; 2003

Rosch, Barry; Luftwaffe Codes, Markings & Units 1939-1945; Schiffer Publishing, Ltd.; Atglen, 1995

French, Gerald M.; Liberal Lady I-V: Reflections of a Military Pilot; Booksurge Publishing, 2007

Minterne, Don: The History of 73rd Squadron RAF (Part 3), Tutor Publications, 2000

Defenders of Liberty: 2nd Bombardment Group/Wing, 1918-1993, Turner Publishing Company, 1996

The United States Strategic Bombing Survey, Summary Report, (European War), September 30, 1945, http://www.anesi.com/ussbs02.htm

Krunić, Čedomir; Civilno Vazduhoplovstvo Kraljevine Jugoslavije, Prva knjiga; Beograd; 2010

Richards, Charles W. ; The Second Was The First; Oregon, Maverick Publications, 1999

Ciglić, Boris and Savić, Dragan; Croatian Aces of World War 2; Osprey Publishing; 2002

Cull, Brian: 249 at War, Grub Street, 1997

Combat Chronology Of The Us Army Air Forces; ftp.rutgers.edu in directory pub/wwii/usaf; byrd.mu.wvnet.edu (129.71.32.152) in pub/history/military/airforce/wwii_chronology

Vojnoistoriski institut Jugoslovenske narodne armije, Zbornik dokumenata i podataka o narodnooslobodilačkom ratu jugoslovenskih naroda, Centralna i vojna biblioteka, tom IV, knjiga 14, borbe u Bosni i Hercegovini 1943. godine, Beograd, 1956.

Vojnoistoriski institut Jugoslovenske narodne armije, Zbornik dokumenata i podataka o narodnooslobodilačkom ratu jugoslovenskih naroda, Centralna i vojna biblioteka, tom IV, knjiga 16, borbe u Bosni i Hercegovini 1943. godine, Beograd, 1956.

Vojnoistoriski institut Jugoslovenske narodne armije, Zbornik dokumenata i podataka o narodnooslobodilačkom ratu jugoslovenskih naroda, Centralna i vojna biblioteka, tom IV, knjiga 18, borbe u Bosni i Hercegovini 1943. godine, Beograd, 1956.

Vojnoistoriski institut Jugoslovenske narodne armije, Zbornik dokumenata i podataka o narodnooslobodilačkom ratu jugoslovenskih naroda, Centralna i vojna biblioteka, tom IV, knjiga 21, borbe u Bosni i Hercegovini 1944. godine, Beograd, 1960.

Vojnoistoriski institut Jugoslovenske narodne armije, Zbornik dokumenata i podataka o narodnooslobodilačkom ratu jugoslovenskih naroda, Centralna i vojna biblioteka, tom

IV, knjiga 22, borbe u Bosni i Hercegovini 1944. godine, Beograd, 1960.
Vojnoistoriski institut Jugoslovenske narodne armije, Zbornik dokumenata i podataka o narodnooslobodilačkom ratu jugoslovenskih naroda, Centralna i vojna biblioteka, tom IV, knjiga 24, borbe u Bosni i Hercegovini 1944. godine, Beograd, 1960.
Vojnoistoriski institut Jugoslovenske narodne armije, Zbornik dokumenata i podataka o narodnooslobodilačkom ratu jugoslovenskih naroda, Centralna i vojna biblioteka, tom IV, knjiga 25, borbe u Bosni i Hercegovini 1944. godine, Beograd, 1960.
Vojnoistoriski institut Jugoslovenske narodne armije, Zbornik dokumenata i podataka o narodnooslobodilačkom ratu jugoslovenskih naroda, Centralna i vojna biblioteka, tom IV, knjiga 26, borbe u Bosni i Hercegovini 1944. godine, Beograd, 1960.
Vojnoistoriski institut Jugoslovenske narodne armije, Zbornik dokumenata i podataka o narodnooslobodilačkom ratu jugoslovenskih naroda, Centralna i vojna biblioteka, tom IV, knjiga 30, borbe u Bosni i Hercegovini 1944. godine, Beograd, 1960.
Vojnoistoriski institut Jugoslovenske narodne armije, Zbornik dokumenata i podataka o narodnooslobodilačkom ratu jugoslovenskih naroda, Centralna i vojna biblioteka, tom V, knjiga 19, borbe u Hrvatskoj 1943. godine, Beograd, 1957.
Vojnoistoriski institut Jugoslovenske narodne armije, Zbornik dokumenata i podataka o narodnooslobodilačkom ratu jugoslovenskih naroda, Centralna i vojna biblioteka, tom V, knjiga 20, borbe u Hrvatskoj 1943. godine, Beograd, 1957.
Vojnoistoriski institut Jugoslovenske narodne armije, Zbornik dokumenata i podataka o narodnooslobodilačkom ratu jugoslovenskih naroda, Centralna i vojna biblioteka, tom V, knjiga 21, borbe u Hrvatskoj 1943. godine, Beograd, 1958.
Vojnoistoriski institut Jugoslovenske narodne armije, Zbornik dokumenata i podataka o narodnooslobodilačkom ratu jugoslovenskih naroda, Centralna i vojna biblioteka, tom V, knjiga 22, borbe u Hrvatskoj 1943. godine, Beograd, 1958.
Vojnoistoriski institut Jugoslovenske narodne armije, Zbornik dokumenata i podataka o narodnooslobodilačkom ratu jugoslovenskih naroda, Centralna i vojna biblioteka, tom V, knjiga 25, borbe u Hrvatskoj 1944. godine, Beograd, 1959.
Vojnoistoriski institut Jugoslovenske narodne armije, Zbornik dokumenata i podataka o narodnooslobodilačkom ratu jugoslovenskih naroda, Centralna i vojna biblioteka, tom V, knjiga 27, borbe u Hrvatskoj 1944. godine, Beograd, 1961.
Vojnoistoriski institut Jugoslovenske narodne armije, Zbornik dokumenata i podataka o narodnooslobodilačkom ratu jugoslovenskih naroda, Centralna i vojna biblioteka, Dejstva na jadranu, februar - avgust 1944. god.; dokumenti jedinica mornarice NOVJ; Beograd, 1962
Vladimir Dedijer: Ratni dnevnik
Hans Peter Eisenbach, Fronteinsätze eines Stuka-Fliegers, Mittelmeer und Ostfront 1943-44, Helios,2009
Georg Schlaug, Die deutchen Lastensegler-Verbande 1937-1945, Eine Chronik auc Berichten Tagebuchern Dokumenten, Motorbuch Verlag, 1985
Manfred Griehl, Junkers Ju 87 "Stuka", Sturzkampfbomber, Schlachtflugzeug, Panzerjager; Motorbuch Verlag, 1998
C. A. 446; Ministero Dell'Aeronautica, Direzione Generale Delle Costruzioni E Degli Approvvigionamenti; Istruzioni e Norme Per Il Montaggio, la Regolazione, L'impiego e La Manutenzione Del Velivolo C. R. 42 (Motore F. I. A.T. A. 74 R. 1 C. 38); Roma; 1940; Anno XVIII
Ministero Dell'aeronautica Direzione Generale Delle Costruzioni E Degli Approvvigionamenti Roma, Aeroplano Caproni 314, 2 Motori I.F. Delta Rc. 3514-S, Versioni A. B. C., Istruzione Per L'uso Dell'aeroplano, Relazione Tecnica E Norme Di Montaggio E Regolazione E

Pilotaggio Dell'aeroplano, Roma, 1943
Hs 126A-1 u B-1 Flugzeughandbuch, L.Dv. 564, Berlin, 1939
Bramo Fafnir Baumuster 323 R, Betriebs- und Wartungsworschrift, BMW Flugmotorenwerke Brandenburg G.M.B.H, Berlin-Spandau, 1941
Flugzeug-Handbuch, He 46D (mit motor SAM 22), Berlin, 1937
Flugbuch, Fw. Eisnemanni, 6./LLG 1
Flugbuch, Ofw. Heinz Kallrich, 12./LLG 1
Flugbuch, Heinz Buss, 1./NSGr 7
Flugbuch, Kurt Gelinek, 3./NSGr7
Flugbuch, Horst Abramowski, 3./NSGr7
Flugbuch, Nerman Gade, 1./NSGr 7
Flugbuch, Cuno Wilhelmj, 3. NSGr 7
Oberbefehlshaber Südost daily report for 22nd May, 27th May
National Archives, London, United Kingdom, Ultra intercepts: VL 4066, VL 421, VL 3196, VL 5734, VL 6110, KV 431, KV 1921, KV 4392, KV 5693, KV 6517, KV 7200, KV 6486, HP 2918, HP 3817, HP 4114, HP 4321, HP 4453, HP 6358, BT 611, BT 1042, KO 565, KO 182, KO 1304, HP 3524, VL 806, CX/MSS/379R (E), CX/MSS/377R (E), CX/MSS/202T 104 (E), CX/MSS/T194 79, CX/MSS/204 109, CX/MSS/260R (B), CX/MSS/370R (E), CX/MSS/71R (B), CX/MSS/133R (B), CX/MSS/145R (B), CX/MSS/R141 (B), CX/MSS/200R (B), CX/MSS/75R (B), KV964, HP8467, HP9264, HP9042, HP9273, HP8611, HP8833, HP9092, HP9180, HP8899, CX/MS/R.64(B), CX MSS 68T 121 (B), CX/MSS/R.71(B), CX/MSS/R.141(B), CX/MSS/R.149(B), CX/MSS/R.151(B), CX/MSS/R.169(B), CX/MSS/R.376 (E), KV 470, CX/MSS/T52/50, CX/MSS/T52/75, CX/MSS/T163/68, KV831, CX/MSS/R.150(B), CX/MSS/T152/60, CX/MSS/R.19(B), CX/MSS/T19/7, CX/MSS/R.20(B), CX/MSS/R.68(B), CX/MSS/R166(B), MSS/T165/23, CX/MSS/R.112/(B); CX/MSS/R.183(B), CX/MSS/R.182(B), CX/MSS/R.184(B), CX/MSS/R.185(B), CX/MSS/R.160(B), CX/MSS/T.138/105, CX/MSS/R.194(B), CX/MSS/T.194/79, CX/MSS/T.194/129, CX/MSS/T.196/26, CX/MSS/T.196/76, CX/MSS/T.197/111, CX/MSS/T.197/139, CX/MSS/T.199/50, CX/MSS/T.199/81, CX/MSS/T.344/62, CX/MSS/R.417(E), CX/MSS/R.490(E), CX/MSS/T.509/72, CX/MSS/T.512/80; CX/MSS/R.518(E), CX/MSS/T.521/35; CX/MSS/T.528/90, CX/MSS/R.348(E), CX/MSS/T.439/69, CX/MSS/T.339/22, CX/MSS/T.339/73, CX/MSS/T.295/20, CX/MSS/T.305/29, CX/MSS/T.201/54, CX/MSS/T.201/55, CX/MSS/T.201/56, CX/MSS/T.201/88, CX/MSS/T.201/108, CX/MSS/T.202/51, CX/MSS/T.202/52, CX/MSS/T.202/55, CX/MSS/T.202/73, CX/MSS/T.202/80, CX/MSS/T.202/81, CX/MSS/T.202/89, CX/MSS/R.203(B), CX/MSS/T.203/5, CX/MSS/T.204/17, CX/MSS/T.204/109, CX/MSS/R.333(B), CX/MSS/R.338(B), CX/MSS/R.262(B), CX/MSS/R.205(B), CX/MSS/T.208/52, CX/MSS/T.210/141, CX/MSS/R.105(B), CX/MSS/R.224(B), CX/MSS/T.355/78, CX/MSS/T.176/117, CX/MSS/R.178(B), CX/MSS/T.54/103, CX/MSS/T.147/7, CX/MSS/T.41/92, CX/MSS/T.203/1, CX/MSS/T.151/9, CX/MSS/R.108(B), CX/MSS/R.106(B), CX/MSS/T.108/52, CX/MSS/T.106/66, CX/MSS/R.107(B), CX/MSS/T.102/45
K.22, F.1, D.14/17; K.80, R.br.58/4-1,D.80;
National Archives, London, United Kingdom, Operations Record Books: Air 27/638; Air 27/1499, Air 27/227, Air 27/223, Air 27/634, Air 27/23,
Vojnohistorijski institut: I a 143/44—22/1-1, k.38; K.17, F.3/a, R.30/4;
National Archives and Records Administration, Washington, USA: NAV-T-314; roll 1546, photo 420-430; NAV-T-314; roll 1547, photo 155-157; roll 554; NAW T-313/R-482/S-720; NAW T-313/R-485/S-809; NAW T-311/R-191/S-831, 869; MACR 11816; MACR 11817; MACR 11818; MACR 11819; MACR 11820; MACR 11821; MACR 3881, MACR 4098, MACR 1812, MACR 1813, MACR 2398, MACR 2070, T-313, reel 193, photo 288, T-313

roll 189/7448772 and 793, NAW T-501/R-266/S-1016;
Bundesarchiv Militärarchiv Freiburg/Breisgau, Germany: RL 2 III 1188/309/239, 1188/20/?; VII; RL 2 III 1189/94/44; RL 2 III 1189/94/45; RL 2 III 1194/94/11; RL 2 III 1192/196/47; RL 2 III 776/89/3; RL 2 III 1192/66/40; RL 2 III 1192/97/6; RL 2 III 1192/97/7; (1) RL 2 III 1193/151/8; RL 2 III 1193/104/3; ; RL 2 III 1193/26/16; RL 2 III 1195/88/14; RL 2 III 1195/88/15; RL 2 III 1195/88/13; RL 2 III 1195/74/3, 4; RL 2 III 1195/63/17, 18; RL 2 III 1195/35/14; RL 2 III 1196/99/7; RL 2 III 1196/99/8; RL 2 III 1196/99/9; RL2 III-58, BA-MA RL 2 III-1183 bis 1196,

Internet sources:

http://www.ghostbombers.com
http://www.ww2.dk
http://www.znaci.net
http://www.461st.org/Missions/April1944.htm
http://www.461st.org/History/765th%20History/PDFs/765%20April%201944.pdf
http://www.norfield-publishing.com/449th/Summary/reports/jul44/7jul44.htm
http://www.450thbg.com/real/s2/1944/july/7july.shtml
http://www.450thbg.com/real/biographies/bradley/bradley.shtml
http://www.norfield-publishing.com/449th/Summary/reports/jan44/14jan.htm
http://www.stammkennzeichen.de